FORMULA 1
CAR BY CAR **1950-59**

Published in April 2020

ISBN 978-1-910505-44-1

Published by Evro Publishing
Westrow House, Holwell, Sherborne, Dorset DT9 5LF, UK

Edited by Mark Hughes
Designed by Richard Parsons

Printed and bound in Slovenia by GPS Group

www.evropublishing.com

The author

Peter Higham is a freelance writer who has worked in the motor racing media for over 30 years. A motor
racing enthusiast since watching the 1973 Silverstone International Trophy on television, Higham joined Haymarket
Publishing in 1986 to work in *Autosport*'s advertising department and remained with the company for nearly 30
years. Part of the launch publishing team for football monthly magazine *FourFourTwo*, he was involved with the LAT
Photographic business for 17 years and Publishing Director of Haymarket Consumer Media's motor racing publications
during the 2000s.

He has written seven previous books, including the first three titles in the *Formula 1 Car by Car* series covering the
1960s, 1970s and 1980s. He has been a columnist for *Autosport* and *Motor Sport* and was instrumental in running the
prestigious Autosport Awards for over 25 years.

The photographs

Most of the photographs in this book have been sourced from Motorsport Images (www.motorsportimages.com). This
London-based archive is the largest motoring and motorsport picture collection in the world with over 23 million colour
images and black and white negatives dating back to 1895. It includes the collections of LAT Images and Sutton Images
as well as the work of Rainer Schlegelmilch, Ercole Colombo and Giorgio Piola.

Motorsport Images also photographs today's Formula 1 World Championship, with full-time photographers and
digital technicians at every race. Other events covered include the WRC, World Endurance Championship, Le Mans 24
Hours, IndyCar, NASCAR, ALMS, GP2 Series, GP3 Series, World Series by Renault, DTM and National Championships
including BTCC and British F3. As part of Motorsport Network, Motorsport Images supplies all of the company's
leading media such as *F1 Racing*, *Autosport* and *Motorsport News*.

The cover

The main image on the front shows Juan Manuel Fangio's Maserati 250F (V12) during practice for the 1957 Monaco
GP. The inset photos on the front show (from left) 1950 Alfa Romeo 158 (Giuseppe Farina, British GP), 1952 Ferrari
500 (Alberto Ascari, French GP), 1955 Mercedes-Benz W196 (Stirling Moss, Monaco GP) and 1959 Cooper T51-Climax
(Jack Brabham, Dutch GP). The four photos on the back show (from top left to bottom right) 1951 Ferrari 375 (José
Froilán González, British GP), 1956 Lancia-Ferrari D50 (Peter Collins, Belgian GP), 1957 Vanwall VW1 (Tony Brooks,
1957 German GP) and 1958 Ferrari Dino 246 (Mike Hawthorn, Portuguese GP).

FORMULA 1
CAR BY CAR 1950-59

Peter Higham

CONTENTS

INTRODUCTION

Although Grand Prix racing had been the pinnacle of the sport since 1906, the Formula 1 World Championship only began at Silverstone on 13 May 1950. It eventually took centre stage in motor racing's psyche, but there was scant attention paid to the new series at the time. Indeed, the specialist press seemed more interested in the Grand Prix of Europe courtesy title awarded in the build-up to that inaugural race.

Red was GP racing's predominant colour during the 1950s with Alfa Romeo, Ferrari and Maserati drivers all crowned World Champion. Mercedes-Benz made a brief and successful return in 1954–55 and British Racing Green emerged by the end of the decade as Vanwall and then Cooper challenged, and beat, the Europeans.

This was the era of Juan Manuel Fangio with the great Argentine driver crowned World Champion on five occasions – a record that would remain unbeaten until Michael Schumacher dominated in the 2000s. Alberto Ascari won back-to-back titles with the temporary switch to Formula 2 rules in 1952 and 1953, and these remain the most recent title

successes for an Italian driver at the time of writing. Stirling Moss finished runner-up four years in a row (and third in 1959 and 1960) although Mike Hawthorn had the honour of becoming the first Englishman to win the title – albeit driving for Ferrari. Classic front-engined designs dominated for much of the decade but Jack Brabham's nimble rear-engined Cooper-Climax won in 1959 to indicate the future.

So, the *Formula 1 Car by Car* story begins here. The well-funded factory teams dominated results but privateer outfits such as Rob Walker Racing had their moments. Every driver/car combination that started a championship GP during the decade is pictured. The Indianapolis 500 was officially a World Championship round for the first 11 years but was never more than an anomaly and is well covered by specialist books on the subject. Each chapter concludes with data, race winners (championship and non-championship) and standings for both drivers' and, from 1958, constructors' titles. Drivers were allowed to share cars until 1958 (with any points scored divided) and such details are included after the 'Driver Performance' charts.

Five-time World Champion Juan Manuel Fangio and the Maserati 250F in classic pose during the 1957 French Grand Prix

KEY TO 'DRIVER PERFORMANCE' CHARTS

Qualifying positions are included in superscript next to the race result; underlined results indicate that the driver led the race. Details of shared drives are given at the bottom of the table: the better result is given if a driver is classified twice in the same race; both results are given if both of a driver's cars finished, as in the 1955 Argentine GP.

R	Retired
NC	Not classified
DSQ	Disqualified
F2	Took part in concurrent F2 race
DNP	Practised but did not take part in qualifying
DNQ	Did not qualify
DNS	Did not start
FL	Fastest lap
NT	No time recorded in qualifying

THE GRAND PRIX KEY IS AS FOLLOWS:

B	Belgium
CH	Switzerland
D	Germany
E	Spain
F	France
GB	Great Britain
I	Italy
MA	Morocco
MC	Monaco
NL	Holland
P	Portugal
PES	Pescara
RA	Argentina
USA	United States of America

All photographs were taken in World Championship races except where shown in italics in captions.

ACKNOWLEDGEMENTS

Many thanks to Eric Verdon-Roe and Mark Hughes at Evro Publishing for having the idea for the *Formula 1 Car by Car* series of books. Thanks also to Mark for his diligent editing and Richard Parsons for the design. I am indebted to the team at Motorsport Images for their help in researching the book and retouching the images. In particular, thanks to Kathy Ager, Kevin Wood, Tim Wright, Catherine Benham, Richard Byles, Craig Woollard, Emma Champion and Zoe Schafer. Those who stepped in to fill elusive gaps included The Klemantaski Collection (Peter Sachs), Willy Iacona and the Revs Digital Library. As always, thanks to my immediate family – Françoise, Joe, Luc and Sofia – for their unwavering support.

BIBLIOGRAPHY

MAGAZINES AND ANNUALS
The Autocar (Haymarket, Twickenham, Middlesex)
Autocourse (Icon Publishing, Malvern, Worcestershire)
Autosport (Autosport Media UK, Richmond, Middlesex)
The Motor (Haymarket, Twickenham, Middlesex)
Motor Sport (Motor Sport Magazine, London)

BOOKS
A–Z of Formula Racing Cars by David Hodges (Bay View, Bideford, Devon, 1990)

A–Z of Grand Prix Cars by David Hodges (Crowood, Ramsbury, Wiltshire, 2001)

Autocourse Grand Prix Who's Who (fourth edition) by Steve Small (Icon Publishing, Malvern, Worcestershire, 2012)

BRM Volume 1 by Doug Nye (Motor Racing Publications, Croydon, Surrey, 1994)

The Complete History of Grand Prix Motor Racing by Adriano Cimarosti (Motor Racing Publications, Croydon, Surrey, 1990)

Cooper Cars by Doug Nye (Osprey, London, 1987)

The Encyclopaedia of Motor Sport edited by G.N. Georgano (Ebury Press and Michael Joseph, London, 1971)

Ferrari (sixth edition) by Hans Tanner and Doug Nye (Foulis/Haynes, Sparkford, Somerset, 1984)

Ferrari: Men from Maranello by Anthony Pritchard (Haynes, Sparkford, Somerset, 2009)

Grand Prix Cars 1945–65 by Mike Lawrence (Motor Racing Publications, Croydon, Surrey, 1998)

Grand Prix Data Book by David Hayhoe and David Holland (Haynes, Sparkford, Somerset, 2006)

Grand Prix! Volume 1 by Mike Lang (Haynes, Sparkford, Somerset, 1981)

The History of English Racing Automobiles by David Weguelin (White Mouse Editions, London, 1980)

The History of the Grand Prix Car 1945–65 by Doug Nye (Hazleton, Richmond, Surrey, 1993)

Lotus: All The Cars by Anthony Pritchard (Aston Publications Ltd, Bourne End, Buckinghamshire, 1990 and 1992)

Maserati: A Racing History by Anthony Pritchard (Haynes, Sparkford, Somerset, 2003)

Mercedes-Benz Grand Prix Racing 1934–1955 by George C. Monkhouse (White Mouse Editions, London, 1984)

A Record of Grand Prix and Voiturette Racing, Volumes 5 and 6 (second editions) by Paul Sheldon, Richard Page and Duncan Rabagliati (St Leonards Press, Shipley, West Yorkshire, 2011)

Alfa Romeo to the fore: Juan Manuel Fangio (left) and Giuseppe Farina lead at the start of the French GP at Reims

1950

BIRTH OF THE FORMULA 1 WORLD CHAMPIONSHIP

A mass pile-up at Tabac decimated the field on the opening lap at Monaco

Juan Manuel Fangio lapped the field in Monaco

The Association Internationale des Automobile Clubs Reconnus that had governed motor racing before World War II was revised in 1947 as the Fédération Internationale de l'Automobile (FIA). A subcommittee, the Commission Sportive Internationale (CSI), was appointed to shape new rules as the sport emerged from the dark days of conflict. The CSI met in October of that year and announced new GP rules for 1948–53. Originally known as Formula A but soon renamed Formula 1, these stipulated 4.5-litre normally aspirated or 1.5-litre forced-induction maximum engine capacity.

A motorcycling world championship had been organised in 1949 and, at a meeting in the last week of February 1950, pre-war racing driver Count Antonio Brivio, the Italian delegate to the FIA, suggested an F1 World Championship for drivers. The *Grandes Épreuves* of Britain, Monaco, Switzerland, Belgium, France and Italy, plus the Indianapolis 500, were announced as qualifying rounds with points awarded to the top five finishers on the scale 8–6–4–3–2 and an extra point to whoever set the fastest race lap. Indy meant that the championship extended outside Europe but it had little relevance during the 11 years it was officially included.

The new World Championship began at Silverstone on Saturday 13 May 1950 with the drivers (and the top three

Raymond Mays demonstrates the V16-engined BRM P15 before the British GP at Silverstone – the first World Championship event

in the F3 race) presented to the royal party by Earl Howe before the start. The race was awarded the honorary title of GP of Europe and was flagged off by Brivio. A crowd of up to 100,000 paid between six shillings (general admission in advance) and £2 2s (for the main pit grandstand) to watch a dominant Alfa Romeo 1–2–3. Alfa's thirsty supercharged cars duly won the title but Ferrari exploited the larger-capacity normally aspirated alternative to challenge by the end of the season.

The most disappointing aspect for British fans was British Racing Motors. Equipped with a V16 engine, the BRM type 15 had been unveiled amid much hype at Folkingham airfield on 15 December 1949 and founder Raymond Mays gave a brief demonstration during the 1950 British GP meeting. However, the car did not appear in a championship race and Raymond Sommer broke its transmission at the start of his heat when it finally made its début in Silverstone's non-championship International Trophy. Reg Parnell won a couple of lesser races at a wet Goodwood in September before both he and Peter Walker retired from the non-championship season finale in Barcelona. Goodwood apart, it had been a sorry start for Britain's national team.

Giuseppe Farina celebrates victory at Silverstone

Giuseppe Farina, Alfa Romeo 158 (Monaco GP)

ALFA CORSE (ALFA ROMEO)

Alfa Romeo dominated the first year of the new World Championship with its famous type 158 (1.5-litre, eight cylinders). This 'Alfetta' had been designed by Gioacchino Colombo for *voiturette* racing in 1938, a programme initiated by Enzo Ferrari when he was running Alfa's racing affairs. It had a conventional tubular chassis, independent suspension via trailing arms at the front and swing axle to the rear, four-speed gearbox and double-overhead-camshaft 1,479cc straight-eight supercharged engine.

Emilio Villoresi led an Alfa Romeo 1–2 on the car's début in the 1,500cc race that supported the 1938 Coppa Ciano at Livorno. The cars complied with the new Formula 1 in 1947 and they proved virtually unbeatable that year and the next. A single exhaust pipe had

Luigi Fagioli, Alfa Romeo 158 (Monaco GP)

replaced the original small-diameter twin arrangement and triple-choke Weber carburettors were fitted. However, the team was rocked by the deaths of drivers Achille Varzi (practising for the 1948 Swiss GP), Jean-Pierre Wimille (driving a Simca-Gordini in Buenos Aires's Palermo Park in January 1949) and Count Trossi (from cancer later that year).

Alfa Romeo did not race in 1949 and its participation in 1950 was initially uncertain. In January, *The Autocar* noted that the team's appearance depended 'entirely on the financial situation of the company and… the politics of the situation.' A three-car entry was finally confirmed in March amid talk of a government subsidy. The engine now featured two-stage supercharging and developed 360bhp at 8,500rpm, although such was their initial dominance that revs were normally restricted to 8,000rpm. The team used Pirelli tyres and Shell oil and fuel. Giovanni-Battista Guidotti remained as team manager and Orazio Satta Puliga, who had joined the design department in 1938, began the year as chief engineer.

Rising star Juan Manuel Fangio joined Giuseppe Farina while Luigi Fagioli ended 12 years of retirement to replace Consalvo Sanesi, the intended third driver, when he injured his arm during the Mille Miglia. Fangio drove a singleton 158 to victory in the non-championship race at a wet San Remo on his début for the team, beating Luigi Villoresi's Ferrari by over a minute.

Alfa Romeo's next event was the British GP at Silverstone, the team's first appearance in England. The 'three Fs', as they were inevitably dubbed, were joined by local favourite Reg Parnell in a fourth 158. Ferrari withdrew a couple of weeks before the race and

Juan Manuel Fangio, Alfa Romeo 158 (French GP)

Alfa Romeo duly locked out the four-car front row with Farina on pole. Farina, Fagioli and Fangio swapped the lead during the opening 20 laps with Parnell, who had higher gear ratios, in fourth place. Fangio was running a close second when his oil pipe fractured with eight laps to go, so Farina led home a dominant 1–2–3 with the radiator on Parnell's third-placed car deranged after he hit a hare. The opposition had been lapped at least twice.

Fangio made a great start from pole position eight days later in Monaco but Farina was beaten off the line by José Froilán González's Maserati. The Italian was second by Tabac but lost control on water that had been swept over the harbour wall by a gust of wind. He crashed heavily and his Alfa bounced back into the road, causing half the field to be eliminated in the mayhem. Fagioli retired in the pits after 15 minutes of hammering failed to straighten his bent steering. Fangio squeezed through the crashed cars and was 51.8sec ahead by the end of lap two. He led throughout, lapping the depleted field.

Farina and Fagioli finished 1–2 in Switzerland while Fangio qualified on pole position but retired when running second. The first suggestion that large, normally aspirated engines might be the future came at Spa-Francorchamps, where Raymond Sommer's 4.5-litre Lago-Talbot led for five laps when the Alfas refuelled. With the 158s requiring a second stop and Sommer running non-stop, the whiff of an upset was in the air before the Frenchman's engine failed after 20 laps. Fangio led Fagioli home while Farina pitted to check falling oil pressure before finishing fourth at reduced pace.

Fangio led yet another Alfa 1–2–3 in qualifying for the French GP at Reims. Farina led the opening 16 laps before two lengthy pitstops

Reg Parnell, Alfa Romeo 158 (British GP)

Consalvo Sanesi, Alfa Romeo 158 (Italian GP)

Piero Taruffi/Juan Manuel Fangio, Alfa Romeo 158 (Italian GP)

Alfa entered additional 158s for Sanesi and Piero Taruffi. Company management appeared to favour Farina and he had an upgraded engine that developed an extra 20bhp in what was now dubbed the type 159. They had meaningful opposition at last as Ferrari finally exploited the full 4.5-litre normally aspirated capacity. Fangio qualified on pole position but it was Farina who made the best start. Alberto Ascari's Ferrari led for a couple of laps before both he and Fangio retired, the Argentine driver taking over Taruffi's car until it also broke. Farina continued unchallenged to a victory that clinched the inaugural world title. Fagioli was third while Sanesi, who had qualified on the outside of the front row in a fine fourth place, retired early.

Less than a month later, Farina was injured in a road accident outside Genoa while Fangio, frustrated by ill luck and team orders, returned to Argentina to consider his future.

to cure a fuel-feed problem. He climbed back into third position before coasting to a halt on the back straight with nine laps to go. With Farina classified outside the points, Fangio took a maximum score to move into the championship lead with a round to go. Both Fangio and Fagioli finished three laps clear of the field despite easing their pace in the closing stages.

Non-championship victories followed at Bari (Farina), Geneva, Pescara (both Fangio) and Silverstone (Farina). Fagioli was on course to win at Pescara before his front suspension broke on the last lap; Fangio followed the stricken car as it limped to the finish but sped past within sight of the line when Louis Rosier's fast-closing Lago-Talbot threatened to snatch victory.

With four points covering the regular team-mates at the Italian GP,

SCUDERIA FERRARI

Ferrari represented the main hope for meaningful opposition to Alfa Romeo. Enzo Ferrari originally formed his *Scuderia* in 1929 but it was 1940 before he constructed his own car. Prince Igor Troubetzkoy drove a stripped Ferrari 166 sports car in the 1948 Monaco GP and the first true F1 car was introduced at that year's Italian GP.

Alfa Romeo engineer Gioacchino Colombo joined on 1 January 1948 and designed the short-wheelbase Ferrari 125 with tubular chassis and 1,498cc 60-degree V12 engine with a single Roots-type supercharger and four-speed gearbox. The original 125 had transverse-leaf independent front suspension and torsion-bar

Alberto Ascari, Ferrari 125 (Monaco GP)

Luigi Villoresi, Ferrari 125 (Monaco GP)

Raymond Sommer, Ferrari 166/F2/50 (Swiss GP)

rear axle. It was underpowered and handled badly so Colombo's assistant, Aurelio Lampredi, reworked it for the 1949 Italian GP with two-stage supercharging, twin overhead camshafts, a five-speed gearbox and – to improve handling – modified rear suspension and a longer chassis. Alberto Ascari won that race and both he and Luigi Villoresi remained as works drivers for 1950. Their entries for the British GP were withdrawn just two weeks before the inaugural World Championship race, *The Autocar* reporting that 'there has apparently been the usual disagreement with regard to the amount of starting money to be paid for their attendance.'

Ferrari arrived late for the following week's Monaco GP and so missed the opportunity to qualify in the top five positions as these were decided in first practice. Ascari and Villoresi, who had set a time

that would have been good enough for second on the grid, avoided the opening-lap chaos at Tabac but Villoresi choose the wrong way around the pile-up on the second lap and stalled. He push-started his car but eventually retired when third while Ascari finished second.

Villoresi had a lighter new chassis for the Swiss GP with four-speed gearbox, de Dion rear suspension and wheelbase restored to its original length. Both regulars ran among the Alfas before retiring. Raymond Sommer drove the works V12 Ferrari 166/F2/50 he had used to win the supporting F2 race but its suspension failed before half distance.

As these cars were no match for the Alfas, technical director Lampredi was already experimenting with normally aspirated designs, the first of which appeared at Spa-Francorchamps where Ascari

Alberto Ascari, Ferrari 275 (Belgian GP)

Alberto Ascari, Ferrari 375 *(Penya Rhin GP, Pedralbes)*

Dorino Serafini/Alberto Ascari, Ferrari 375 (Italian GP)

finished fifth despite an early puncture. His old long-wheelbase chassis was fitted with the atmospheric 60-degree single-overhead-cam 3,322cc V12 sports car engine. The renamed Ferrari 275 remained underpowered and lacked the Lago-Talbots' fuel range. No supercharged works cars were taken to the French GP, where Ascari and Villoresi shared the Ferrari 275 during practice but the car was withdrawn.

Engine capacity was stretched to 4,101cc for the non-championship GP des Nations in Geneva and two new 4,494cc Ferrari 375s were introduced at the Italian GP. These had a redesigned tubular chassis, four-speed gearbox, independent front suspension via wishbones and transverse leaf springs, and a de Dion rear end. Ascari qualified second and led a couple of laps before his engine failed. Villoresi had been injured at Geneva so Dorino Serafini drove the second Ferrari 375 at Monza. He qualified sixth and handed his car to Ascari, who finished second. With Alfa Romeo absent, Ascari completed 1950 by leading a Ferrari 1–2–3 in the Penya Rhin GP at Barcelona to confirm that normally aspirated engines represented Ferrari's immediate future.

PETER WHITEHEAD

The first privateer to buy an F1 Ferrari, Peter Whitehead used his short-wheelbase, single-stage 125 to win the 1949 Czech GP at Brno. Ferrari also withdrew Whitehead's car from the 1950 British GP when it decided not to send its works cars and Whitehead was disappointed when the organisers refused his request to drive an

Peter Whitehead, Ferrari 125 (French GP)

ERA B-type instead. A non-starter in Monaco following three engine failures during practice, the British Racing Green car returned to Modena for an overhaul. Last on the French GP grid having missed practice, Whitehead finished third despite a blown head gasket right at the end. With future sports car team manager David Yorke in charge, Whitehead won non-championship races in Jersey and at Dundrod and finished seventh in the final GP at Monza.

AUTOMOBILES TALBOT-DARRACQ

Venetian-born Major Antonio Lago acquired Automobiles Talbot and its Suresnes factory when Sunbeam-Talbot-Darracq collapsed in 1935. New large-capacity GP cars, including the 1939 offset *monoplace*, were introduced before World War II. These formed the basis for new chief engineer Carlo Marchetti's Talbot-Lago T26C (it would later be renamed Lago-Talbot) when it was introduced in 1948. Unable to finance a planned supercharged V16, Talbot retained Walter Becchia's normally aspirated 4,483cc straight-six engine with revised valves and twin camshafts, driven through a four-speed Wilson pre-selector gearbox. The cross-section tubular chassis, transverse leaf spring/wishbone front suspension and outdated rigid rear axle were based on the 1939 car. Lago-Talbot was the only leading marque without hydraulic brakes. The T26C weighed over 900kg and the engine now produced just 240bhp at 4,700rpm; but it was reliable, cost-effective and far more fuel efficient than its Italian rivals.

Lago-Talbot introduced two plugs per cylinder on Philippe

Yves Giraud-Cabantous, Lago-Talbot T26C-DA (British GP)

Eugène Martin, Lago-Talbot T26C-DA (British GP)

Philippe Étancelin/Eugène Chaboud, Lago-Talbot T26C-DA (French GP)

Étancelin's car at the 1949 GP de France and this arrangement was standard on the works cars in 1950. With increased compression ratio, Duplex magnetos and three Zenith carburettors mounted horizontally (with air intake moved from the top of the engine cover to the right-hand side), 280bhp was now claimed from the redesignated Lago-Talbot T26C-DA (*double allumage*).

Despite strikes in France, two works T26C-DAs were sent to Silverstone for the opening World Championship GP with Yves Giraud-Cabantous and Eugène Martin nominated as drivers. The 'best-of-the-rest' behind the dominant Alfa Romeos, Martin retired from sixth when his oil pressure faded during the early laps while Giraud-Cabantous finished fourth, two laps behind.

The team missed the following week's Monaco GP but three cars arrived at Bremgarten for the Swiss GP where Louis Rosier finished third. Giraud-Cabantous crashed into the trees without injury on the opening lap at Eymatt corner but sixth-placed Martin broke his leg and suffered head injuries when he did likewise at half distance. Eugène Chaboud replaced Martin at Spa-Francorchamps with Étancelin also included in an expanded four-car works line-up. On a day when Raymond Sommer's private T26C led for five laps, Giraud-Cabantous, Étancelin and Chaboud all suffered engine problems but Le Mans winner Rosier finished third once more.

Sommer was added to the line-up for the French GP driving a lighter T26C-GS chassis with central transmission and sports car mudguards removed. It proved a chastening experience because an issue with their scavenge pumps caused chronic overheating in the oppressive heat. Chaboud did not start and Giraud-Cabantous, Rosier and Sommer all pitted by lap eight. Giraud-Cabantous finished 12 laps down in last place having 'used almost more water than fuel' according to *The Autocar*. Étancelin, whose hot radiator had burned his leg, handed his car to Chaboud when he pitted for rear tyres and water after 28 laps and the substitute driver claimed a distant fifth at the finish.

Rosier used the T26C-DA's superior fuel consumption to beat the works Ferraris in the non-championship Dutch GP on the team's final F1 appearance as Lago considered his diminishing resources. Rosier was fourth in the inaugural World Championship thanks to his third-place finishes in Switzerland and Belgium and a couple of scores as a privateer, but the works team closed when Talbot entered voluntary liquidation in March 1951.

RAYMOND SOMMER

Famed pre-war driver Raymond Sommer drove a variety of machinery during the 1950 F1 season, scoring points on one occasion and briefly threatening the established order in Belgium.

He privately entered his short-chassis, single-stage supercharged Ferrari 125 for the British GP but this plan was abandoned when the works team decided not to go to Silverstone. Sommer made his championship début in Monaco, where he narrowly avoided the first-lap mêlée at Tabac to run second before poor handling restricted him to fourth place at the end. He drove for the works Ferrari and Lago-Talbot teams in Switzerland and France respectively, retiring on both occasions.

Raymond Sommer, Ferrari 125 (Monaco GP)

With Ferrari now developing a new normally aspirated engine, Sommer drove his old Lago-Talbot T26C in Belgium and proved the sensation of the race. He qualified fifth, ahead of the twin-plug works cars, and on lap eight of the race he passed Luigi Villoresi's Ferrari at Burnenville to run fourth behind the Alfa Romeos. The non-stopping Sommer led for five glorious laps when the Alfas refuelled for the first time and lay third when his engine failed after 20 of the 35 laps.

Sommer continued in the T26C at Albi, where he passed Fangio's ailing Maserati on the curved finish line to win heat one of the non-championship event. Unfortunately, he was travelling too fast and crashed into the straw bales and a photographer. The car was repaired for the Italian GP, where Sommer qualified eighth and ran fourth before the gearbox failed. That was Sommer's final GP as he was killed a week later during an F2 race at Cadours.

ECURIE ROSIER

Louis Rosier had been expected to join the factory Lago-Talbot team but he began 1950 driving the prototype Lago-Talbot T26C that had won the 1949 Belgian GP. Fifth at Silverstone, he was among those to crash on the opening lap in Monaco. Rosier drove a works T26C-DA for the next three rounds so made a late arrangement for Harry Schell to drive his car in Switzerland, the entry officially made in the name of Schell's Ecurie Bleue. The Franco-American challenged Emmanuel de Graffenried for sixth before fading brakes restricted him to eighth at the finish.

Raymond Sommer, Lago-Talbot T26C (Italian GP)

Harry Schell, Lago-Talbot T26C (Swiss GP)

Louis Rosier, Lago-Talbot T26C (British GP)

Charles Pozzi/Louis Rosier, Lago-Talbot T26C (French GP)

Charles Pozzi drove the car in the French GP but handed it to Rosier after the latter's works car retired, Rosier finishing sixth. With Automobiles Talbot-Darracq absent, Rosier won the non-championship Albi and Dutch GPs on successive weekends and almost beat the Alfa Romeos at Pescara. Juan Manuel Fangio tried to shadow Luigi Fagioli's crippled leading car to the finish but sped up when he saw Rosier approaching in his mirrors. Second that day, Rosier was fourth in the Italian GP where he also entered his Le Mans-winning Lago-Talbot T26C-GS for Henri Louveau, who retired with failing brakes. Rosier scored points on four occasions, including two third places for the works team, to clinch a distant fourth in the championship.

ECURIE BELGE

The old-fashioned Lago-Talbot T26C was popular among privateers in 1950, the old-style six-plug cars fitted with Solex carburettors. An ever-present example during the inaugural championship was the yellow Ecurie Belge car of band leader Johnny Claes. He started all six qualifying GPs and the best of his four classified finishes was seventh (and last) in Monaco. It was during practice for the non-championship International Trophy at Silverstone that Claes caused a surprise by matching Giuseppe Farina's Alfa Romeo for the quickest practice lap, a feat that *Motor Sport* felt was 'almost too good to believe'. Unfortunately, there was no opportunity to dispel that cynicism for Claes crashed at Abbey on the opening lap of his heat while avoiding Yves Giraud-Cabantous.

Henri Louveau, Lago-Talbot T26C-GS (Italian GP)

Johnny Claes, Lago-Talbot T26C (Monaco GP)

Philippe Étancelin, Lago-Talbot T26C (British GP)

OTHER LAGO-TALBOT PRIVATEERS

A real veteran at 54 years old, Philippe Étancelin began the season driving an old Lago-Talbot T26C. Eighth in the British GP when a mid-race plug change did not cure his down-on-power engine, he qualified fourth and ran sixth in Monaco before retiring. He held an impressive fourth in Switzerland – 'thundering around with the big Talbot in his own inimitable style, which always looks wrong, but produces results' according to *The Autocar* – before the gearbox failed. Étancelin drove a works car in Belgium and France but returned to the privateer ranks to finish fourth at Pescara. Fifth in the Italian GP when lapped five times, he was a similarly distant

fourth in the non-championship Penya Rhin GP.

'Pierre Levegh' (otherwise known as Pierre Bouillon) was another to use a Lago-Talbot T26C for GP starts in Belgium, France and Italy. Seventh at Spa-Francorchamps despite a mid-race change of spark plugs, he was placed in non-championship races at Pau, Bari, Albi and Pescara.

There were seven private Lago-Talbots in the Italian GP field, including Guy Mairesse in Yves Giraud-Cabantous's privately entered T26C. Mairesse qualified respectably in the midfield but made a poor start and ran among the backmarkers before an oil pipe fractured at half distance.

'Pierre Levegh', Lago-Talbot T26C (*International Trophy, Silverstone*)

Guy Mairesse, Lago-Talbot T26C-GS (*Penya Rhin GP, Pedralbes*)

Louis Chiron, Maserati 4CLT/48 (Monaco GP)

OFFICINE ALFIERI MASERATI

Spark-plug manufacturer Adolfo Orsi acquired Maserati on 1 January 1937 and moved the company from Bologna to Modena. Initially retained on 10-year contracts, Ernesto, Ettore and Bindo Maserati all left in 1947 and new designer Alberto Massimino was responsible for the Maserati 4CLT when it was introduced in June of that year. This was a development of the pre-war 4CL *voiturette* with lower tubular chassis and sleek body shape. The independent front suspension was via rocker arms and coil springs while the old-fashioned rigid rear axle was retained. The existing 1,489cc four-cylinder engine now featured four valves per cylinder and a Roots-type supercharger. It was reworked in 1948 as the 4CLT/48,

Franco Rol, Maserati 4CLT/48 (Monaco GP)

with two-stage supercharger boosting power to 260bhp at 7,000rpm. Alberto Ascari's victory on the car's début in San Remo led to it being colloquially named after the Mediterranean resort.

Italy was gripped by industrial unrest in 1949 with management at Orsi's Modena factory locked out that February. The protests led to tragedy in January 1950 when six workers were killed after police lost control and opened fire. It was therefore unsurprising that development of the 4CLT/48 was limited, although *Motor Sport* noted that the engine had been stressed 'almost to bursting point'.

Unlike in previous seasons, Maserati entered a works team in 1950 with Monégasque veteran Louis Chiron as lead driver. His clutch failed during the British GP after an oil leak had covered driver and cockpit. A distant third in Monaco, he only qualified on the final row in Switzerland where unscheduled stops for fuel (the mechanics forgot to top up on the grid) and spark plugs restricted him to ninth. The works team missed the Belgian GP and Chiron was an early retirement from the final two GPs of the season in France and Italy.

Franco Rol drove a second car at three World Championship GPs and selected non-championship events. A distant fifth in San Remo after changing plugs, Rol was the slowest qualifier for the Monaco GP, where he injured his wrist in the first-lap accident. Forced to miss the next two GPs, he qualified seventh on his return at the French GP, although a suspect batch of fuel caused both works cars to blow their engines on lap eight. Rol was running seventh at Monza until halted by another engine failure.

Emmanuel de Graffenried, Maserati 4CLT/48 (British GP)

SCUDERIA ENRICO PLATÉ

Former racing driver and mechanic Enrico Platé was born in Milan but it was from a base in Switzerland that he ran private Maseratis during the late 1940s. A Maserati 4CLT/48 was acquired in 1949 and two such cars were fielded for the aristocratic pairing of Baron Emmanuel de Graffenried and Prince Birabongse Bhanudej Bhanubandh, better known as 'B. Bira'.

Using a new chassis with modified steering, 'Bira' was the fastest non-Alfa Romeo driver during practice for the British GP and he chased the dominant red cars until being slowed by problems with the fuel system, eventually coasting to a halt at Club corner. De Graffenried had a new engine for the race which he ran in during F3 practice, but his run in the top 10 came to a smoky end when it threw a con rod. Giuseppe Farina crashed on the opening lap of the Monaco GP, delaying 'Bira' and eliminating de Graffenried. Slowed by braking issues, 'Bira' was lapped five times on the way to fifth at the finish.

The Platé 4CLT/48s were again the fastest Maseratis in Switzerland, where 'Bira' qualified eighth and enjoyed a fine race into fourth, despite an unscheduled pitstop and an oil leak, with de Graffenried sixth. They missed the next two GPs but non-championship success included de Graffenried's third-place finishes in the British Empire Trophy and Jersey Road Race. Both qualified for the Italian GP in the midfield, where 'Bira' blew an engine after a single lap and de Graffenried finished sixth once more. They were second ('Bira') and fourth in the Goodwood Trophy

and de Graffenried completed 1950 by finishing fifth in the non-championship Penya Rhin GP.

Successive points scores in Monaco and Switzerland helped 'Bira' claim eighth in the inaugural drivers' standings.

'B. Bira', Maserati 4CLT/48 (Monaco GP)

David Murray, Maserati 4CLT/48 (British GP)

David Hampshire, Maserati 4CLT/48 (British GP)

Reg Parnell, Maserati 4CLT/48 (French GP)

SCUDERIA AMBROSIANA

Founded before the war by Count 'Johnny' Lurani and friends in Milan, Scuderia Ambrosiana had been Maserati's leading team during 1948. Luigi Villoresi and Alberto Ascari finished 1–2 in that year's British GP at Silverstone but their defection to Ferrari for 1949 effectively ended Ambosiana's short tenure as a leading GP team.

It continued to field a pair of Maserati 4CLT/48s sporadically during the 1950 World Championship. Regular driver Reg Parnell guested for Alfa Romeo in the British GP so David Murray joined David Hampshire at Silverstone. They qualified on the penultimate row and ran in the midfield until Murray's engine failed, while Hampshire made several late pitstops and was classified ninth. Scuderia Ambrosiana missed the next three GPs before returning at the French GP where both Hampshire and Parnell were victims of Maserati's engine maladies before the end of lap 10. Parnell was second in the Jersey Road Race and Hampshire beat a limited field in another minor race at Gamston. A single car was sent to Monza for the championship finale, where Murray ran at the back before retiring after 56 laps.

SCUDERIA MILANO

Brothers Arnaldo and Arialdo Ruggeri of Milan took advantage of the 1949 Italian GP organisers' incentive for new machinery by modifying two Maserati 4CLT/48s and entering them as Maserati-Milanos. The wheelbase was shortened and drum brakes enlarged, but the key changes were to the engine. Mario Speluzzi increased the two-stage supercharger boost pressure by 25 per cent to develop an extra 20bhp. Normally known as the Maserati 4CLT/50-Milano or 4CLT/50-Speluzzi, this was enough for the Automobile Club of Milan to pay the six million lire additional starting money.

Two new chassis were planned for 1950 but limited funds slowed development so the 1949 hybrid car initially appeared. Entries were secured for the first two GPs of the season, for Felice Bonetto at Silverstone and Clemente Biondetti at Monaco, but neither arrived. Scuderia Milano finally made its championship bow in Switzerland, where Bonetto's 4CLT/50 finished fifth after an early 'off' and a mid-race refuelling disaster; *The Motor* noted that 'they overdid the pressure of the hose and blew the pits to pieces.' Bonetto was fourth in France before his over-stressed engine failed.

The new car – Milano '01' – was finally ready for the non-championship GP des Nations in Geneva. The chassis had a ladder frame with double wishbone/longitudinal torsion bar front suspension and de Dion/transverse leaf spring rear, while the radiator grille was wider and oval. The Speluzzi-developed engine now had a large single-stage Roots-type blower and two plugs per cylinder featured for the Italian GP. Gianfranco Comotti's engine failed on the car's championship début and Bonetto's 4CLT/50 did not start after a troubled practice. Local amateurs Juan Jover and Chico Godia drove in Barcelona's non-championship race, the former finishing 10th and last in the Milano. A second Milano chassis was later sold and refettled as the ill-starred Arzani-Volpini in 1955.

Felice Bonetto, Maserati 4CLT/50-Milano (Swiss GP)

Gianfranco Comotti, Milano 01 (Italian GP)

José Froilán González, Maserati 4CLT/48 (Monaco GP)

SCUDERIA ACHILLE VARZI

The Automóvil Club Argentina continued to enter Argentine drivers in its pale blue-and-yellow Maserati 4CLT/48s. Little-known José Froilán González and Alfredo Pián were chosen as the mainstay of the team with 1949 revelation Juan Manuel Fangio driving when his Alfa Romeo commitments allowed. Renamed Scuderia Achille Varzi in honour of the fallen Italian star, it was based in Varzi's former workshop in Galliate.

Fangio began 1950 by winning at Pau and Pián finished third on his début in San Remo, albeit lapped twice. The team missed the British GP and Monaco was a disaster as Pián crashed on oil on the climb from Ste Dévote during practice and was thrown clear, breaking his leg to end his short European career. González qualified on the outside of the three-car front row but he hit Giuseppe Farina's Alfa when the Italian crashed on the opening lap,

rupturing the fuel tank and causing it to burst into flames moments later at the Gasworks hairpin. González suffered second-degree burns before he was able to leap from the moving car.

A single 4CLT/48 was sent to the Swiss GP with Nello Pagani replacing González and Pián. The reigning motorcycle world champion passed Harry Schell to claim seventh on his only F1 championship appearance. González returned at the French GP where his was the first Maserati to retire, with piston failure after just four laps of the Reims-Gueux circuit.

With Alfa Romeo absent, Fangio led non-championship races at Albi and Zandvoort before retiring. González won a heat at Albi and inherited second overall, but in the Dutch GP he was lucky to escape further burns when his car caught fire during his second refuelling stop. The team missed the Italian GP and did not return in 1951.

Alfredo Pián, Maserati 4CLT/48 (Monaco GP)

Nello Pagani, Maserati 4CLT/48 (Swiss GP)

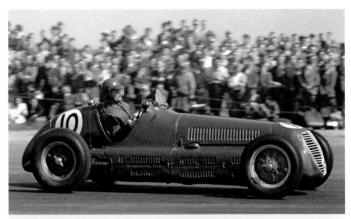

Joe Fry/Brian Shawe-Taylor, Maserati 4CL (British GP)

Antonio Branca, Maserati 4CL (Swiss GP)

OTHER MASERATI PRIVATEERS

Joe Fry entered his ex-Emmanuel de Graffenried Maserati 4CL in the British GP at Silverstone. This conventional *voiturette* was designed by Ernesto Maserati in 1939 with a double-overhead-cam four-cylinder engine that also formed the basis of the 4CLT/48. A single-stage Roots supercharger was initially fitted with 220bhp claimed. Fry was the penultimate qualifier after engine problems during Thursday practice. With the cylinder block resleeved, he ran at the back of the field before others were delayed. Brian Shawe-

Taylor, whose ERA B-type had been refused, took over when Fry pitted and finished 10th, six laps behind the winning Alfas.

Antonio Branca also raced an old 4CL during 1950, finishing last in Switzerland and Belgium. He lost several laps on his début at Bremgarten while pushing his car back to the pits after he had spun and stalled. Magazine proprietor and pre-war works driver Paul Pietsch entered a Maserati 4CLT/48 in the Italian GP; he was the slowest qualifier after a troubled practice and his engine failed at the start.

Paul Pietsch, Maserati 4CLT/48 *(Freiburg hillclimb)*

Robert Manzon, Simca-Gordini 15 (Monaco GP)

Maurice Trintignant, Simca-Gordini 15 *(Penya Rhin GP, Pedralbes)*

EQUIPE GORDINI

Amédée Gordini introduced the nimble, ladder-frame Simca-Gordini 15 in 1947 with the production-based straight-four engine enlarged to 1,490cc a year later. The four-speed gearbox and suspension were also derived from Simca parts. A single Wade supercharger was fitted for 1950 although its 160bhp made this the least powerful Formula 1 contender. Poor reliability and limited finances did not help either. The same chassis ran in Formula 2 races that year with the supercharger removed. Équipe Gordini made its championship bow at Monaco where both Robert Manzon and Maurice Trintignant were eliminated in the first-lap accident. They missed the next two races before Manzon finished the French GP in a surprise fourth. Trintignant was third in Albi and both had retired by lap 14 of the Italian GP.

ENGLISH RACING AUTOMOBILES (ERA)

English Racing Automobiles was formed on 6 November 1933 by Raymond Mays, Peter Berthon and original backer Humphrey Cook. A mainstay of *voiturette* racing for the rest of the decade, these upright old cars were now eligible for the new F1 and historic racing simultaneously. Keen to sell the company, Cook moved ERA from its original base in Bourne to Dunstable by the end of 1945 and Leslie Johnson acquired it three years later.

Two ERA E-types, Johnson's works car and Peter Walker's dark green privately owned machine, were entered in the 1950 British GP. The original example of this streamlined *voiturette* was introduced in 1939 while the second chassis was eventually completed after the war. It had a conventional tubular chassis with independent front suspension and de Dion rear axle. The 1,488cc straight-six engine originally had a large single-stage Zoller supercharger although Walker, who had acquired the original chassis in 1949, replaced his with a two-stage Roots blower. The E-type was an unhappy and unreliable project and the appearances at Silverstone mirrored that sorry record. As *The Autocar* noted in its race report, 'the complete failure of the E-types was disappointing, if not entirely novel.'

With Johnson's aluminium bodywork still unpainted, practice was plagued by gearbox issues and he retired from the race as he passed the pits for the second time with supercharger aflame. Having cracked a cylinder head on Thursday and broken the transmission on Friday, Walker struggled to engage a gear at the start of the race and after a couple of slow laps handed over to

Leslie Johnson, ERA E-type (British GP)

Peter Walker/Tony Rolt, ERA E-type (British GP)

Tony Rolt, whose Delage and *Bimotore* Alfa Romeo had been refused an entry; the problem could not be fixed and they retired with just five laps completed.

Those fortunes were in stark contrast to the two older ERAs in the British GP field. The original ERA A-type was introduced in March 1934 to Reid Railton's design, with input from Berthon. Murray Jamieson designed the Roots-type supercharger. The 1,488cc straight-six was driven through a four-speed Wilson pre-selector gearbox with 170bhp at 6,500rpm claimed. Semi-elliptic springs were fitted front and rear. The nervous handling was improved by a stiffened chassis and modified suspension when production of the B-type began in the winter of 1934. The new C-type followed for 1937 with Zoller supercharger now standard (boosting power to 225bhp), redesigned con rods (to improve reliability), new brakes and Porsche independent front suspension.

Bob Gerard and Cuth Harrison enjoyed a spirited duel in a pair of old ERA *voiturettes* at Silverstone. Gerard's car (R14B) had a B-type chassis and suspension and an uprated C-type engine and Zoller supercharger. Harrison's ex-Earl Howe chassis (R8B) was converted to C specification in 1938 and he rebuilt the car again in 1949 with revised radiator and Jamieson supercharger. Gerard beat his compatriot into sixth place by just 0.4sec after a late stop

Bob Gerard, ERA B-type (British GP)

Bob Gerard, ERA A-type (Monaco GP)

Cuth Harrison, ERA C-type (Monaco GP)

for fuel, winning the Fred Craner Memorial Trophy for the first British car to finish. Both travelled to Monaco with Gerard now driving his older A-type, which dated back to 1935. Harrison was eliminated in the Tabac pile-up but Gerard squeezed through and snatched another sixth-place finish from Johnny Claes with five laps to go. Both enjoyed success in national races with Harrison fourth in the International Trophy at Silverstone. The Sheffield-based car dealer made a third World Championship appearance a week later at Monza but retired.

ALTA

Alta Car & Engineering was based in Tolworth, Surrey and owner Geoffrey Taylor announced plans for a GP car in 1945. Money was in short supply so it was three years before the appearance of a prototype, which proved heavy with inconsistent handling. Its independent suspension included rubber blocks in the springs and its elegant aluminium bodywork was the work of Leacroft of Egham. The twin-overhead-cam 1,485cc straight-four engine was mated to a four-speed synchromesh gearbox, both of Alta design.

Two Alta GPs, the second and third cars to be built, appeared at Silverstone: Geoffrey Crossley drove the second chassis, which had been built in 1949 with the original Roots-type single-stage blower; Irishman Joe Kelly acquired the third chassis, with two-stage supercharging, which was only completed in the paddock. Crossley was unclassified following numerous pitstops and Kelly's clutch slipped until his transmission failed. Crossley was ninth in

Geoffrey Crossley, Alta GP (British GP)

the Belgian GP and both finished the Jersey Road Race, Crossley sixth and Kelly eighth. Kelly was fourth in the Ulster Trophy at Dundrod against another national field.

HORSCHELL RACING CORPORATION

The Cooper Car Company ended the decade as World Champions but its F1 story began with a short-lived and low-key appearance in the 1950 Monaco GP. Franco-American Harry Schell raced a Cooper T12-JAP in the Prix de Monte Carlo F3 support race, winning his heat and finishing second behind Stirling Moss in the final. He then fitted a 1,097cc JAP (J.A. Prestwich) vee-twin engine for the following day's main event, lining up at the back as he had not practised with the F1 cars. The underpowered car was already moving when the signal was given to start but Schell crashed into Robert Manzon's Simca-Gordini when Giuseppe Farina triggered the opening lap pile-up at Tabac.

Joe Kelly, Alta GP (British GP)

CLEMENTE BIONDETTI

Clemente Biondetti, a 52-year-old Italian veteran, produced an odd 'special' that he raced in the autumn F1 races at Pescara and Monza. He acquired a Ferrari 166I sports car chassis, bodywork and running gear from Count Soave Besana and installed the 3.4-litre six-cylinder twin-cam engine and gearbox from a Jaguar XK120. The resulting offset single-seater lacked rigidity and was not a success. Biondetti retired from his only World Championship appearance, in the Italian GP, when the engine failed after 17 laps.

Clemente Biondetti, Ferrari 166I-Jaguar (Italian GP)

Harry Schell, Cooper T12-JAP (*Monaco GP, F3 race*)

1950 RESULTS

DRIVER PERFORMANCE (EXCLUDING INDIANAPOLIS 500)

DRIVER	CAR-ENGINE	GB	MC	CH	B	F	I
Alberto Ascari	Ferrari 125	–	⁷2	⁵R	–	–	–
	Ferrari 275	–	–	–	⁷5	NT DNS	–
	Ferrari 375	–	–	–	–	–	²**2**
Clemente Biondetti	Ferrari 166I-Jaguar	–	–	–	–	–	²⁵R
'B.Bira'	Maserati 4CLT/48	⁵R	¹⁴5	⁸4	–	–	¹⁵R
Felice Bonetto	Maserati 4CLT/50-Milano	–	–	¹²5	–	¹¹R	²³DNS
Antonio Branca	Maserati 4CL	–	–	¹⁷11	¹³10	–	–
Eugène Chaboud	Lago-Talbot T26C-DA	–	–	–	¹¹R	¹⁰5	–
Louis Chiron	Maserati 4CLT/48	¹¹R	⁸3	¹⁶9	–	¹⁴R	¹⁹R
Johnny Claes	Lago-Talbot T26C	²¹11	¹⁹7	¹⁴10	¹⁴8	¹⁵R	²²R
Gianfranco Comotti	Milano 01	–	–	–	–	–	²⁶R
Geoffrey Crossley	Alta GP	¹⁷R	–	–	¹²9	–	–
Emmanuel de Graffenried	Maserati 4CLT/48	⁸R	¹¹R	¹¹6	–	–	¹⁷6
Philippe Étancelin	Lago-Talbot T26C	¹⁴8	⁴R	⁶R	–	–	¹⁶5
	Lago-Talbot T26C-DA	–	–	–	⁶R	⁴5	–
Luigi Fagioli	Alfa Romeo 158	²**2**	⁵R	³**2**	³**2**	³2	⁵**3**
Juan Manuel Fangio	Alfa Romeo 158	³**R**	¹**1** FL	¹R	²**1**	¹**1** FL	¹R FL
Giuseppe Farina	Alfa Romeo 158	¹**1** FL	²R	²**1** FL	⁴**4** FL	²**7**	–
	Alfa Romeo 159	–	–	–	–	–	³**1**
Joe Fry	Maserati 4CL	²⁰10	–	–	–	–	–
Bob Gerard	ERA B-type	¹³6	–	–	–	–	–
	ERA A-type	–	¹⁵6	–	–	–	–
Yves Giraud-Cabantous	Lago-Talbot T26C-DA	⁶4	–	⁷R	⁹R	⁵8	–
José Froilán González	Maserati 4CLT/48	–	³R	–	–	⁸R	–
David Hampshire	Maserati 4CLT/48	¹⁶9	–	–	–	¹⁸R	–
Cuth Harrison	ERA C-type	¹⁵7	¹³R	–	–	–	²¹R
Leslie Johnson	ERA E-type	¹²R	–	–	–	–	–
Joe Kelly	Alta GP	¹⁹NC	–	–	–	–	–
'Pierre Levegh'	Lago-Talbot T26C	–	–	–	¹⁰7	⁹R	²⁰R
Henri Louveau	Lago-Talbot T26C-GS	–	–	–	–	–	¹⁴R
Guy Mairesse	Lago-Talbot T26C	–	–	–	–	–	¹¹R
Robert Manzon	Simca-Gordini 15	–	¹⁶R	–	–	¹³4	¹⁰R
Eugène Martin	Lago-Talbot T26C-DA	⁷R	–	⁹R	–	–	–
David Murray	Maserati 4CLT/48	¹⁸R	–	–	–	–	²⁴R
Nello Pagani	Maserati 4CLT/48	–	–	¹⁵7	–	–	–
Reg Parnell	Alfa Romeo 158	⁴3	–	–	–	–	–
	Maserati 4CLT/48	–	–	–	–	¹²R	–
Alfredo Pián	Maserati 4CLT/48	–	¹⁸DNS	–	–	–	–
Paul Pietsch	Maserati 4CLT/48	–	–	–	–	–	²⁷R
Charles Pozzi	Lago-Talbot T26C	–	–	–	–	¹⁶6	–
Franco Rol	Maserati 4CLT/48	–	¹⁷R	–	–	⁷R	⁹R
Tony Rolt	ERA E-type	NT R	–	–	–	–	–
Louis Rosier	Lago-Talbot T26C	⁹5	¹⁰R	–	–	NT 6	¹³4
	Lago-Talbot T26C-DA	–	–	¹⁰3	⁸3	⁶R	–

DRIVER PERFORMANCE CONTINUED

DRIVER	CAR-ENGINE	GB	MC	CH	B	F	I
Consalvo Sanesi	Alfa Romeo 158	–	–	–	–	–	[4] R
Harry Schell	Cooper T12-JAP	–	[20] R	–	–	–	–
	Lago-Talbot T26C	–	–	[18] 8	–	–	–
Dorino Serafini	Ferrari 375	–	–	–	–	–	[6] 2
Brian Shawe-Taylor	Maserati 4CL	[NT] 10	–	–	–	–	–
Raymond Sommer	Ferrari 125	–	[9] 4	–	–	–	–
	Ferrari 166/F2/50	–	–	[13] R	–	–	–
	Lago-Talbot T26C	–	–	–	[5] R	–	[8] R
	Lago-Talbot T26C-GS	–	–	–	–	[17] R	–
Piero Taruffi	Alfa Romeo 158	–	–	–	–	–	[7] R
Maurice Trintignant	Simca-Gordini 15	–	[12] R	–	–	–	[12] R
Luigi Villoresi	Ferrari 125	–	[6] R	[4] R	[4] 6	–	–
	Ferrari 275	–	–	–	–	[NT] DNS	–
Peter Walker	ERA E-type	[10] R	–	–	–	–	–
Peter Whitehead	Ferrari 125	–	[21] DNS	–	–	[19] 3	[18] 7

SHARED DRIVES British GP: Joe Fry/Brian Shawe Taylor (Maserati 4CL) 10; Peter Walker/Tony Rolt (ERA E type) R. French GP: Philippe Étancelin/Eugène Chaboud (Lago Talbot T26C DA) 5; Charles Pozzi/Louis Rosier (Lago Talbot T26C) 6. Italian GP: Dorino Serafini/Alberto Ascari (Ferrari 375) 2; Piero Taruffi/Juan Manuel Fangio (Alfa Romeo 158) R.

FORMULA 1 RACE WINNERS

ROUND	RACE (CIRCUIT)	DATE	WINNER
–	Grand Prix de Pau (Pau)	Apr 10	Juan Manuel Fangio (Maserati 4CLT/48)
–	Richmond Trophy (Goodwood)	Apr 10	Reg Parnell (Maserati 4CLT/48)
–	Gran Premio di San Remo (San Remo)	Apr 16	Juan Manuel Fangio (Alfa Romeo 158)
–	Grand Prix de Paris (Montlhéry)	Apr 30	Georges Grignard (Lago-Talbot T26C)
1	**British and European Grand Prix (Silverstone)**	**May 13**	**Giuseppe Farina (Alfa Romeo 158)**
2	**Grand Prix de Monaco (Monte Carlo)**	**May 21**	**Juan Manuel Fangio (Alfa Romeo 158)**
3*	**Indianapolis 500 (Indianapolis)**	**May 30**	**Johnnie Parsons (Kurtis-Offenhauser)**
4	**Grand Prix de Suisse (Bremgarten)**	**Jun 4**	**Giuseppe Farina (Alfa Romeo 158)**
–	British Empire Trophy (Douglas)	Jun 15	Bob Gerard (ERA B-type)
5	**Grand Prix de Belgique (Spa-Francorchamps)**	**Jun 18**	**Juan Manuel Fangio (Alfa Romeo 158)**
6	**Grand Prix de l'Automobile Club de France (Reims)**	**Jul 2**	**Juan Manuel Fangio (Alfa Romeo 158)**
–	Gran Premio di Bari (Bari)	Jul 9	Giuseppe Farina (Alfa Romeo 158)
–	JCC Jersey Road Race (St Helier)	Jul 13	Peter Whitehead (Ferrari 125)
–	Grand Prix d'Albi (Albi)	Jul 16	Louis Rosier (Lago-Talbot T26C)
–	Grote Prijs van Nederland (Zandvoort)	Jul 23	Louis Rosier (Lago-Talbot T26C-DA)
–	Grand Prix des Nations (Geneva)	Jul 30	Juan Manuel Fangio (Alfa Romeo 158)
–	Johore Grand Prix (Johore)	Aug 6	J.M. Patterson (MG TC)
–	Nottingham Trophy (Gamston)	Aug 7	David Hampshire (Maserati 4CLT/48)
–	Ulster Trophy (Dundrod)	Aug 12	Peter Whitehead (Ferrari 125)
–	Gran Premio di Pescara (Pescara)	Aug 15	Juan Manuel Fangio (Alfa Romeo 158)
–	Sheffield Telegraph Trophy (Gamston)	Aug 19	Cuth Harrison (ERA C-type)
–	Daily Express International Trophy (Silverstone)	Aug 26	Giuseppe Farina (Alfa Romeo 158)
7	**Gran Premio d'Italia (Monza)**	**Sep 3**	**Giuseppe Farina (Alfa Romeo 159)**
–	Goodwood Trophy (Goodwood)	Sep 30	Reg Parnell (BRM P15)
–	Gran Premio do Penya Rhin (Pedralbes)	Oct 29	Alberto Ascari (Ferrari 375)

*Run to AAA National Championship rules

DRIVERS' CHAMPIONSHIP

DRIVERS		POINTS
1	Giuseppe Farina	30
2	Juan Manuel Fangio	27
3	Luigi Fagioli	24 (28)*
4	Louis Rosier	13
5	Alberto Ascari	11
6	Johnnie Parsons	9
7	Bill Holland	6
8	'B. Bira'	5
9=	Louis Chiron	4
	Reg Parnell	4
	Mauri Rose	4
	Peter Whitehead	4
13=	Philippe Étancelin	3
	Yves Giraud Cabantous	3
	Cecil Green	3
	Robert Manzon	3
	Dorino Serafini	3
	Raymond Sommer	3
19	Felice Bonetto	2
20=	Tony Bettenhausen	1
	Eugène Chaboud	1
	Joie Chitwood	1

*Best six results count

Juan Manuel Fangio's Alfa Romeo 159 coasts into the pits after his victory in the Spanish GP clinched the 1951 World Championship

1951

FANGIO'S FIRST TITLE AS ALFA ROMEO BOW OUT

Alfa Romeo's Sanesi, Farina, Bonetto, Fangio and Guidotti (from left)

This was the year in which large-capacity normally aspirated engines eclipsed the thirsty high-boost blown rivals. The Ferrari 375 was the quickest car by mid-season and José Froilán González delivered the marque's maiden World Championship GP victory at Silverstone in July. The title developed into a straight fight between Alfa Romeo and Ferrari but an incorrect choice of wheel size at the final race thwarted Alberto Ascari's challenge. So Alfa Romeo successfully retained the World Championship with Juan Manuel Fangio crowned for the first time.

There were seven World Championship GPs this year with the Automobilclub von Deutschland adopting F1 rules for its race and Barcelona included for the first time. The Monaco GP was not held and remained absent for the next four years, a sports car event being preferred in 1952. There were fears that the 1951 British GP would be the

José Froilán González and Juan Manuel Fangio (standing) on the grid before the British GP

Alberto Ascari leads Ferrari team-mate José Froilán González at the start of the decisive Spanish GP

last to be held at Silverstone for the Royal Automobile Club announced on 17 May that it would not renew its lease at the end of the year. However, the British Racing Drivers' Club finally agreed a four-year lease in October, guaranteeing the event's immediate future.

Mercedes-Benz considered a return to GP racing and in February sent three 1939 W163s to Argentina, where Fangio, Hermann Lang and Karl Kling were beaten by González's locally entered 2-litre Ferrari V12. Then on 27 May, Alfred Neubauer announced that the company would enter the Italian GP, with a development of the 1.5-litre supercharged W165 *voiturette* that had dominated the 1939 Tripoli GP expected to be used. That intriguing prospect never materialised, although Neubauer and Lang visited the French GP.

Alfa Romeo mechanics in the paddock in France

Juan Manuel Fangio, Alfa Romeo 159 (Spanish GP)

ALFA CORSE (ALFA ROMEO)

Alfa Romeo confirmed that it would defend its world title at the start of 1951 with a regular three-car team. Despite his misgivings at the end of 1950, Juan Manuel Fangio remained alongside new World Champion Giuseppe Farina with Consalvo Sanesi and Felice Bonetto also signed. Giaocchino Colombo returned to the engineering department in February.

Alfa Romeo had not lost a race since 1946 but the Ferrari 375 was threatening victory by the end of 1950 and a serious challenge was expected. Alfa responded by fitting auxiliary fuel tanks to the existing 159 to extend its range between pitstops. The most

extreme example supplemented the standard tank behind the driver with one under each elbow, another alongside the engine and a fifth above the scuttle, all of which allowed 70 gallons to be carried. Engine power was boosted to 425bhp at 9,300rpm but average fuel consumption was just 1.6mpg.

Fangio and Farina led a 1–3 and 1–2 respectively in the heats for the non-championship International Trophy at Silverstone but the final was lost when torrential rain and hail forced it to be abandoned after six laps with Fangio's third-placed (or fourth – the visibility was bad!) car the leading Alfa. Four 159s were again entered for the opening championship race in Switzerland. Farina

Giuseppe Farina, Alfa Romeo 159 (Spanish GP)

Felice Bonetto, Alfa Romeo 159 (British GP)

Consalvo Sanesi, Alfa Romeo 159 (French GP)

intended to run non-stop in the long-range car, Fangio and local guest driver Emmanuel de Graffenried each had a single extra tank under their right elbows while Sanesi was handed an experimental 159 with de Dion rear axle and standard fuel tank. Fangio excelled in the appalling conditions and converted pole position into his first victory of the season after refuelling at half distance. Slow off the line and a handful in the wet due to its heavy fuel load, Farina's 159 was passed by Piero Taruffi's Ferrari in the closing stages and the reigning champion survived a final lap spin at Forsthaus to finish third. Sanesi and de Graffenried, who continued after spinning into the straw bales at one stage, finished fourth and fifth respectively.

All three Alfas were fitted with extra tanks from Belgium where Fangio drove the de Dion car with 19in (rather than the normal 17in) wheels after excessive tyre wear in practice. He qualified on pole position but lost 15 minutes when his left rear wheel jammed at his pitstop, Fangio standing impassively by his car. Farina, who had dominated the non-championship Ulster Trophy at Dundrod, led for all bar three laps and beat Alberto Ascari's Ferrari by almost three minutes. Sanesi retired with a holed radiator.

On pole again in France, Fangio's swing axle car misfired from lap nine and he fell out of contention when he stopped to change a magneto. Recalled to the team for this one race, Luigi Fagioli handed his smaller-capacity car to Fangio at his regular pitstop. Fourth after returning to the track, Fangio then inherited

victory when Farina punctured a front tyre and Ascari pitted. Farina and Sanesi (in the de Dion chassis) were both delayed by further magneto problems but finished fifth and 10th respectively, the latter having pushed his broken car nearly a mile to the finish. Fagioli came home 11th once Fangio's car had been repaired.

Bonetto took over the fourth 159 at the British GP and jumped into the lead from the second row but the race soon developed into a battle between Argentina's Fangio and José Froilán González. Try as he might, Fangio could not beat his compatriot, who scored Ferrari's first victory in a World Championship GP. Fangio, the misfiring Bonetto and Sanesi, whose wheel also jammed at his

Emmanuel de Graffenried, Alfa Romeo 159 (Spanish GP)

Luigi Fagioli/Juan Manuel Fangio, Alfa Romeo 159 (French GP)

Paul Pietsch, Alfa Romeo 159 (German GP)

pitstop, finished 2–4–6 while Farina retired when the de Dion car caught fire at Abbey.

With Ferrari now in the ascendency, Fangio prevented total humiliation in Germany by finishing second despite stalling at his pitstop. Both Farina and Bonetto retired while Paul Pietsch, who was a late entry in the fourth car, crashed over the wall at the North turn, without injury. Fangio beat the Ferraris at Bari but Sanesi and a mechanic were badly burned when his car was engulfed in flames during testing at Monza. Fangio, Farina and Bonetto all had rebodied cars for the Italian GP with de Dion rear axles, strengthened chassis, improved brakes, twin exhausts and high-boost engines; de Graffenried replaced Sanesi in the old swing-axle car. Fangio and Ascari battled for the lead before the Alfa stopped for tyres while de Graffenried and Farina retired early. Fangio's piston failed at half distance but Farina finished in a fine third after taking over Bonetto's car. Any hope of catching González's second-placed Ferrari was lost when a fuel leak forced an extra stop.

Title favourites before the final race in Barcelona, Ferrari chose the wrong wheel size and suffered a succession of early punctures. Fangio took the lead on lap four and eased to victory and his first World Championship. Farina, who had won the previous month's Goodwood Trophy, Bonetto and de Graffenried finished 3–5–6.

Faced with the need to develop a completed new normally aspirated engine, Alfa Romeo confirmed it was quitting F1 in March 1952 and would not return until 1979.

SCUDERIA FERRARI

Encouraged by progress made in the second half of 1950, Ferrari introduced an upgraded version of the atmospheric 4.5-litre type 375. This now had two plugs per cylinder in the single-overhead-cam V12 engine with improved cooling to new brakes. Luigi Villoresi won the opening non-championship races at Syracuse and Pau with a 1950-specification Ferrari 375 before Alberto Ascari dominated on the new car's début at San Remo.

Three cars were entered for the Swiss GP, where Ascari, who should have been in hospital having burned his left arm during the previous week's F2 race at Genoa, and Piero Taruffi were entrusted with the twin-ignition models while Villoresi had an old-style 375. Taruffi excelled in the heavy rain and finished second but the off-form Ascari trailed home in sixth place and Villoresi crashed through a hedge at Forsthaus. All three cars had the latest engine at Spa-Francorchamps where they ran non-stop to finish second (Ascari) and third (Villoresi).

The 375s were fitted with curved windscreens and temporarily switched from the team's regular Pirelli tyres to Englebert in France, where José Froilán González replaced an unwell Taruffi. Ascari led the opening laps in France before his gearbox broke after 10 laps. He took over González's car at the pitstops and finished second, with Villoresi third. Ferrari had challenged the supercharged Alfa Romeos but so far victory remained elusive.

Back on Pirelli tyres for the British GP, González used a 1950-specification 375 (with flat windscreen) to set the first 100mph lap of Silverstone and qualify on pole position. He then

Luigi Villoresi, Ferrari 375 (French GP)

out-duelled compatriot Juan Manuel Fangio to score Ferrari's first victory in a World Championship GP. He ran wide at Becketts while lapping Consalvo Sanesi's Alfa and even had time to offer his car to Ascari at his 23-second fuel stop, the Italian having broken another gearbox. Villoresi spun at Copse but completed a historic day for the *Scuderia* by finishing third once more.

That Ferrari had taken a decisive lead over Alfa Romeo was confirmed at the Nürburgring, where four cars were entered with Taruffi back in the fold. All four finished in the top five while just one Alfa, Fangio's second-placed car, lasted the distance. Using the old-specification engine, Ascari beat Fangio to victory by 30.5sec despite a precautionary stop for rear tyres. Stirling Moss met with Enzo Ferrari at Maranello at this time and discussed driving in Bari

Alberto Ascari, Ferrari 375 (Spanish GP)

José Froilán González, Ferrari 375 (British GP)

and at the Italian GP. Unfortunately, Ferrari preferred Taruffi at Bari and Moss was committed to Jaguar and the RAC Tourist Trophy on the Italian GP weekend.

González won at Pescara and finished second to Fangio in Bari before five Ferraris were entered for the Italian GP at Monza. Three 24-plug 375s for Ascari, Villoresi and González had new bodywork that incorporated the windscreen and headrest plus modified brakes, while Taruffi had an old model. Brazilian Francesco 'Chico' Landi drove the prototype 2.5-litre Ferrari 625 four-cylinder car in practice but for the race switched to a single-ignition 375 that dropped out after one lap when its transmission failed. Ascari and Fangio disputed the lead once more before the Argentinian retired, leaving Ascari and

González to finish 1–2 for Ferrari with Villoresi and Taruffi also placed.

That result left Ascari two points behind Fangio but with fewer scores to drop before the final round on the streets of Barcelona's Pedralbes district. Ascari qualified on pole position as Ferrari attempted to run without pitting. However, Ferrari crucially choose 16in wheels that placed extra strain on the tyres, especially with a heavy fuel load. Taruffi, Villoresi and Ascari all punctured tyres by lap eight and González was in on lap 15. 'This was a gamble by Ferrari,' The Autocar reported, 'that just did not come off.' González switched to 17in wheels at his stop and finished second while Ascari made two more stops before finally changing to the larger wheels. He finished fourth but the title was lost.

Piero Taruffi, Ferrari 375 (Spanish GP)

Chico Landi, Ferrari 625 (Italian GP, practice)

Reg Parnell, Ferrari 375 (French GP)

VANDERVELL PRODUCTS (THINWALL)

Previously a prominent supporter of BRM, industrialist Tony Vandervell acquired an ex-works 12-plug Ferrari 375 (its chassis originally from a type 125) and had it repainted British Racing Green and renamed it the Thinwall Special to promote his bearing company. Second behind Juan Manuel Fangio's Alfa Romeo in the opening heat for the International Trophy at Silverstone, Reg Parnell was leading the final when it was abandoned after six laps due to a flooded track.

Winner of the following week's *Formule Libre* Festival of Britain Trophy at Goodwood and second at Dundrod, Parnell was due to drive for BRM in the French GP so Brian Shawe-Taylor practised the Thinwall 375. However, Shawe-Taylor was dropped when he criticised the brakes and Parnell became available when BRM withdrew. Parnell qualified ninth and drove a fine race into fourth place, limping across the line when the transmission broke on the last lap.

Parnell raced for BRM in the British GP (finishing fifth from the back of the grid) so Peter Whitehead drove Vandervell's car. He switched from Dunlops to Pirellis for the race and finished ninth after losing three minutes in the pits having the brakes adjusted. Parnell was second in the Goodwood Trophy before dominating another *Formule Libre* race against a national field at Winfield in the Scottish Borders.

Parnell was 10th in the final World Championship standings thanks to his points scores at Reims and Silverstone.

Peter Whitehead, Ferrari 375 (British GP)

Rudolf Fischer, Ferrari 212 *(Dutch GP)*

ECURIE ESPADON

Zürich-based restaurateur Rudolf Fischer formed Ecurie Espadon ('Team Swordfish') at the start of 1951. He acquired a normally aspirated 2,562cc Ferrari 212 and ran it in red with a pronounced white vee on the bonnet. The car was very reliable and Fischer finished every F1 race he started, with best results of second at Bordeaux and third at Syracuse and San Remo. He finished the Dutch GP in fourth position when denied another podium by a puncture. In addition to that non-championship success, Fischer started the Swiss and German GPs, finishing sixth at the Nürburgring; he also entered the Italian GP but did not start after crashing in practice. Fischer also entered cars for fellow Swiss amateurs such as Peter Hirt, whose Veritas Meteor retired on the opening lap of the Swiss GP when its fuel pump failed.

PETER WHITEHEAD

The handling of the original short-wheelbase Ferrari 125 had always been unpredictable so Peter Whitehead sold his car at the end of 1950 and bought an ex-works long-wheelbase chassis fitted with a single-overhead-cam, two-stage supercharged engine and swing-axle rear suspension. Early non-championship success included third on the streets of Bordeaux, fourth in the curtailed International Trophy at Silverstone and fifth in Bari, but three World Championship appearances with the car ended in retirement. He suffered light injuries when he crashed out of sixth during the closing stages of the Swiss GP. In the French GP his engine twice blew a head gasket, in practice and on the opening lap, while a similarly brief Italian GP ended with a holed piston.

Peter Hirt, Veritas Meteor *(Prix de Berne, 1950)*

Peter Whitehead, Ferrari 125 (Italian GP)

BRITISH RACING MOTORS (BRM)

BRM's faltering start to F1 continued in 1951 amid poor management, production delays and financial uncertainty. The British Motor Racing Research Trust had been launched by former ERA directors Raymond Mays and Peter Berthon in February 1947 and Mays demonstrated the Mark 1 BRM P15 to the press at Folkingham on 15 December 1949. Test driver Ken Richardson spent the following year pounding around the Lincolnshire airfield but the cars only appeared in late-season non-championship races.

Berthon's high-revving 135-degree V16 engine was an overly complicated, double-overhead-cam unit with a Rolls-Royce-developed centrifugal two-stage supercharger and it drove through a transverse-mounted five-speed gearbox. The car's tubular frame was braced by steel sheet and the suspension used unusual Lucas pneumatic struts and a de Dion rear axle. It was hoped that power would exceed 500bhp, but 330bhp at 10,250rpm was more likely in 1951; drivability was compromised by excessive wheelspin at any speed. Planned fuel injection was abandoned. The car overheated in testing and the resulting large radiator increased drag. BRM raced on Dunlop tyres.

Reg Parnell and 'B. Bira' were announced as drivers on 4 April 1951 but the team's entry for the Swiss GP was cancelled on 16 May following a test at Silverstone. It was not until France that BRM again appeared on an entry list only for Parnell to arrive direct from Le Mans to find an apologetic telegram informing him that the team had scratched once more. There was considerable scepticism when the

Peter Walker, BRM P15 (British GP)

BRMs failed to arrive for British GP practice but two light green cars were delivered at 7am on race morning. Peter Walker replaced 'Bira' in the line-up but the Royal Automobile Club refused Richardson's nomination as reserve due to his lack of racing experience. Instructed not to exceed 10,000rpm, the drivers withstood excessively high cockpit temperatures to climb from the back of the grid and finish in a morale-boosting fifth (Parnell) and seventh (Walker). Both suffered burns but their 'heroism' was celebrated in the British press.

Three days after the race, Stirling Moss tested at Folkingham as BRM tried to woo the young Englishman. Two cars were sent to Monza, where BRM suffered another disappointing weekend. As

Reg Parnell, BRM P15 (British GP)

Ken Richardson, BRM P15 (Italian GP)

Robert Manzon, Simca-Gordini 15 (Spanish GP)

Walker was still recovering from his Silverstone burns, Richardson was entered alongside Parnell. Again the RAC refused the test driver the necessary licence to race, so Hans Stuck tried the BRM on race morning only for the gearbox to fail and render the car a non-starter. Parnell qualified eighth but similar problems with the gearbox's lubrication system meant that he non-started too.

Post-race BRM remained at Monza for prolonged testing. Moss, who had been prematurely announced as the team's star signing for 1952, participated in these tests and endured a frustrating time as repeated failures were diagnosed and fixed. *Motor Sport* reported that BRM was 'in a state of utter dejection and appeared to have blinded themselves with their own science.' The team did not enter the Spanish GP.

EQUIPE GORDINI

Amédée Gordini persevered with his Simca-Gordini 15 during 1951. A new 1,496cc four-cylinder engine featured five bearings and twin overhead camshafts but remained underpowered and unreliable in F1 trim. Robert Manzon and Maurice Trintignant were retained with André Simon added to an expanded three-car line-up.

Trintignant was fifth in Bordeaux after pushing his car over the line following gearbox failure on the last lap. Juan Manuel Fangio made a guest appearance in a Simca-Gordini 15 in the Paris GP in the Bois de Boulogne and both he and Manzon led before all five Simca-Gordinis retired with clutch or valve failures. Simca severed all ties with Gordini and the team withdrew from the Swiss GP. It returned at Reims with Amédée's son Aldo driving a fourth car,

André Simon, Simca-Gordini 15 (Spanish GP)

Maurice Trintignant, Simca-Gordini 15 (Spanish GP)

Aldo Gordini, Simca-Gordini 11 (French GP)

Jean Behra, Simca-Gordini 15 (Italian GP); driven by Maurice Trintignant in practice

an old Simca-Gordini 11. All four retired once more and the team withdrew from the British GP.

Trintignant and Simon blew engines during the German GP but Manzon's smoking Simca-Gordini 15 held together long enough to finish seventh. The Italian teams did not attend the non-championship race at Albi where Trintignant converted pole position into a surprise victory – the first for a supercharged Simca-Gordini. He fell ill after qualifying for the Italian GP so French motorcycle champion Jean Behra started in his place, wearing Trintignant's helmet to disguise the switch. Just one Simca-Gordini finished in Italy and Spain as the engine woes continued: Simon was lapped

six times on the way to sixth at Monza while Manzon was ninth at Pedralbes, seven laps off the pace.

Simca-Gordini did not score points during 1951. A 4.5-litre OSCA V12 engine was acquired by the end of the year but never raced.

HERSHAM & WALTON MOTORS (HWM)

George Abecassis and John Heath formed Hersham & Walton Motors in post-war Surrey and a new F2 car was introduced by the end of February 1951. Rather than the previous offset cars, this was the company's first true single-seater. The 1,960cc twin-cam Alta

George Abecassis, HWM 51-Alta (*Madgwick Cup, Goodwood*)

straight-four engine was retained, with Weber carburettors fitted; SUs were tried but never raced. Heath modified front suspension from an MG TD while designing a new de Dion rear axle with quarter-elliptic springs. The rear of the frame was lowered by a couple of inches, Leacroft of Egham supplied the bodywork and Armstrong Siddeley the four-speed pre-selector gearboxes. The cars were prepared by chief mechanic Alf Francis.

The Swiss GP organisers invited HWM to enter two such cars at Bremgarten with Abecassis – only recently recovered from injuries sustained while testing at Goodwood – and team regular Stirling Moss making their GP débuts. Abecassis retired at half distance while Moss lost seventh to Louis Chiron on the last lap when he ran out of fuel approaching the finishing line.

The 21-year-old Moss enjoyed an impressive campaign during 1951. Winner of the Lavant Cup on the début of the new car at Easter Monday Goodwood, he was third in the non-championship F1 Dutch GP, only losing second on the last lap when a loose magneto wire needed to be fixed. The F2 season ended with Moss leading an HWM 1–2–3 in Goodwood's Madgwick Cup and at Winfield.

ECURIE ROSIER

Antonio Lago closed the works Talbot team in March but these large-capacity machines continued to prove popular among privateers with as many as eight examples on GP grids during 1951. Prime among those to enter Lago-Talbots was Louis Rosier, who acquired an ex-

Stirling Moss, HWM 51-Alta (Swiss GP)

Louis Rosier, Lago-Talbot T26C-DA (Spanish GP)

Louis Chiron, Lago-Talbot T26C (French GP)

works T26C-DA and drove it in all seven GPs, finishing on all but one occasion, each time as the highest-placed Lago-Talbot. His best performance in a championship round came at Spa-Francorchamps where he ran non-stop into fourth place, his only points-scoring result of the year. Six podium finishes in non-championship races included victories on the streets of Bordeaux and in the Dutch GP at Zandvoort.

Ecurie Rosier entered a second car for Henri Louveau at the start of the season but he rolled the original T26C at both Pau and in the Swiss GP. The car hit a telegraph pole at Bremgarten and Louveau suffered concussion and a broken leg, prompting his retirement from motor racing. He was replaced by Louis Chiron from the next GP in Belgium and the Monégasque veteran finished the French GP a distant sixth but retired from his five other championship appearances with the car. Third in the non-championship Albi GP, Chiron was denied that position in Pescara when he lost his brakes and spun at the final chicane.

Henri Louveau, Lago-Talbot T26C (Swiss GP)

ECURIE BELGE

Johnny Claes traded his six-plug Lago-Talbot for an ex-works T26C-DA and again organised a full GP campaign. He crashed into the crowd at San Remo following brake failure during practice and a spectator died from his injuries. Brake failure also caused him to crash out of both the French and Spanish GPs. Seventh in his home race at Spa-Francorchamps despite a misfire was as close as Claes came to scoring points.

Johnny Claes, Lago-Talbot T26C-DA (Spanish GP)

André Pilette, Lago-Talbot T26C (*Dutch GP*)

ECURIE BELGIQUE

Jacques Swaters, André Pilette, Charles de Tornaco and Roger Laurent joined forces and formed Ecurie Belgique to run an ex-Georges Grignard Lago-Talbot T26C in 1951. Pilette recovered from crashing at La Source during practice for the Belgian GP to finish sixth on his championship début. He qualified on the outside of the three-car front row for the non-title Dutch GP at Zandvoort and, having run second for the opening five laps, looked set for third place when a puncture led to his car rolling over, causing injuries that ended his season. His replacement, Swaters, finished 10th in the German GP and retired from the Italian GP when running last. Laurent finished Albi's non-championship race in seventh place.

OTHER LAGO-TALBOT PRIVATEERS

Yves Giraud-Cabantous acquired Raymond Sommer's Lago-Talbot T26C and started six GPs. He finished fifth in Belgium when lapped twice and ran in the top six at the Nürburgring before crashing. During the Spanish GP he hit a dog, an incident that, according to *The Autocar*, 'irretrievably damaged the radiator – and the dog'. He also prepared Guy Mairesse's T26C during 1951 and the road haulage company owner finished both GPs he entered, 14th after changing plugs in Switzerland and ninth in France.

Philippe Étancelin bought the Lago-Talbot T26C-DA he had raced in the 1950 Belgian and French GPs and entered five championship races without troubling the front runners, a distant eighth in Spain

Jacques Swaters, Lago-Talbot T26C (German GP)

Yves Giraud-Cabantous, Lago-Talbot T26C (French GP)

Guy Mairesse, Lago-Talbot T26C (French GP)

Georges Grignard, Lago-Talbot T26C-DA (Spanish GP)

Philippe Étancelin, Lago-Talbot T26C-DA (French GP)

Duncan Hamilton, Lago-Talbot T26C (British GP)

'Pierre Levegh', Lago-Talbot T26C (*Dutch GP*)

José Froilán González, Lago-Talbot T26C-GS (Swiss GP)

Eugène Chaboud, Lago-Talbot T26C-GS (French GP)

his best result when points were on offer. He was a lapped second at Zandvoort despite puncturing a tyre and at Pescara he passed Louis Chiron's brakeless T26C at the last corner to snatch third place. Georges Grignard drove an ex-works T26C-DA in the final race in Spain, where his engine failed.

'Pierre Levegh' raced his T26C in Belgium, Germany and Italy and finished eighth in the first of these. Meanwhile, Duncan Hamilton sold his ex-'B. Bira' ERA B-type ('Remus') and bought Johnny Claes's T26C. Second when torrential rain forced the International Trophy final to be abandoned, he gained an entry when F1 returned to Silverstone for the British GP, in which he stopped for oil and a glass of beer, spun at Stowe and was lapped nine times before finishing 12th. After taking fifth place in the non-championship Dutch GP, his was the only speck of green on the German GP grid. Having changed his broken gearbox casing after practice, Hamilton suffered from fading brakes and an overheating engine before retiring after 12 laps of the Nürburgring.

A couple of two-seater Lago-Talbot T26C-GS sports cars were entered during 1951 with fenders and lights removed. Having beaten a trio of Mercedes-Benz W163s in the Argentine *Temporada* during February with a 2-litre Ferrari 166 entered by the Automóvil Club Argentina, José Froilán González's European season began in his own T26C-GS, with which he finished second in the Paris GP in the Bois de Boulogne. He retired from the following week's Swiss GP when the oil pump failed and then

Harry Schell, Maserati 4CLT/48 (*International Trophy, Silverstone*)

accepted Ferrari's offer to join the *Scuderia* from the French GP. A week after he retired a T26C-GS from the Le Mans 24 Hours, Eugène Chaboud stripped the car of mudguards and ancillaries and finished eighth in the French GP.

SCUDERIA ENRICO PLATÉ

Enrico Platé continued to enter a pair of Maserati CLT/48s at selected races with Harry Schell becoming a regular driver alongside Emmanuel de Graffenried.

The Swiss amateur lost third place at Pau when oil pressure faded

and Schell finished fourth in San Remo. De Graffenried was offered a works Alfa Romeo for the Swiss GP so Louis Chiron deputised and finished seventh. José Froilán González did not take up his entry for the Belgian GP, both Schell and de Graffenried retired in France, and the team missed the British GP.

The single Maserati run for de Graffenried in Germany suffered engine failure. Paul Pietsch had been his intended team-mate at the Nürburgring but instead accepted Alfa Romeo's late offer of a drive in a fourth entry at his home race. Schell finished seventh at Pescara and de Graffenried was ninth in Bari, lapped eight times and last on the team's final appearance of 1951.

Emmanuel de Graffenried, Maserati 4CLT/48 (*San Remo GP*)

Louis Chiron, Maserati 4CLT/48 (Swiss GP)

David Murray, Maserati 4CLT/48 (British GP)

Onofre Marimón, Maserati 4CLT/50-Milano (French GP)

SCUDERIA AMBROSIANA

David Murray hired 'Wilkie' Wilkinson as mechanic and drove a
Maserati 4CLT/48 under the Scuderia Ambrosiana banner in the
British and German GPs, plus selected non-championship races,
the best of which, at Dundrod, yielded sixth place. His engine failed
during the British GP and Murray rolled in practice at the Nürburgring,
writing off the car but escaping serious injury.

SCUDERIA MILANO

The Ruggeri brothers' Scuderia Milano made a couple of World
Championship appearances in 1951 without making an impression.
Juan Manuel Fangio's protégé, Onofre Marimón, lasted just two laps

of the French GP before the Maserati 4CLT/50's Speluzzi engine
failed. Two red-and-yellow Maseratis entered for the Spanish GP in
Barcelona have been listed in many sources as standard 4CLT/48s,
but according to the book *A Record of GP and Voiturette Racing*
Chico Godia's was a 4CLT/50 and Juan Jover's Milano '01'. While
Jover did not start, Godia had an eventful race: he almost collided
with Felice Bonetto's Alfa Romeo at a pitstop, then crashed with
two laps to go but limped on, the car battered and without its
bonnet, to claim 10th place.

Scuderia Milano withdrew at the end of the season. World
Champion Giuseppe Farina drove a Maserati 4CLT/48 in five non-
championship races when his Alfa Romeo commitments allowed,
winning the Paris GP.

Chico Godia, Maserati 4CLT/48 (Spanish GP)

John James, Maserati 4CLT/48 (British GP)

OTHER MASERATI PRIVATEERS

Antonio Branca drove Vicomtesse de Walckiers's ex-works Maserati 4CLT/48 in four F1 races, including the German GP in which his engine failed after three laps. Sixth at Pescara was his best result in non-championship events.

John James acquired a 4CLT/48 from Reg Parnell and entered the British GP, retiring after 23 laps. Parnell had advertised the car in *Autosport* on 3 November 1950, describing it as 'virtually an English production of the 4CLT Maserati' due to its new British-built tubular chassis, bodywork and engine.

Following Joe Fry's death at Blandford hillclimb in July 1950, Duncan Hamilton and Philip Fotheringham-Parker acquired the Maserati 4CL that he had raced in that year's British GP. Fotheringham-Parker drove the four-year-old car in the 1951 British GP, retiring at half distance when an oil pipe fractured. A week later, he beat a 10-car field to win the Scottish GP at Winfield.

Philip Fotheringham-Parker, Maserati 4CL (British GP)

Antonio Branca, Maserati 4CLT/48 (German GP)

Franco Rol, OSCA 4500G (Italian GP)

OFFICINE SPECIALIZZATE COSTRUZIONE AUTOMOBILI (OSCA)

Ernesto, Ettore and Bindo Maserati left the company that bore their name in 1947 and formed Officina Specializzata Costruzione Automobili (OSCA) in San Lazzaro di Saverna in Bologna's south-western suburbs. With the Maserati 4CLT/48 no longer competitive, Ernesto Maserati designed a new 4,472cc unsupercharged V12 engine with two valves per cylinder and the brothers hoped that 4CLT/48 owners would be customers for it. This engine was also installed in the unique OSCA 4500G that Franco Rol drove in the 1951 Italian GP; this car had a new tubular chassis, double wishbones/coil spring front suspension and a de Dion/torsion bar rear end. The V12 engine developed 295bhp at 7,500rpm, compared with the Ferrari 375's 350bhp. A distant ninth at Monza, Rol drove the car in the 1952 Valentino GP in Turin but it was rendered obsolete when F2 rules were adopted for that year's World Championship.

ECURIE SIAM

'B. Bira' took delivery of the first OSCA V12 engine to be built and fitted it into his existing Maserati 4CLT/48. With the car painted in Siamese blue and yellow, 'Bira' won the 12-lap Richmond Trophy on début at Goodwood's Easter Monday meeting and finished fourth in Bordeaux. His engine failed during a *Formule Libre* race at Goodwood and, with no replacement available, he missed most of the World Championship season, only reappearing for the final race in Spain, where the V12 refused to run cleanly and expired after just one lap of the race.

'B. Bira', Maserati 4CLT/48-OSCA (*Richmond Trophy, Goodwood*)

Bob Gerard, ERA B-type (British GP)

ENGLISH RACING AUTOMOBILES (ERA)

Brian Shawe-Taylor bought Cuth Harrison's ERA C-type in April and entered selected British races. He was third in the Ulster Trophy after a mighty scrap with Bob Gerard's B-type, then finished the British GP in eighth position when six laps off the pace. On the second lap of the *Daily Graphic* Trophy at Goodwood in September, he spun at St Mary's and was hit by Antonio Branca's Maserati, which caused the ERA to roll and throw out its driver; although Shawe-Taylor was in a coma for weeks, he made a full recovery but decided not to race again. Gerard qualified 10th for the British GP with his B-type (still fitted with C-type engine) and finished 11th.

Brian Shawe-Taylor, ERA C-type (British GP)

JOE KELLY

Dubliner Joe Kelly returned to Silverstone for the 1951 British GP, where his Alta was the slowest qualifier, a full 35sec adrift of José Froilán González's pole-position time. The Alta misfired from the start and was unclassified after an afternoon at the tail of the field. The contrasting strengths of F1 fields were emphasised by the following week's non-championship Scottish GP at Winfield where Kelly set the fastest race lap before retiring from second position.

Kelly did not enter another World Championship GP but used the Alta chassis as the basis for a new F2 car in 1953. Fitted with a Bristol straight-six engine, his renamed IRA (Irish Racing Automobiles) competed in a couple of lesser F2 races that year without success.

Joe Kelly, Alta GP (British GP)

1951 RESULTS

DRIVER PERFORMANCE (EXCLUDING INDIANAPOLIS 500)

DRIVER	CAR-ENGINE	CH	B	F	GB	D	I	E
George Abecassis	HWM 51-Alta	[20] R	–	–	–	–	–	–
Alberto Ascari	Ferrari 375	[7] 6	[4] 2	[3] **2**	[4] R	[1] **1**	[3] **1**	[1] **4**
Jean Behra	Simca-Gordini 15	–	–	–	–	–	[12] R	–
'B.Bira'	Maserati 4CLT/48-OSCA	–	–	–	–	–	–	[19] R
Felice Bonetto	Alfa Romeo 159	–	–	–	[7] **4**	[10] R	[7] 3	[8] 5
Antonio Branca	Maserati 4CLT/48	–	–	–	–	[17] R	–	–
Eugène Chaboud	Lago-Talbot T26C-GS	–	–	[14] 8	–	–	–	–
Louis Chiron	Maserati 4CLT/48	[19] 7	–	–	–	–	–	–
	Lago-Talbot T26C	–	[9] R	[8] 6	[13] R	[13] R	[17] R	[12] R
Johnny Claes	Lago-Talbot T26C-DA	[18] 13	[11] 7	[12] R	[14] 13	[18] 11	[21] R	[15] R
Emmanuel de Graffenried	Alfa Romeo 159	[5] 5	–	–	–	–	[9] R	[6] 6
	Maserati 4CLT/48	–	–	[16] R	–	[16] R	–	–
Philippe Étancelin	Lago-Talbot T26C-DA	[12] 10	[10] R	[10] R	–	[21] R	–	[13] 8
Luigi Fagioli	Alfa Romeo 159	–	–	[7] 1	–	–	–	–
Juan Manuel Fangio	Alfa Romeo 159	[1] **1** FL	[1] **9** FL	[1] **1** FL	[2] **2**	[3] **2** FL	[1] **R**	[2] **1** FL
Giuseppe Farina	Alfa Romeo 159	[2] **3**	[2] **1**	[2] **5**	[3] R FL	[4] R	[2] 3 FL	[4] 3
Rudolf Fischer	Ferrari 212	[10] 11	–	–	–	[8] 6	[23] DNS	–
Philip Fotheringham-Parker	Maserati 4CL	–	–	–	[16] R	–	–	–
Bob Gerard	ERA B-type	–	–	–	[10] 11	–	–	–
Yves Giraud-Cabantous	Lago-Talbot T26C	[15] R	[8] 5	[11] 7	–	[11] R	[14] 8	[14] R
Chico Godia	Maserati 4CLT/48	–	–	–	–	–	–	[17] 10
José Froilán González	Lago-Talbot T26C-GS	[13] R	–	–	–	–	–	–
	Ferrari 375	–	–	[6] 2	[1] **1**	[2] **3**	[4] 2	[3] 2
Aldo Gordini	Simca-Gordini 11	–	–	[17] R	–	–	–	–
Georges Grignard	Lago-Talbot T26C-DA	–	–	–	–	–	–	[16] R
Duncan Hamilton	Lago-Talbot T26C	–	–	–	[11] 12	[20] R	–	–
Peter Hirt	Veritas Meteor	[16] R	–	–	–	–	–	–
John James	Maserati 4CLT/48	–	–	–	[17] R	–	–	–
Juan Jover	Maserati 4CLT/48	–	–	–	–	–	–	[18] DNS
Joe Kelly	Alta GP	–	–	–	[18] NC	–	–	–
Chico Landi	Ferrari 375	–	–	–	–	–	[16] R	–
'Pierre Levegh'	Lago-Talbot T26C	–	[13] 8	–	–	[19] 9	[20] R	–
Henri Louveau	Lago-Talbot T26C	[11] R	–	–	–	–	–	–
Guy Mairesse	Lago-Talbot T26C	[21] 14	–	[19] 9	–	–	–	–
Robert Manzon	Simca-Gordini 15	–	–	[23] R	–	[9] 7	[13] R	[9] 9
Onofre Marimón	Maserati 4CLT/50-Milano	–	–	[15] R	–	–	–	–
Stirling Moss	HWM 51-Alta	[14] 8	–	–	–	–	–	–
David Murray	Maserati 4CLT/48	–	–	–	[15] R	[23] DNS	–	–
Reg Parnell	Ferrari 375	–	–	[9] 4	–	–	–	–
	BRM P15	–	–	–	[20] 5	–	[8] DNS	–
Paul Pietsch	Alfa Romeo 159	–	–	–	–	[7] R	–	–
André Pilette	Lago-Talbot T26C	–	[12] 6	–	–	–	–	–
Ken Richardson	BRM P15	–	–	–	–	–	[10] DNS	–
Franco Rol	OSCA 4500G	–	–	–	–	–	[18] 9	–

DRIVER PERFORMANCE CONTINUED

DRIVER	CAR-ENGINE	CH	B	F	GB	D	I	E
Louis Rosier	Lago-Talbot T26C-DA	[8] 9	[7] 4	[13] R	[9] 10	[15] 8	[15] 7	[20] 7
Consalvo Sanesi	Alfa Romeo 159	[4] 4	[6] R	[5] 10	[6] 6	—	—	—
Harry Schell	Maserati 4CLT/48	[17] 12	—	[22] R	—	—	—	—
Brian Shawe-Taylor	Ferrari 375	—	—	[NT] DNP	—	—	—	—
	ERA C-type	—	—	—	[12] 8	—	—	—
André Simon	Simca-Gordini 15	—	—	[21] R	—	[12] R	[11] 6	[10] R
Hans Stuck	BRM P15	—	—	—	—	—	[NT] DNS	—
Jacques Swaters	Lago-Talbot T26C	—	—	—	—	[22] 10	[22] R	—
Piero Taruffi	Ferrari 375	[6] 2	[5] R	—	—	[6] 5	[6] 5	[7] R
Maurice Trintignant	Simca-Gordini 15	—	—	[18] R	—	[14] R	[12] DNS	[11] R
Luigi Villoresi	Ferrari 375	[3] R	[3] 3	[4] 3	[5] 3	[5] 4	[5] 4	[5] R
Peter Walker	BRM P15	—	—	—	[19] 7	—	—	—
Peter Whitehead	Ferrari 125	[9] R	—	[20] R	—	—	[19] R	—
	Ferrari 375	—	—	—	[8] 9	—	—	—

SHARED DRIVES French GP: Luigi Fagioli/Juan Manuel Fangio (Alfa Romeo 159) 1; José Froilán González/Alberto Ascari (Ferrari 375) 2; Juan Manuel Fangio/Luigi Fagioli (Alfa Romeo 159) 11. Italian GP: Felice Bonetto/Giuseppe Farina (Alfa Romeo 159) 3.

FORMULA 1 RACE WINNERS

ROUND	RACE (CIRCUIT)	DATE	WINNER
–	Gran Premio di Siracusa (Syracuse)	Mar 11	Luigi Villoresi (Ferrari 375)
–	Richmond Trophy (Goodwood)	Mar 26	'B. Bira' (Maserati 4CLT/48-OSCA)
–	Grand Prix de Pau (Pau)	Mar 26	Luigi Villoresi (Ferrari 375)
–	Gran Premio di San Remo (San Remo)	Apr 22	Alberto Ascari (Ferrari 375)
–	Grand Prix de Bordeaux (Bordeaux)	Apr 29	Louis Rosier (Lago-Talbot T26C-DA)
–	Daily Express International Trophy (Silverstone)	May 5	Reg Parnell (Ferrari 375)
–	Grand Prix de Paris (Bois de Boulogne)	May 20	Giuseppe Farina (Maserati 4CLT/48)
1	**Grand Prix de Suisse (Bremgarten)**	**May 27**	**Juan Manuel Fangio (Alfa Romeo 159)**
2*	**Indianapolis 500 (Indianapolis)**	**May 30**	**Lee Wallard (Kurtis-Offenhauser)**
–	News of the World Ulster Trophy (Dundrod)	Jun 2	Giuseppe Farina (Alfa Romeo 159)
3	**Grand Prix de Belgique (Spa-Francorchamps)**	**Jun 17**	**Giuseppe Farina (Alfa Romeo 159)**
4	**Grand Prix de l'Automobile Club de France et d'Europe (Reims)**	**Jul 1**	**Luigi Fagioli/Juan Manuel Fangio (Alfa Romeo 159)**
5	**British Grand Prix (Silverstone)**	**Jul 14**	**José Froilán González (Ferrari 375)**
–	Scottish Grand Prix (Winfield)	Jul 21	Philip Fotheringham-Parker (Maserati 4CL)
–	Grote Prijs van Nederland (Zandvoort)	Jul 22	Louis Rosier (Lago-Talbot T26C-DA)
6	**Grosser Preis von Deutschland (Nürburgring)**	**Jul 29**	**Alberto Ascari (Ferrari 375)**
–	Grand Prix d'Albi (Albi)	Aug 5	Maurice Trintignant (Simca-Gordini 15)
–	Johore Grand Prix (Johore)	Aug 6	Bill Ferguson (Cooper-JAP)
–	Gran Premio di Pescara (Pescara)	Aug 15	José Froilán González (Ferrari 375)
–	Gran Premio di Bari (Bari)	Sep 2	Juan Manuel Fangio (Alfa Romeo 159)
7	**Gran Premio d'Italia (Monza)**	**Sep 16**	**Alberto Ascari (Ferrari 375)**
–	Goodwood Trophy (Goodwood)	Sep 29	Giuseppe Farina (Alfa Romeo 159)
–	Jubilee Woodside Formula 1 Race (Woodside)	Oct 8	Stan Jones (Maybach Special)
8	**Gran Premio de España (Pedralbes)**	**Oct 28**	**Juan Manuel Fangio (Alfa Romeo 159)**

*Run to AAA National Championship rules

DRIVERS' CHAMPIONSHIP

DRIVERS		POINTS
1	Juan Manuel Fangio	31 (37)*
2	Alberto Ascari	25 (28)*
3	José Froilán González	24 (27)*
4	Giuseppe Farina	19 (22)*
5	Luigi Villoresi	15 (18)*
6	Piero Taruffi	10
7	Lee Wallard	9
8	Felice Bonetto	7
9	Mike Nazaruk	6
10	Reg Parnell	5
11	Luigi Fagioli	4
12=	Andy Linden	3
	Louis Rosier	3
	Consalvo Sanesi	3
15=	Manuel Ayulo	2
	Bobby Ball	2
	Yves Giraud Cabantous	2
	Emmanuel de Graffenried	2
	Jack McGrath	2

*Best four results count

The all-conquering Ferrari 500s of Alberto Ascari and Giuseppe Farina lead Gordini's Robert Manzon and Jean Behra on the opening lap at Rouen

1952

F2 RULES SEE ASCARI AND FERRARI DOMINATE

World Champion Alberto Ascari moments after winning the French GP

Mechanics work on Paul Frère's HWM at the Nürburgring

Alfa Romeo confirmed that it was concentrating on sports car racing in March 1952 and Gordini withdrew rather than continue supercharging its cars, so just Ferrari and BRM remained as active F1 constructors.

In January, the French authorities dropped F1 in favour of F2 for its new (and ultimately one-off) eight-race Grands Prix de France championship, which offered 60 million Francs in prize money. F2 rules stipulated 2-litre normally aspirated or 500cc blown engines. Other European organisers wavered until the opening non-championship F1 race of the year in Turin's Valentino Park. BRM was testing at Monza at that time but, rather than enter, it sent its V16 cars back to Folkingham for Juan Manuel Fangio and José Froilán González to try. As Stirling Moss later wrote, 'the BRM management were clearly star-struck by the interest shown by these two experienced drivers…'

Ferraris finished 1–2–3–4 in Turin and the result of BRM's no-show was immediate. Remaining GP promotors switched to F2 and the FIA announced that the smaller category would decide the next two World Champions. BRM had effectively rendered its own V16 project obsolete.

Photographers take close-ups of Luigi Villoresi's third-placed Ferrari 500 during the Italian GP

The Automobile Club de Monaco switched to sports cars and the GP was marred by the fatal injuries sustained by veteran Luigi Fagioli. There was rumour of a race in New York City – surely motor racing's most persistent non-event – and when the World Championship calendar was published by the FIA in October 1951 it included the Rio de Janeiro GP on 14 December. That would have been on the tortuous Gávea road course but the race was downgraded to a minor national meeting when it went ahead on that date. Rouen-les-Essarts held the French GP for the first time and the challenging venue boasted an impressive double-tier pit complex and three-storey timing and press building. The British GP was organised by Silverstone's new leaseholders, the British Racing Drivers' Club, with the *Daily Express* newspaper. The circuit had been renovated with start-line and new brick pits moved to the straight between Woodcote and Copse. *Motor Sport* gave 'full praise for the proper lavatory accommodation'. The championship finale in Barcelona (26 October) was cancelled with six weeks' notice. The Italian GP organisers upset many by inviting 36 entries but only allowing the fastest 24 to start.

Second-placed Piero Taruffi and Tony Vandervell at the British GP

Alberto Ascari, Ferrari 500 (French GP)

Giuseppe Farina, Ferrari 500 (Belgian GP)

SCUDERIA FERRARI

Ferrari was the pre-season favourite irrespective of which rules were chosen. Simplicity and speed were key to Aurelio Lampredi's Ferrari 500 when Alberto Ascari lapped the field on its début at Modena on 23 September 1951 and he would dominate the championship's F2 era.

The uncomplicated 1,984cc monobloc straight-four engine had two valves per cylinder and double overhead camshafts. With impressive low-speed torque and developing 165bhp at 7,200rpm in 1952, it featured fewer parts than the 166/F2/50's V12, bringing reduced weight and improved reliability. The engine was mounted well back, immediately ahead of the driver, to optimise weight distribution, with the four-speed gearbox attached to the final-drive casing. The lightweight tubular chassis and suspension layout were retained from the Ferrari 375. Four single-choke Weber carburettors replaced the original twin-choke units and the radiator was revised for 1952.

Ascari remained in a three-car team, although he would miss the Swiss GP while qualifying a modified Ferrari 375 for the Indianapolis 500. Giuseppe Farina signed at the start of January and Piero Taruffi was confirmed by the end of the month. Long-term Ferrari associate Nello Ugolini replaced Federico Giberti as team manager.

Luigi Villoresi, Ferrari 500 (Italian GP)

Pre-season form was ominous with Ascari leading a Scuderia Ferrari 1–2–3 in Syracuse before lapping the field time and again at Pau and Marseille, where Farina crashed out of the lead. Luigi Villoresi was part of the team at the start of the season but was injured in a road accident returning from Marseille. Ferrari missed the International Trophy to race in Naples, where Farina beat Taruffi when five laps clear of another local field.

With Ascari in America and Villoresi convalescing, André Simon was the late choice to join Farina and Taruffi for the Swiss GP. Farina qualified on pole, led until his magneto failed and suffered an identical failure when he took over Simon's car. So Taruffi won the opening championship round by almost a lap and repeated that success in a French championship race at Montlhéry. Ascari retired from the Indy 500 when his right rear wheel collapsed when running eighth. Ferrari wanted to enter 1950 Indy 500 winner Johnnie Parsons in the British, Italian and Spanish GPs, so he travelled to Maranello but could not agree terms.

Farina and Simon finished 1–2 in the non-championship Monza GP and Ascari, Farina and Taruffi locked out the Belgian GP front row only for Jean Behra's Gordini to take a shock lead on the opening lap. Ascari and Farina soon passed the Frenchman and eased to a 1–2 victory in heavy rain, 27 years after Antonio Ascari – Alberto's father – had won the race. The perfect result was denied

when the slow-starting Taruffi crashed into Behra at Malmedy while disputing third.

Behra scored a surprise victory at Reims so, according to *Autosport*, 'Ugolini and Lampredi immediately went in search of the missing rpm', with Ascari and Farina driving modified cars at the following week's French GP. Two Marelli magnetos originally placed to the rear of the cylinder head were prone to overheating so these were replaced by a single unit in front of the engine, which as a consequence could be moved three inches further

Piero Taruffi, Ferrari 500 (British GP)

André Simon, Ferrari 500 (Italian GP)

back. With Taruffi preferred to the recovered Villoresi in an old-specification car, Ferraris filled the three-car front row and Ascari led a dominant 1–2–3. Villoresi won a minor race at Les Sables d'Olonne, where Ascari and Farina crashed into Harry Schell's Maserati-Platé in a five-car pile-up.

New cars were readied for the British GP, where Ascari lapped second-placed Taruffi and Farina finished sixth after losing three minutes to change plugs. Ascari lost the lead at the Nürburgring with two laps to go when he pitted because oil had leaked into the cockpit and the engine needed replenishment; 19 seconds behind Farina when he resumed, he retook the lead by the end of the penultimate lap to score his third successive German GP victory. Farina was second but Taruffi lost third when his car's de Dion tube

broke on the last lap. He waited for Ascari to take the chequered flag before limping across the line in fourth place.

Ascari retired from the French championship Comminges GP so took over Simon's car to lead Farina in yet another 1–2 and he won the final such race at La Baule. Ascari, Farina and Villoresi lapped the field at least twice in Holland, where Ascari's fifth successive GP victory was enough to clinch the World Championship with a race to spare and despite missing the opening GP.

Five works Ferrari 500s were entered for the final championship race at Monza. Starting from pole position as normal, the non-stopping Ascari eased to victory once José Froilán González's Maserati refuelled. Villoresi and Farina finished third and fourth, Simon sixth and Taruffi a delayed seventh. Ferrari's successful season ended with its local non-championship race in Modena: González threatened a rare Maserati victory but Villoresi snatched victory when the Argentinian was baulked while lapping Piero Carini on the penultimate lap.

The dominant Ascari won all six GPs he entered and claimed both the World Championship and the French title with Farina runner-up in both.

ECURIE ESPADON

Ecurie Espadon team owner Rudolf Fischer acquired a Ferrari 500 and fitted his existing Ferrari 212 with a 2-litre V12 from the type 166/F2/50. Some customers criticised Ferrari for imposing a lower rev limit than the works machines, but Fischer enjoyed

Rudolf Fischer/Peter Hirt, Ferrari 212 (French GP)

an exceptional privateer season with his type 500. Fourth at Syracuse (having led at the start) and in the International Trophy at Silverstone, he finished the Swiss GP in a fine second position after running non-stop. He beat Stirling Moss's HWM in the following week's Eifelrennen and was third on aggregate in another non-championship race at Monza in June.

Despite that success, Ecurie Espadon was not invited to enter the Belgian GP and Fischer blew his engine practising in France, so the 500 did not start. Strangely off the pace at the British GP, Fischer raced among the works cars in Germany and passed Piero Taruffi's ailing 500 to claim third in what *Autosport* described as the 'race of his life'. Espadon missed the Dutch GP and Fischer retired from the final round at Monza. He was fifth at Modena and won the wet Avusrennen with ease.

Peter Hirt began the year in the Ferrari 212 and finished seventh in Switzerland when lapped six times. With the Ferrari 500 a non-starter in France, Fischer started in the 212 and at half distance handed it to Hirt, who finished 11th after spinning and stalling the engine. Hirt's brakes failed during the British GP and he was replaced for the German GP by 50-year-old Rudolf Schoeller, who retired. Hans Stuck drove the Ferrari 212 at Monza but could not qualify when slowest of those to record a time. The pre-war GP winner then finished ninth at Modena and fifth at Avus.

Fischer's two podium finishes were rewarded with joint fourth place in the World Championship, so it was a surprise when he sold Ecurie Espadon to Schoeller at the end of the season and retired from racing.

Peter Hirt, Ferrari 212 (Swiss GP)

Rudolf Schoeller, Ferrari 212 (German GP)

Rudolf Fischer, Ferrari 500 (Italian GP)

Louis Rosier, Ferrari 500 (French GP)

ECURIE ROSIER

French champion for the previous four years, Louis Rosier ordered a pair of Ferrari 500s in November but suffered a frustrating campaign. A distant second in Pau, he retired from the opening three World Championship rounds, the Swiss GP bringing a narrow escape from being run over when he was thrown into the road during an accident on lap three. Rosier missed the next three GPs and success was confined to third-place finishes at Caen and La Baule. He returned to the World Championship in Italy where the blue car was lapped five times on the way to 10th place. Rosier beat a national field at Cadours to win his final race of 1952.

The second Ferrari 500 was not ready for the start of the season so Maurice Trintignant, who signed in February, drove an old Ferrari 166/F2/50; it did not start the Swiss GP due to engine problems. Tired of waiting for his new car to arrive, he returned to Gordini for his next championship appearance.

ECURIE FRANCORCHAMPS

Garage owner Jacques Swaters renamed Ecurie Belgique as Ecurie Francorchamps for 1952. He acquired a Ferrari 500 that was finished in Belgian yellow when it was completed on 31 May and delivered direct to Chimay, where Roger Laurent crashed into Johnny Claes on the opening lap of the non-championship GP des

Charles de Tornaco, Ferrari 500 (Italian GP)

Roger Laurent, Ferrari 500 (German GP)

Gianfranco Comotti, Ferrari 166/F2/50 (French GP)

Frontières. Charles de Tornaco retired from the Monza Autodrome GP before passing Claes's Simca-Gordini in the closing stages at Spa-Francorchamps to claim seventh. Laurent was sixth when lapped twice in Germany. De Tornaco then retired from the Dutch GP and did not qualify at Monza.

SCUDERIA MARZOTTO

The Marzotto family was among the richest in Italy thanks to its Valdagno-based textile company. The four brothers were successful

amateur sports car drivers with Giannino a two-time Mille Miglia winner. His Ferrari 166/F2/50 had won the 1951 Rouen GP on a rare single-seater appearance and they continued to enter these cars in selected F2 races during 1952. Gianfranco Comotti finished third in Naples and two cars were sent to Rouen-les-Essarts for the French GP. Piero Carini's Ferrari 125 chassis was powered by a 166/F2/50 engine that blew a gasket after two laps while Comotti finished 12th and last. A single entry was accepted for the German GP at the Nürburgring, where Carini's 166/F2/50 brakes failed after a single lap.

Piero Carini, Ferrari 166/F2/50 (German GP)

Roy Salvadori, Ferrari 500 (British GP)

BOBBY BAIRD/G. CAPRARA

The son of the *Belfast Telegraph* newspaper proprietor, Bobby Baird acquired a green Ferrari 500 and finished fourth in his heat for the International Trophy. For the British GP he entered Roy Salvadori, who qualified the unfamiliar car 19th and finished a creditable eighth. Salvadori won the late-season Joe Fry Memorial Trophy at Castle Combe.

EQUIPE GORDINI

With its association at an end, the last Simca parts (the coil-spring front suspension) were discarded in the new Gordini 16. Amédée Gordini denied rumours that his cash-strapped company was closing in November 1951 and confirmed that he had abandoned supercharging, so this was a 2-litre unblown double-overhead-cam F2 design. A three-car team was entered in both the World Championship and Grands Prix de France series.

The type 16 had a light and simple steel tubular frame, 1,989cc straight-six monobloc engine with two valves per cylinder, three twin-choke Weber carburettors and five-speed synchromesh gearbox. The independent front suspension was by torsion bars and double wishbones while a rigid rear axle was retained. The water and oil radiators were mounted in the nose. The Gordini 16 was second only to Ferrari on sheer speed but reliability continued to be suspect, with the transmission a particular weakness. André Simon was originally announced alongside Robert Manzon and Jean Behra,

so 'B. Bira' was a surprise third driver when the French GP entries were published in April.

Having qualified on the front row for the type 16's début at Marseille, Manzon won his heat at the International Trophy only for the transmission to fail in the final. The second type 16 was completed on the Thursday before the Swiss GP and Behra drove it from Gordini's Paris workshops to Berne on the open road. He finished third despite a couple of stops to replace a broken exhaust. Manzon harried the Ferraris at the start before losing a water pipe while 'Bira' also retired an old 1.5-litre Simca-Gordini 15. Manzon started the Paris GP from pole position but lost victory to another transmission failure. Behra won at Aix-les-Bains.

Robert Manzon, Gordini 16 (Italian GP)

Jean Behra, Gordini 16 (Belgian GP)

'B. Bira', Gordini 16 (French GP)

Behra shocked the Ferraris by leading the opening lap of the Belgian GP. Passed by both Alberto Ascari and Giuseppe Farina on lap two, he survived a spin at La Source to challenge Piero Taruffi's Ferrari for third before they crashed into each other at Malmedy. Manzon qualified fourth and recovered from a slow start to inherit a third-place finish. Johnny Claes had lent his private car to a mysterious American so drove the factory's ill-handling Gordini 16S sports car into eighth place; 'Bira' finished 10th despite spinning his elderly car in the Ardennes rain.

The following week's non-championship event at Reims provided the highlight of Gordini's racing history for Behra soundly beat a high-quality field that included three works Ferraris; 'Bira'

was fourth on his first appearance with his own type 16. Behra's Reims success proved a glorious one-off as the French GP saw Manzon, who had injured his arm during the sports car race at Reims, finish fourth behind three Ferraris. Behra spun into a ditch when running fourth during the early stages but recovered from a lengthy pitstop to snatch seventh. Maurice Trintignant's Simca-Gordini 15 claimed fifth while 'Bira' retired after persistent gear-selection difficulties.

Behra broke his shoulder practising at Les Sables d'Olonne so Trintignant deputised for the next two GPs. Manzon qualified on the four-car front row at Silverstone and both he and Trintignant split the Ferraris during practice at the Nürburgring, although they

Maurice Trintignant, Gordini 16 (Italian GP)

'B. Bira', Simca-Gordini 15 (Belgian GP)

Maurice Trintignant, Simca-Gordini 15 (French GP)

Paul Frère, Simca-Gordini 15 (Dutch GP)

Johnny Claes, Gordini 16S (Belgian GP)

retired on both occasions. 'Bira' was 11th in Britain before quitting the team. Trintignant led a Gordini 1–2 at Caen against a limited field with the not fully fit Behra second on his return. Behra was fifth in Germany and third at St Gaudens, where Manzon retired from the lead. Manzon and Trintignant finished the Dutch GP fifth and sixth but the gearbox on Paul Frère's Simca-Gordini 15 failed. The three works Gordinis ran in the top five during the early laps of the Italian GP before inevitable gremlins, although Manzon's car was still circulating slowly on five cylinders at the finish.

Amédée Gordini was awarded the *Légion d'Honneur* in August. The season finished badly for Behra as he suffered serious head and chest injuries during the Carrera Panamericana when his Gordini crashed into a ravine following a puncture.

Johnny Claes, Simca-Gordini 15 (British GP)

ECURIE BELGE

Winner of the 1951 GP des Frontières with a Simca-Gordini 11, Johnny Claes acquired Antonio Branca's newer type 15 chassis and 1.5-litre engine from Vicomtesse de Walckiers and entered it under his Ecurie Belge moniker. Having lent the yellow car to Robert O'Brien for the Belgian GP, Claes retired in France and finished 15th at Silverstone. Third at Les Sables d'Olonne, he did not qualify for the Italian GP.

SIMCA-GORDINI PRIVATEERS

Max de Terra retired Alfred Dattner's old Simca-Gordini 11 after just a lap of the Swiss GP. Unknown American Robert O'Brien hired Johnny Claes's 1.5-litre Simca-Gordini 15 for the Belgian GP, his first race in Europe. A full 83sec off pole, O'Brien was lapped six times on his way to 14th at the finish.

Max de Terra, Simca-Gordini 11 (Swiss GP)

OFFICINE ALFIERI MASERATI

Fresh capital led Adolfo Orsi to build the new F2 Maserati A6GCM and enter a three-car works team in 1952. However, an accident at Monza threw his plans into disarray.

Alberto Massimino and Vittorio Bellentani based the 1,988cc double-overhead-cam straight-six engine on Ernesto Maserati's final sports car design for the company. Developing 160bhp, it was offset to the left in a conventional twin-tube chassis and featured three twin-choke Weber carburettors with single-plug-per-cylinder

Robert O'Brien, Simca-Gordini 15 (Belgian GP)

José Froilán González, Maserati A6GCM (Italian GP)

ignition and a Marelli magneto. The independent front suspension had rubber blocks, double wishbones and coil springs while the rigid rear axle and quarter-elliptic springs/radius rods from the 4CLT were retained. Former Ferrari engineer Valerio Colotti was responsible for the constant-mesh four-speed gearbox. The A6GCM was shorter and wider than its predecessor but the pretty bodywork followed Maserati lines.

Maserati celebrated a coup when Juan Manuel Fangio signed following Alfa Romeo's withdrawal. José Froilán González was tempted away from Ferrari and Felice Bonetto drove the third car. Nello Pagani raced a singleton A6GCM in the Argentine

Temporada races in March but it was clear that development was required. Maserati withdrew from the Swiss GP and it was the non-championship Monza Autodrome GP on 8 June before the cars were deemed ready. Fangio had raced a BRM in the previous day's Ulster Trophy and his connecting flight from Paris to Milan was cancelled due to fog. He borrowed Louis Rosier's road car and drove through the night, arriving at Monza just two hours before the start. Perhaps overcome by fatigue, Fangio crashed at Lesmo and was thrown clear when the car rolled. He suffered a broken neck and concussion and did not race again that year. Having led at the start, Bonetto pushed his car across the line to claim seventh after the fuel pump failed.

Felice Bonetto, Maserati A6GCM (Italian GP)

Franco Rol, Maserati A6GCM (Italian GP); driven by José Froilán González in practice

Fangio was in a Rome hospital for two months and the works team withdrew until a lone A6GCM, complete with revised exhausts and carburation, was sent to the German GP for Bonetto. Initially fourth, he spun in front of the pack on the opening lap, changed a punctured rear tyre and was disqualified for a push start.

Massimino modified the A6GCM's engine for the Italian GP with a second magneto and twin-plug ignition helping generate another 10bhp. Anti-roll bars were now fitted front and rear. Suddenly competitive, González light-fuelled and led the opening 36 laps before pitting. He charged back to finish second, 61.8sec behind Alberto Ascari's winning Ferrari. Bonetto was fifth but the engine in Franco Rol's third car failed. In the following week's non-title race at Modena, González passed Luigi Villoresi for the lead with nine laps to go but lost victory when held up lapping Piero Carini's HWM on the penultimate lap. González's successive second-place finishes confirmed Maserati's late-season improvement and he was ninth in the World Championship.

ESCUDERIA BANDEIRANTES

Uruguayan Eitel Cantoni formed Escuderia Bandeirantes in 1952 and ordered a couple of Maserati A6GCMs, with a third car delivered in August. The light brown livery did not impress the British press, with *Motor Sport* noting that the cars were 'painted in a very odd colour' and *Autosport* describing it as a 'rather dingy buff'.

The first cars were ready for June's non-championship race at Monza where Brazilians Francesco 'Chico' Landi and 'Gino

'Gino Bianco', Maserati A6GCM (Italian GP)

Eitel Cantoni, Maserati A6GCM (Italian GP)

Philippe Étancelin, Maserati A6GCM (French GP)

Chico Landi, Maserati A6GCM (Italian GP)

Bianco' (an Italian émigré whose real name was Luigi Bertetti) failed to impress. A single entry was accepted for the French GP on the proviso that local hero Philippe Étancelin drove. Awarded with the *Légion d'Honneur* by Secretary of State Jean Manson before the start, Étancelin was eighth on his final GP appearance despite poor

acceleration and four spins in the rain.

'Bianco' raced in the last four GPs of the season, 18th at Silverstone and a non-finisher thereafter. Cantoni himself made three GP starts from mid-season and was 11th in Italy after pushing his car across the line when it ran out of fuel. Landi drove the third car at Zandvoort and Monza and finished in the top 10 on both occasions. At Zandvoort, Cantoni gave his car to Dutch 500cc F3 driver Jan Flinterman, who retired early but maintained local interest when he took over Landi's car to finish ninth despite losing 46sec changing a broken rear wheel.

SCUDERIA ENRICO PLATÉ

Enrico Platé planned to acquire at least one new Maserati A6GCM but the manufacturer could not confirm its delivery date so he rebuilt his existing 4CLT/48s as normally aspirated 2-litre F2 cars, using a new cylinder block, camshaft, con rods and pistons, and twin Weber carburettors as well as a new radiator. The tubular chassis was lightened and the wheelbase was reduced by 7in. Renamed Maserati-Platés, the cars were lighter than the Ferrari 500 but only developed 140bhp at 7,000rpm.

Emmanuel de Graffenried was confirmed in February with Louis Chiron his team-mate for the opening non-championship race in Syracuse. During practice Chiron was burned when his car caught fire, his injuries exacerbated by his nylon overalls, and he was unable to race for the rest of the year. Nello Pagani and Franco Cortese joined the team for early Grands Prix de France events

Jan Flinterman, Maserati A6GCM (Dutch GP)

Emmanuel de Graffenried, Maserati-Platé (British GP)

at Pau and Marseille, where de Graffenried finished sixth and fourth respectively, before Harry Schell returned to the fold for the International Trophy, which brought third place for de Graffenried while Schell retired from the final having briefly held eighth.

Schell cut his face when his engine seized during the Swiss GP while de Graffenried finished sixth. At Aix-les-Bains they were third (de Graffenried) and fourth (Schell), but did not receive an entry for the Belgian GP. Schell's gearbox broke after seven laps in France so he took over de Graffenried's car, which suffered brake failure (a particular Achilles' heel of the Maserati-Platé) at half distance. With just six days before the British GP and both battered cars requiring repairs, the team started from the back after missing practice and ran among the tail enders throughout. After that Schell quit.

De Graffenried was fifth at St Gaudens in a singleton entry before being joined by Alberto Crespo for the final French round at La Baule. Sixth that day, Crespo was the quicker driver during practice for the Italian GP but neither qualified. Scuderia Platé's final race of 1952 was at Cadours, where de Graffenried finished third and Crespo retired.

ECURIE RICHMOND

Jimmy Richmond's independent team was the first to order a pair of new F2 Cooper T20-Bristols. Charles and John Cooper, along with designer Owen Maddock, chose a simple front-engine layout with its box-section chassis stiffened by a tubular frame. The T20 (or Mark 1) had the BMW 328-based 1,971cc six-cylinder power

Harry Schell, Maserati-Platé (British GP)

Alan Brown, Cooper T20-Bristol (British GP)

Eric Brandon, Cooper T20-Bristol (Belgian GP)

The pale green T20s were assembled at Cooper's Hollyfield Road, Surbiton works by mechanics Ginger Devlin and Bernie Rodger in time for Alan Brown and Eric Brandon to race at Goodwood on Easter Monday. They finished second and third in the Lavant Cup to complete a Cooper-Bristol 1–2–3 behind Mike Hawthorn. Both were classified in the opening two GPs of the season with Brown fifth in Switzerland and sixth at Spa-Francorchamps. Slipping fan belts and other maladies ruined their British GP but Brown's was the second F2 car to finish the *Daily Mail* Trophy at Boreham. They missed the German and Dutch GPs and finished outside the top 10 at Monza following another troubled run.

LESLIE HAWTHORN

Mike Hawthorn graduated to F2 in 1952 after just one full racing season. The 23-year-old tested a Connaught and HWM before family friend Bob Chase bought him a Cooper T20-Bristol that was run by his father Leslie Hawthorn and mechanic Brit Pearce from the family's Tourist Trophy Garage in Farnham. Its engine was converted to use nitromethane fuel additive, which gave it a distinct edge over other Cooper-Bristols.

Hawthorn made his début in the unpainted T20 at Goodwood's Easter Monday meeting and shocked the establishment by winning F2 and *Formule Libre* races, and finishing second in the F1 Richmond Trophy. Winner at Ibsley and second in the F1 Ulster Trophy (driving Archie Bryde's prototype T20),

unit and four-speed gearbox from the Bristol 401 saloon. The radiator arrangement for water and oil was reminiscent of a 1951 Ferrari with bonnet-mounted intake directing air to three Solex carburettors. A pair of side fuel tanks supplemented another in the tail, increasing capacity to 28 gallons. Suspension followed standard Cooper thinking with transverse leaf springs, wishbones and hydraulic dampers. Dunlop tyres were normally fitted. The car was underpowered (130bhp at 5,800rpm) but fuel consumption and road-holding were excellent.

Mike Hawthorn, Cooper T20-Bristol (Belgian GP)

Ken Wharton, Cooper T20-Bristol (Italian GP)

Hawthorn's now dark green T20 won a heat for the International Trophy and led the final before the gear lever broke. Hawthorn made an impressive continental début when fourth in the Belgian GP despite a couple of unscheduled fuel stops due to a leaking tank. While his car was repaired, he borrowed Bryde's T20 for the next two French races, finishing seventh at Reims but retiring from the French GP at Rouen-les-Essarts having run fifth.

Back in Chase's car for the British GP, Hawthorn finished third despite trying not to over-stress the engine. He missed the German GP in favour of an F1 race at Boreham, where he finished third after leading during a rain shower. His impressive rookie campaign continued at Zandvoort, where he qualified on the outside of the three-car front row and finished fourth behind the dominant Ferraris. He was unclassified in the Monza finale after losing an hour having a faulty distributor drive changed.

Ferrari team manager Nello Ugolini was among the impressed onlookers and invited Britain's new star to try a Ferrari 500 during practice for the following week's non-championship race in Modena. Hawthorn transferred to his Cooper-Bristol for comparison and promptly rolled when he tried to match the Ferrari's braking point, pulling himself in hospital with a compressed lung and light concussion. Roy Salvadori drove the Cooper-Bristol in the race but he too crashed.

Mike Hawthorn scored points in three of his five GP starts and the impressive newcomer was fourth equal in the final standings.

ECURIE ECOSSE

David Murray, Ian Stewart, Sir James Scott-Douglas and Bill Dobson formed Ecurie Ecosse in 1952 to field Jaguar XK120s. As Murray's wife demanded he stopped driving following his Nürburgring injuries in 1951, he managed the operation with Merchiston Motors partner 'Wilkie' Wilkinson responsible for preparation. Ecurie Ecosse also acquired a Cooper T20-Bristol that was delivered in July and painted in the team's navy blue colours with white cross of St Andrew on the radiator. Murray defied his wife's wishes to début the car in the British GP where a change of spark plugs failed to cure a chronic misfire. Ken Wharton then qualified midfield for the Italian GP and finished ninth.

David Murray, Cooper T20-Bristol (British GP)

Reg Parnell, Cooper T20-Bristol (British GP)

A.H.M. BRYDE

Archie Bryde acquired the original Cooper T20-Bristol and lent it to the Hawthorns for a few races, including the French GP. Reg Parnell drove the car a fortnight later in the British GP, qualifying sixth and finishing seventh, three laps behind the unbeatable Ferraris.

Ken Wharton, Frazer Nash FN48-Bristol (Belgian GP)

FRAZER NASH (SCUDERIA FRANERA AND T.A.D. CROOK)

Frazer Nash of London Road, Isleworth offered an F2 variant of its successful Le Mans Replica sports car in 1952. This shared the same 4in diameter ladder-frame chassis as the sports car with three tubular cross members. The independent front suspension had lower wishbones and transverse leaf springs while the car's live rear axle was fixed by an 'A' locating bracket and longitudinal torsion bars. George Gray of Emsworth fabricated its unattractive aluminium bodywork, which had a bonnet-mounted air intake for the three Solex carburettors that fed its Bristol six-cylinder engine. The old-fashioned rear suspension compromised handling and performance was disappointing because the car was heavier than the similarly powered Cooper T20.

Peter Bell, Ken Wharton's backer, ordered a Frazer Nash FN48-Bristol and planned to run his ERA B-type in hillclimbs, these two choices of machinery giving rise to the team's name, Scuderia Franera. Wharton finished seventh on his début in the International Trophy in what *Motor Sport* termed 'the ugly monoposto, yellow-wheeled, dark green Frazer Nash'. He then survived a race of attrition and the Swiss rain to claim a surprise fourth in the opening World Championship race at Bremgarten. Third in the Eifelrennen, Wharton lost his shirt and suffered lacerations to his back when he crashed through a barbed wire fence during the Belgian GP, only avoiding a worse outcome because he ducked. He was sidelined until the Dutch GP, where he qualified seventh and ran among the backmarkers before the rear axle seized with three laps to go.

Tony Crook, Frazer Nash LMR-BMW (British GP)

Having driven Ecurie Ecosse's Cooper-Bristol at Monza, Wharton took the Frazer Nash to second place in the Joe Fry Memorial Trophy at Castle Combe.

Tony Crook was one of those to enter a stripped Frazer Nash Le Mans Replica sports car in F2 events during 1952. He finished 17th in the International Trophy before being accepted for the British GP after three cars withdrew. He qualified 25th and was lapped 10 times on his way to 21st place.

HERSHAM & WALTON MOTORS (HWM)

Bolstered by F2 success in 1951, HWM undertook an ambitious continental campaign that included entering at least three cars in all seven World Championship GPs. Stirling Moss moved to ERA although he did begin 1952 with HWM while his new car was being completed. Lance Macklin was promoted to team leader and promising F3 driver Peter Collins signed after arriving uninvited at a March test at Lindley (later the Motor Industry Research Association test track). Yves Giraud-Cabantous concentrated on the French championship and a series of drivers shared the third, and sometimes, fourth HWM.

Designed by Eugene Dunn, HWM's new car was introduced at the start of the year. It featured a triangulated steel tubular frame that proprietor John Heath claimed was a third lighter but also stiffer than its predecessor. The rear brake drums were moved inboard, rear bodywork revised, and the new ZF differential and de Dion rear axle were suspended by torsion bars. Engineer Robin Jackson modified

Stirling Moss, HWM 52-Alta (Swiss GP)

Lance Macklin, HWM 52-Alta (French GP)

Paul Frère, HWM 51/52-Alta (Belgian GP)

Peter Collins, HWM 52-Alta (British GP)

Yves Giraud-Cabantous, HWM 52-Alta (French GP)

George Abecassis, HWM 52-Alta (Swiss GP)

Johnny Claes, HWM 52-Alta (German GP)

Duncan Hamilton, HWM 51/52-Alta (British GP)

the Alta twin-overhead-camshaft engine with a new cylinder head, Laystall crankshafts and con rods, boosting power to 140bhp. The main tank in the tail and smaller panniers either side of the cockpit carried 31 gallons of fuel while the oil tank was beneath the driver's seat. Two twin-choke Weber carburettors and Armstrong Siddeley four-speed gearbox were retained. However, budget was limited and HWM's exhausting schedule took its toll on reliability, especially as respected chief mechanic Alf Francis left before the season.

Macklin scored the biggest victory of his career by leading Tony Rolt's upgraded 1951 car in an HWM 1–2 at Silverstone's International Trophy after quicker cars encountered mechanical problems in the final. Moss and George Abecassis completed the four-car line-up for the Swiss GP, where Collins and Abecassis (running fifth) crashed simultaneously when rear wheels fell off following transmission failure, Abecassis lucky to escape injury when thrown clear; Moss ran third in the early laps but both he and Macklin were withdrawn as a precaution. Second at Aix-les-Bains, Macklin was 11th in the wet Belgian GP following a spin while Collins retired early. Moss was second in the Eifelrennen despite his fire extinguisher going off in the cockpit. Collins narrowly beat Jean Behra's Gordini into sixth in the French GP, his gearbox breaking as he crossed the finishing line. Macklin and Giraud-Cabantous, making his only World Championship appearance of 1952, also finished in the top 10 on a rare day when all the HWMs completed the course.

After a much-delayed second place at Les Sables d'Olonne, Collins found his British GP ruined by a misfire but Macklin finished 13th. Johnny Claes replaced Macklin for the German GP and finished 10th

Roger Laurent, HWM 52-Alta (Belgian GP)

Dries van der Lof, HWM 52-Alta (Dutch GP)

despite a broken rear-axle bearing. The organisers refused to allow Collins to start as did not complete enough practice laps following crankshaft failure. HWM had arrived late at the Nürburgring and *Motor Sport* noted that 'it was obvious that John Heath was trying to do too much with insufficient equipment; cars and mechanics were all sadly in need of a slight break from working virtually non-stop since the beginning of the season.' Macklin was eighth in Holland but neither he nor Collins qualified for the Italian GP at Monza.

Paul Frère's 1951 works car snatched victory on the last lap of the GP des Frontières at Chimay and the Belgian journalist was Walton's leading contender at Spa-Francorchamps, finishing fifth to score HWM's only points of the season. Roger Laurent hired the fourth car that day to finish 12th after being lapped four times. Duncan Hamilton took over the 1951 car for the British GP and was the quickest HWM in practice but the engine expired after 44 laps in the midfield. Hamilton was handed a new car for the Dutch GP, which he finished in a career-best seventh. HWM pleased the race organisers at Zandvoort by replacing Collins with local amateur Dries van der Lof, who was unclassified following several stops to fix a faulty magneto.

TONY GAZE

Tony Gaze acquired an ex-works 1951 HWM and fitted the engine and gearbox from his Alta. The Australian World War II fighter pilot made his World Championship début at Spa-Francorchamps, where

he ran at the back throughout and finished 15th, needing medical treatment after being hit in the face by a bird. He retired from the British and German GPs. He was quicker than the works cars during practice for the Italian GP but no HWMs qualified.

CONNAUGHT ENGINEERING

In contrast to HWM chasing starting money across Europe, Connaught concentrated on British events. Rodney Clarke established Continental Cars in Send, Surrey after being invalided out of the Royal Air Force in 1943. Former customer and fellow RAF officer Mike Oliver joined after World War II and industrialist Kenneth McAlpine approached them to prepare his ex-Whitney Straight Maserati 8CM. A Lea-Francis-based sports car was built in 1949 and McAlpine backed the renamed Connaught Engineering to introduce the F2 A-type in 1950. These were sturdy, well-made, handsome cars with conventional tubular frame and wishbone/ torsion bar suspension front and rear; a new de Dion rear end was introduced for 1951. The dry-sump in-line four-cylinder Lea-Francis engine was retained, bored out from its initial 1,767cc to 1,960cc and fitted with four Amal carburettors. The car used a four-speed Wilson pre-selector gearbox.

Initial non-championship results were not particularly impressive although Ken Downing used the first customer car to finish second at Chimay after being passed by Paul Frère on the last lap. The

Kenneth McAlpine, Connaught A-Lea-Francis (Italian GP)

Ken Downing, Connaught A-Lea-Francis (British GP)

Tony Gaze, HWM 51/52-Alta (British GP)

Dennis Poore, Connaught A-Lea-Francis (British GP)

exhaust system had been revised by the time four Connaught A-types were entered for the British GP and *The Autocar* reported that they had 'far more speed than they had hitherto displayed'. Dennis Poore and Eric Thompson joined McAlpine and Downing after rival cars withdrew and all bar McAlpine qualified in the top 10. Poore ran in the top four all day and survived a spin at Copse Corner and swollen tongue (due to a bee sting) to finish fourth. Thompson passed Giuseppe Farina's ailing Ferrari to take fifth, much to the pleasure of the Silverstone crowd, with Downing a delayed ninth and McAlpine 16th.

Downing retired from the Dutch GP and Mike Hawthorn borrowed the original A-type to win a minor race at Turnberry. A three-car team was sent to the Italian GP and Stirling Moss did a late deal to join McAlpine and Poore when ERA withdrew. Moss used a tow from Alberto Ascari's Ferrari to qualify ninth but only McAlpine's Connaught was classified, 12th after its driver pushed the broken car across the line. Downing led a 1–2 in the Madgwick Cup at Goodwood and Poore headed a 1–2–3 at the final non-championship race of the season at Charterhall.

ENGLISH RACING AUTOMOBILES (ERA)

ERA owner Leslie Johnson persuaded Stirling Moss to sign for his Dunstable-based concern in February and announced the company's first post-war design a month later. Team manager Dick Wilkins arrived from the Velocette motorcycle team while Ken Gregory resigned from the Half Litre Club to manage Moss's

Eric Thompson, Connaught A-Lea-Francis (British GP)

Stirling Moss, Connaught A-Lea-Francis (Italian GP)

Stirling Moss, ERA G-type-Bristol (Belgian GP)

commercial affairs. Moss drove for HWM in Switzerland before the ERA G-type was ready to test at Silverstone and Lindley before the Belgian GP. *Autosport* described David Hodkin's design as 'a far from handsome machine with its almost square-fronted, squat, quasi-two-seater body and odd-looking wheels'. Two large-diameter oval tubes and four cross members were magnesium, which resulted in an exceptionally light and rigid frame. The front suspension was via coil springs and wishbones while the de Dion rear axle was sprung by coil springs. It had inboard rear brakes and Bristol supplied the 1,971cc straight-six engine (which was converted to dry sump) and four-speed gearbox. Hodkin placed the drivetrain on the left-hand side with driver offset to the right. The high engine led to poor frontal area and inadequate straight-line speed. Three cars were planned but only one was ever built.

Moss was happy with the matt green G-type's handling at Spa-Francorchamps but a piston failed during practice so a new engine was flown over from England and fitted overnight. Moss made a great start from 10th only to crash heavily when the hastily fitted engine seized on the opening lap. ERA's entry for the French GP was refused and in the British GP Moss's G-type misfired its way to another retirement. Having missed practice for the Dutch GP due to racing in the Goodwood Nine Hours, Moss lay seventh when his engine failed in the closing stages.

ERA withdrew from the Italian GP and Johnson sold the entire project to Bristol at the end of the year. The marque did not start another GP.

ALTA (PETER WHITEHEAD)

When acquiring his long-chassis Ferrari 125 in 1951, Peter Whitehead also took delivery of a normally aspirated 1,995cc type 166 V12 that he fitted for F2 races. A new Alta was ordered from Geoffrey Taylor's Tolworth-based concern but Whitehead raced the Ferrari 166/F2/50 while that car was being built. Quality preparation was assured as Alf Francis joined from HWM. Fifth in early non-championship events at Syracuse and Silverstone, Whitehead was placed in the F1 races in Turin and Albi with the blown 1.5-litre unit refitted.

The Alta F2 was delivered in May, Taylor having kept rubber in the suspension, fitted new alloy wheels and reworked the straight-four engine and exhaust system. The 1,970cc power unit retained

Peter Whitehead, Alta F2 (French GP)

Graham Whitehead, Alta F2 (British GP)

double overhead camshafts and had two plugs per cylinder. Shorter exhausts were introduced and the original SU carburettors replaced by Weber twin-choke versions after a failure during the Autodrome GP at Monza. Reliability was suspect, especially with the gearbox, and Whitehead retired at both Reims (the non-championship GP de la Marne) and Rouen-les-Essarts (the French GP).

He lent the Alta to half-brother Graham Whitehead for the British GP and reverted to the Ferrari. Both finished, albeit only 10th (Peter's Ferrari) and 12th (Graham on the last championship appearance of an Alta). Graham was a distant fourth in St Gaudens with the Alta but Peter broke its engine after a lap at La Baule. Peter Whitehead's Ferrari did not qualify for the Italian GP.

ASTON-BUTTERWORTH

British amateur Bill Aston drew inspiration from his F2 Cooper to build two elegant and lightweight new cars for 1952. The Aston had a box-section frame with front suspension by transverse leaf springs and wishbones, and a swing rear axle. A deal with Küchen for engines fell through so Aston acquired two air-cooled 1,983cc flat-four engines from Enfield-based Archie Butterworth. This unit's compact dimensions allowed for low front bodywork although the driver sat upright and so negated any aerodynamic benefits. Four Amal carburettors were fitted and the gearbox was an MG four-speed. Borrani wire wheels were fitted to the original chassis (NB41) but Dunlop alloys were used when Robin Montgomerie-

Peter Whitehead, Ferrari 166/F2/50 (Italian GP)

Robin Montgomerie-Charrington, Aston NB41-Butterworth (Belgian GP)

Bill Aston, Aston NB41-Butterworth (Italian GP)

Charrington ordered the second car (NB42). Reliability was poor and limited funds hindered development.

A veteran of World War I, Aston made his début in NB41 at Goodwood on Easter Monday. Both cars were ready for the International Trophy at Silverstone but retired in the heats. Montgomerie-Charrington drove NB41 to third place in the non-championship race at Chimay despite running out of fuel at the end. With the car painted blue and white (due to his American wife's nationality) for the Belgian GP, he ran as high as seventh before incorrect fuel added at a pitstop caused a terminal misfire.

Aston drove the car at the British GP but did not start after troubled practice days. The engine had revised carburettors and new Allard/Steyr cylinder heads for the German GP, where Aston started in the midfield, was ninth by the end of lap one and retired following clutch failure after two more tours of the *Nordschleife*. The 52-year-old did not qualify for the Italian GP when the engine refused to run cleanly.

In 1953 Aston raced the car in lesser F2 races but Montgomerie-Charrington moved to America and did not appear again.

VERITAS

Motor racing quickly returned to post-war Germany with Veritas key to that regeneration. In 1947 BMW engineers Ernst Loof and Lorenz Dietrich used the 1,971cc engine and parts from the BMW 328

to build the first Veritas at Messkirch. In 1950 Veritas introduced its own 1,988cc single-overhead-camshaft engine, which closely followed the BMW but used Heinkel alloy heads and three Solex carburettors, and gave a power increase from 125bhp to 140bhp running on methanol fuel. With resources stretched, Dietrich left but the stubborn Loof relocated to the Nürburgring that year.

The offset Veritas RS was introduced in 1948 with a ladder chassis frame, double wishbone/torsion bar independent suspension, BMW hydraulic brakes and five-speed Veritas gearbox. The Veritas Meteor was displayed at the 1950 Paris Salon and featured a de Dion rear axle. Fast circuits such as Avus and the Grenzlandring were prevalent in Germany, so these models were offered as open-wheelers or with all-enveloping streamlined bodywork as required.

Toni Ulmen drove an open-wheel Veritas Meteor-BMW in two World Championship races plus selected lesser events during 1952. After finishing 11th in the International Trophy and fifth in the Eifelrennen, his fuel tank split just four laps into the Swiss GP and he came home eighth on his return to the Nürburgring for the German GP. The car was fitted with streamlined bodywork to win the following month's flat-out blast around the Grenzlandring, a flat-out blast round the ring road of Wegberg on the Dutch border. Ulmen was crowned West German F2 champion in his last full season.

Belgian veteran Arthur Legat, *Motor Presse* proprietor Paul Pietsch and Hans Klenk all raced open-wheel Meteors fitted with

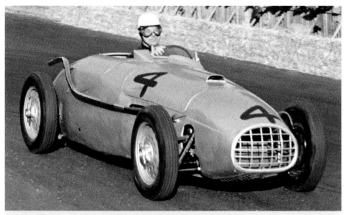

Toni Ulmen, Veritas Meteor-BMW (Swiss GP)

Paul Pietsch, Veritas Meteor (German GP)

Arthur Legat, Veritas Meteor (Belgian GP)

Theo Helfrich, Veritas RS-BMW (German GP)

Hans Klenk, Veritas Meteor (German GP)

Loof's proprietary engine. Legat was a leisurely 13th in the Belgian GP after spinning at La Source. Pietsch experimented with Weber carburettors at the German GP, where he qualified seventh, the quickest local, only for his gearbox to break on lap two. Klenk finished the German GP in 11th position and was second at Avus. Fritz Riess, Theo Helfrich, Adolf Brudes and Josef Peters all entered Veritas RS-BMWs in the German GP, Le Mans winner Riess finishing a creditable seventh while the engines on the other three cars all failed. Riess beat Helfrich to win a non-championship race at Dessau and was third at Avus.

Loof finally gave up the unequal struggle and Veritas closed in 1953. He returned to work for BMW but died on 3 March 1956 from a brain tumour.

Josef Peters, Veritas RS-BMW (German GP)

Adolf Brudes, Veritas RS-BMW (German GP)

Fritz Riess, Veritas RS-BMW (German GP)

Willi Heeks, AFM 8-BMW (German GP)

ALEX VON FALKENHAUSEN MOTORENBAU (AFM)

Another former BMW engineer, Alex von Falkenhausen, opened workshops in Munich and cannibalised BMW 328s to build a sports car, with the first single-seater AFM following in 1949. By 1952, 130bhp was available from the straight-six BMW 328 engine, and suspension was independent at the front via coil springs and double wishbones while a de Dion axle and torsion bars were employed at the back. Alloy wheels contained the brake drums and the prop shaft was lowered so the driver sat low in the conventional tubular chassis.

In addition to the BMW-powered cars, von Falkenhausen fitted a works car with a 1,993cc V8 engine built by Richard Küchen to an Abarth design. This had one Amal carburettor per cylinder although two twin-choke Webers were soon substituted. Power of 150bhp at 5,900rpm was claimed but reliability was suspect, with the valve gear a particular weakness. Hans Stuck beat Alberto Ascari's Ferrari 166/F2/50 in a heat at the 1950 Monza Autodrome GP and both Willi Heeks and Fritz Riess won national F2 races that year.

Stuck drove the works AFM-Küchen at the start of 1952, including in the opening World Championship race at Bremgarten. The troublesome V8 engine was detuned in the hope of finishing but that

Hans Stuck, AFM 4-Küchen (Swiss GP)

Helmut Niedermayr, AFM 6-BMW (German GP)

Ernst Klodwig, Heck-BMW (German GP)

Günther Bechem, BMW Eigenbau (German GP)

just made it slow as well as unreliable, so much so that Stuck was running last when a piston failed after five laps. With a BMW engine, however, Stuck returned to the circuits to win a national race on the streets of Leipzig in August. Four private AFM-BMWs entered the German GP although two, belonging to Willi Krakau and Ludwig Fischer, did not start. Helmut Niedermayr finished ninth in Krakau's car after crashing his Veritas during practice. Heeks started ninth and held an early seventh place before plug trouble intervened.

BMW SPECIALS

The post-war F2 boom in Germany was powered by the straight-six engine from the BMW 328 road car. In addition to the Veritas and AFM marques, a number of independent drivers built one-off 'specials' (or *Eigenbau*) and five such cars were entered in the 1952 German GP.

East Berliner Ernst Klodwig's self-built Heck-BMW lined up on the last row and was still circulating at leisurely pace at the finish when 12th and last. This was a rear-engine design (*Heck* meaning 'rear') with large front-mounted radiator and Volkswagen suspension and gearbox. Paul Greifzu had been East Germany's leading engineer/driver with his front-engine 'special', beating western rivals in the 1951 Avusrennen. He was killed while practising at Dessau on 10 May 1952 but the car was entered at the Nürburgring by former rival Rudolf Krause, whose engine broke after three laps in the midfield. 'Bernhard Nacke' (Günther Bechem was his real name) started at the back and stopped repeatedly to change plugs before giving up.

Rudolf Krause, Greifzu-BMW (German GP)

Marcel Balsa, BMW Spéciale (German GP)

Harry Merkel was unable to set a qualifying time in Willi Krakau's *Eigenbau* so did not start. Finally, Marcel Balsa brought his strange French-built Spéciale across the border and was running 14th when the rear axle failed.

OFFICINE SPECIALIZATE COSTRUZIONE AUTOMOBILI (OSCA)

Elie Bayol entered a stripped 1,340cc OSCA MT4 sports car in the F2 Grands Prix de France races. It proved somewhat breathless on fast circuits and he was frequently lapped but placed at Pau, Marseille and Montlhéry.

Bayol had a brand-new OSCA 20 for the GP du Comminges where he ran fourth before being disqualified for a pit infraction. *Motor Sport* described the car as 'very pretty' with 1,987cc double-overhead-cam straight-six engine, 'normal OSCA independent front suspension' (double wishbones and coil springs) and de Dion rear with quarter-elliptic springs. The rear brakes were inboard with four-speed gearbox mounted on the differential. Although 155bhp at 6,000rpm was claimed, weight was an issue. Bayol took the car to Monza and did well to qualify 10th for the Italian GP, only for the gearbox to break on the first lap. Sixth a week later in Modena made him the highest-placed privateer.

CISITALIA

Piero Dusio, formerly a footballer with Juventus, and Piero Taruffi founded Cisitalia (Consorzio Industriale Sportiva Italia) in 1946 with ex-FIAT engineer Dante Giacosa hired to design a cost-effective car for new single-make races. The Cisitalia D46 had a ground-breaking multi-tubular spaceframe chassis and independent suspension derived from the Fiat 500 Topolino. The series soon foundered and the subsequent rear-engine F1 Cisitalia 360 was delayed and overly complicated. That brought Cisitalia to the brink of financial oblivion in 1950 but did not deter Dusio, who entered the 1952 Italian GP with a D46 powered by a 2-litre BPM (Botta e Puricelli, Milano) four-cylinder marine engine with an overhead camshaft and four Dell'Orto motorcycle carburettors. It was a disaster as the engine blew itself to pieces on the first day of practice, so Dusio did not qualify.

Elie Bayol, OSCA 20 (Italian GP)

1952 RESULTS

DRIVER PERFORMANCE (EXCLUDING INDIANAPOLIS 500)

DRIVER	CAR-ENGINE	CH	B	F	GB	D	NL	I
George Abecassis	HWM 52-Alta	[10] R	–	–	–	–	–	–
Alberto Ascari	Ferrari 500	–	[1] 1 FL	[1] 1 FL	[2] 1 FL	[1] 1 FL	[1] 1 FL	[1] 1 FL
Bill Aston	Aston NB41-Butterworth	–	–	–	[30] DNS	[21] R	–	[31] DNQ
Marcel Balsa	BMW Spéciale	–	–	–	–	[25] R	–	–
Elie Bayol	OSCA 20	–	–	–	–	–	–	[10] R
Günther Bechem	BMW Eigenbau	–	–	–	–	[30] R	–	–
Jean Behra	Gordini 16	[7] 3	[5] R	[4] 7	–	[11] 5	[6] R	[11] R
'Gino Bianco'	Maserati A6GCM	–	–	–	[28] 18	[16] R	[12] R	[24] R
'B.Bira'	Simca-Gordini 15	[11] R	[18] 10	–	–	–	–	–
	Gordini 16	–	–	[8] R	[10] 11	–	–	–
Felice Bonetto	Maserati A6GCM	–	–	–	–	[10] DSQ	–	[13] 5
Eric Brandon	Cooper T20-Bristol	[17] 8	[12] 9	–	[18] 20	–	–	[20] 13
Alan Brown	Cooper T20-Bristol	[15] 5	[9] 6	–	[13] 22	–	–	[21] 15
Adolf Brudes	Veritas RS-BMW	–	–	–	–	[19] R	–	–
Eitel Cantoni	Maserati A6GCM	–	–	–	[27] R	[26] R	–	[23] 11
Piero Carini	Ferrari 166/F2/50	–	–	[19] R	–	[27] R	–	–
Johnny Claes	Gordini 16S	–	[19] 8	–	–	–	–	–
	Simca-Gordini 15	–	–	[20] R	[23] 15	–	–	[34] DNQ
	HWM 52-Alta	–	–	–	–	[32] 10	–	–
Peter Collins	HWM 52-Alta	[6] R	[11] R	[7] 6	[14] R	[33] DNS	–	[28] DNQ
Gianfranco Comotti	Ferrari 166/F2/50	–	–	[18] 12	–	–	–	–
Alberto Crespo	Maserati-Platé	–	–	–	–	–	–	[26] DNQ
Tony Crook	Frazer Nash LMR-BMW	–	–	–	[25] 21	–	–	–
Emmanuel de Graffenried	Maserati-Platé	[8] 6	–	–	[11] R	[31] 19	–	[27] DNQ
Max de Terra	Simca-Gordini 11	[21] R	–	–	–	–	–	–
Charles de Tornaco	Ferrari 500	–	[13] 7	–	–	–	[17] R	[25] DNQ
Ken Downing	Connaught A-Lea-Francis	–	–	–	[5] 9	–	[13] R	–
Piero Dusio	Cisitalia D46-BPM	–	–	–	–	–	–	[35] DNQ
Philippe Étancelin	Maserati A6GCM	–	–	[16] 8	–	–	–	–
Giuseppe Farina	Ferrari 500	[1] R	[2] 2	[2] 2	[1] 6	[2] 2	[2] 2	[3] 4
Ludwig Fischer	AFM 1-BMW	–	–	–	–	[31] DNS	–	–
Rudolf Fischer	Ferrari 500	[5] 2	–	–	[15] 14	[6] 3	–	[14] R
	Ferrari 212	–	–	[17] 11	–	–	–	–
Jan Flinterman	Maserati A6GCM	–	–	–	–	–	[15] 9	–
Paul Frère	HWM 51/52-Alta	–	[8] 5	–	–	[13] R	–	–
	Simca-Gordini 15	–	–	–	–	–	[11] R	–
Tony Gaze	HWM 51/52-Alta	–	[16] 15	–	[26] R	[14] R	–	[30] DNQ
Yves Giraud-Cabantous	HWM 52-Alta	–	–	[10] 10	–	–	–	–
José Froilán González	Maserati A6GCM	–	–	–	–	–	–	[5] 2 FL
Duncan Hamilton	HWM 51/52-Alta	–	–	–	[11] R	–	–	–
	HWM 52-Alta	–	–	–	–	–	[10] 7	–
Mike Hawthorn	Cooper T20-Bristol	–	[6] 4	[15] R	[7] 3	–	[3] 4	[12] NC
Willi Heeks	AFM 8-BMW	–	–	–	–	[9] R	–	–
Theo Helfrich	Veritas RS-BMW	–	–	–	–	[18] R	–	–
Peter Hirt	Ferrari 212	[19] 7	–	NT 11	[24] R	–	–	–
Hans Klenk	Veritas Meteor	–	–	–	–	[8] 11	–	–
Ernst Klodwig	Heck-BMW	–	–	–	–	[29] 12	–	–
Willi Krakau	AFM 7-BMW	–	–	–	–	[28] DNS	–	–
Rudolf Krause	Greifzu-BMW	–	–	–	–	[23] R	–	–
Chico Landi	Maserati A6GCM	–	–	–	–	–	[16] 9	[18] 8
Roger Laurent	HWM 52-Alta	–	[20] 12	–	–	–	–	–
	Ferrari 500	–	–	–	–	[17] 6	–	–
Arthur Legat	Veritas Meteor	–	[21] 13	–	–	–	–	–
Lance Macklin	HWM 52-Alta	[12] R	[14] 11	[14] 9	[29] 13	–	[9] 8	[32] DNQ
Robert Manzon	Gordini 16	[3] R	[4] 3	[5] 4	[4] R	[4] R	[8] 5	[7] 14
Kenneth McAlpine	Connaught A-Lea-Francis	–	–	–	[17] 16	–	–	[22] R
Harry Merkel	BMW Eigenbau	–	–	–	–	[34] DNS	–	–
Robin Montgomerie-Charrington	Aston NB41-Butterworth	–	[15] R	–	–	–	–	–
Stirling Moss	HWM 52-Alta	[9] R	–	–	–	–	–	–
	ERA G-type-Bristol	–	[10] R	–	[16] R	–	[18] R	–
	Connaught A-Lea-Francis	–	–	–	–	–	–	[9] R
David Murray	Cooper T20-Bristol	–	–	–	[22] R	–	–	–
Helmut Niedermayr	AFM 6-BMW	–	–	–	–	[22] 9	–	–
Robert O'Brien	Simca-Gordini 15	–	[22] 14	–	–	–	–	–
Reg Parnell	Cooper T20-Bristol	–	–	–	[6] 7	–	–	–
Josef Peters	Veritas RS-BMW	–	–	–	–	[20] R	–	–
Paul Pietsch	Veritas Meteor	–	–	–	–	[7] R	–	–
Dennis Poore	Connaught A-Lea-Francis	–	–	–	[8] 4	–	–	[19] 12
Fritz Riess	Veritas RS-BMW	–	–	–	–	[12] 7	–	–
Franco Rol	Maserati A6GCM	–	–	–	–	–	–	[16] R
Louis Rosier	Ferrari 500	[20] R	[17] R	[9] R	–	–	–	[17] 10
Roy Salvadori	Ferrari 500	–	–	[19] 8	–	–	–	–

DRIVER PERFORMANCE CONTINUED

DRIVER	CAR-ENGINE	CH	B	F	GB	D	NL	I
Harry Schell	Maserati-Platé	[18] R	–	[12] R	[32] 17	–	–	–
Rudolf Schoeller	Ferrari 212	–	–	–	–	[24] R	–	–
André Simon	Ferrari 500	[4] R	–	–	–	–	–	[8] 6
Hans Stuck	AFM 4-Küchen	[14] R	–	–	–	–	–	–
	Ferrari 212	–	–	–	–	–	–	[33] DNQ
Piero Taruffi	Ferrari 500	[2] 1 FL	[3] R	[3] 3	[3] 2	[5] 4	–	[6] 7
Eric Thompson	Connaught A-Lea-Francis	–	–	–	[9] 5	–	–	–
Maurice Trintignant	Ferrari 166/F2/50	[22] DNS	–	–	–	–	–	–
	Simca-Gordini 15	–	–	[6] 5	–	–	–	–
	Gordini 16	–	–	–	[21] R	[3] R	[5] 6	[4] R
Toni Ulmen	Veritas Meteor-BMW	[16] R	–	–	–	[15] 8	–	–
Dries van der Lof	HWM 52-Alta	–	–	–	–	–	[14] NC	–
Luigi Villoresi	Ferrari 500	–	–	–	–	–	[4] 3	[2] 3
Ken Wharton	Frazer Nash FN48-Bristol	[13] 4	[7] R	–	–	–	[7] R	–
	Cooper T20-Bristol	–	–	–	–	–	–	[15] 9
Graham Whitehead	Alta F2	–	–	–	[12] 12	–	–	–
Peter Whitehead	Alta F2	–	–	[13] R	–	–	–	–
	Ferrari 166/F2/50	–	–	–	[20] 10	–	–	[29] DNQ

SHARED DRIVES Swiss GP: André Simon/Giuseppe Farina (Ferrari 500) R. French GP: Rudolf Fischer/Peter Hirt (Ferrari 212) 11; Emmanuel de Graffenried/Harry Schell (Maserati-Platé) R. Dutch GP: Chico Landi/Jan Flinterman (Maserati A6GCM) 9.

FORMULA 2 RACE WINNERS

ROUND	RACE (CIRCUIT)	DATE	WINNER
–	Gran Premio di Siracusa (Syracuse)	Mar 16	Alberto Ascari (Ferrari 500)
–	Lavant Cup (Goodwood)	Apr 14	Mike Hawthorn (Cooper T20-Bristol)
–	Grand Prix de Pau (Pau)	Apr 14	Alberto Ascari (Ferrari 500)
–	West Hampshire & Dorset Car Club Formula 2 Race (Ibsley)	Apr 19	Mike Hawthorn (Cooper T20-Bristol)
–	Rostock Osthafen Kurs (Rostock-Ost)	Apr 20	Paul Greifzu (Greifzu-BMW)
–	Grand Prix de Marseille (Marseille-Parc Borély)	Apr 27	Alberto Ascari (Ferrari 500)
–	Aston Martin Owners Club Formula 2 Race (Snetterton)	May 3	Dickie Stoop (Frazer Nash Mille Miglia)
–	Bernau Autobahn-Schleife (Bernau)	May 4	Rudolf Krause (BMW Eigenbau)
–	Daily Express International Trophy (Silverstone)	May 10	Lance Macklin (HWM 52-Alta)
–	Gran Premio di Napoli (Posillipo)	May 11	Giuseppe Farina (Ferrari 500)
–	Dessau Autobahn-Spinne (Dessau)	May 11	Fritz Riess (Veritas RS-BMW)
1	**Grand Prix de Suisse (Bremgarten)**	**May 18**	**Piero Taruffi (Ferrari 500)**
–	Eifelrennen (Nürburgring)	May 25	Rudolf Fischer (Ferrari 500)
–	Grand Prix de Paris (Montlhéry)	May 25	Piero Taruffi (Ferrari 500)
2*	**Indianapolis 500 (Indianapolis)**	**May 30**	**Troy Ruttman (Kuzma-Offenhauser)**
–	Grand Prix des Frontières (Chimay)	Jun 1	Paul Frère (HWM 51/52-Alta)
–	Leipzig Stadtpark-Rennen (Leipzig)	Jun 2	Edgar Barth (EMW-BMW)
–	Strassen-Rennen Halle-Saale (Halle-Saale)	Jun 8	Edgar Barth (EMW-BMW)
–	Circuit du Lac (Aix-les-Bains)	Jun 8	Jean Behra (Gordini 16)
–	Gran Premio dell'Autodromo di Monza (Monza)	Jun 8	Giuseppe Farina (Ferrari 500)
–	West Essex Car Club Formula 2 Race (Boreham)	Jun 21	Reg Parnell (Cooper T20-Bristol)
3	**Grand Prix de Belgique et d'Europe (Spa-Francorchamps)**	**Jun 22**	**Alberto Ascari (Ferrari 500)**
–	Grand Prix de la Marne (Reims)	Jun 29	Jean Behra (Gordini 16)
4	**Grand Prix de l'Automobile Club de France (Rouen-les-Essarts)**	**Jul 6**	**Alberto Ascari (Ferrari 500)**
–	Grand Prix des Sables d'Olonne (Les Sables d'Olonne)	Jul 13	Luigi Villoresi (Ferrari 500)
5	**British Grand Prix (Silverstone)**	**Jul 19**	**Alberto Ascari (Ferrari 500)**
–	Grand Prix de Caen (Caen)	Jul 27	Maurice Trintignant (Gordini 16)
6	**Grosser Preis von Deutschland (Nürburgring)**	**Aug 3**	**Alberto Ascari (Ferrari 500)**
–	Grand Prix du Comminges (St Gaudens)	Aug 10	André Simon/Alberto Ascari (Ferrari 500)
–	Strassen-Rennen Leipzig (Leipzig)	Aug 17	Hans Stuck (AFM 4-BMW)
7	**Grote Prijs van Nederland (Zandvoort)**	**Aug 17**	**Alberto Ascari (Ferrari 500)**
–	National Trophy (Turnberry)	Aug 23	Mike Hawthorn (Connaught A-Lea-Francis)
–	Grand Prix de la Baule (La Baule)	Aug 24	Alberto Ascari (Ferrari 500)
–	Grenzlandring-Rennen (Grenzlandring)	Aug 31	Toni Ulmen (Veritas RS-BMW)
–	Sachsenring-Rennen (Sachsenring)	Sep 7	Edgar Barth (EMW-BMW)
8	**Gran Premio d'Italia (Monza)**	**Sep 7**	**Alberto Ascari (Ferrari 500)**
–	Circuit de Cadours (Cadours)	Sep 14	Louis Rosier (Ferrari 500)
–	Gran Premio di Modena (Modena Aerautodromo)	Sep 14	Luigi Villoresi (Ferrari 500)
–	Madgwick Cup (Goodwood)	Sep 27	Ken Downing (Connaught A-Lea-Francis)
–	Avusrennen (Avus)	Sep 28	Rudolf Fischer (Ferrari 500)
–	Joe Fry Memorial Trophy (Castle Combe)	Oct 4	Roy Salvadori (Ferrari 500)
–	Newcastle Journal Trophy (Charterhall)	Oct 11	Dennis Poore (Connaught A-Lea-Francis)

*Run to AAA National Championship rules

DRIVERS' CHAMPIONSHIP

	DRIVERS	POINTS
1	Alberto Ascari	36 (53.5)*
2	Giuseppe Farina	24 (27)*
3	Piero Taruffi	22
4=	Rudolf Fischer	10
	Mike Hawthorn	10
6	Robert Manzon	9
7=	Troy Ruttman	8
	Luigi Villoresi	8
9	José Froilán González	6.5
10=	Jean Behra	6
	Jim Rathmann	6
12	Sam Hanks	4
13=	Duane Carter	3
	Dennis Poore	3
	Ken Wharton	3
16=	Felice Bonetto	2
	Alan Brown	2
	Art Cross	2
	Paul Frère	2
	Eric Thompson	2
	Maurice Trintignant	2
22	Bill Vukovich	1

*Best four results count

Giuseppe Farina, Alberto Ascari, Juan Manuel Fangio and Onofre Marimón in close quarters at Monza; Fangio eventually won at the last corner

1953

FERRARI SUPREME AS ASCARI RETAINS TITLE

Juan Manuel Fangio's Maserati A6GCM (A6SSG) takes the lead at the start of the Swiss GP at Bremgarten

Stirling Moss and Mike Hawthorn before the Dutch GP

Ferrari won all but the final race of the F2 World Championship years but switching categories had been an undoubted success. The variety and sheer number of F2 cars provided interesting and large grids at most races, with a record 34 cars starting the 1953 German GP. Alberto Ascari retained the world title having won nine GPs in a row from Belgium 1952 to the same race a year later. That remarkable run came to an end in the epic 1953 French GP at Reims, where Ferrari team-mate Mike Hawthorn beat Maserati's Juan Manuel Fangio after a slipstreaming classic. It was Fangio who finally gave Maserati its first World Championship GP win after another outstanding contest at Monza.

Published in the first week of October 1952, the 1953 World Championship calendar included a new race at the impressive Autódromo 17 de Octubre in Buenos Aires. Unfortunately, crowd control was appalling as an estimated 350,000 spectators lined the track. The race should not have started and two serious accidents followed as spectators encroached onto the road with at least 10 killed and many more injured. The Dutch GP organisers resurfaced Zandvoort a week before the race and the surface broke up dangerously as a consequence.

The German GP was originally awarded the Grand Prix of Europe courtesy title but the organisers declined, preferring to defer until 1954. The final championship round in Barcelona was then given that honour but, for the second year in a row, this race was cancelled at short notice so no European GP was held in 1953. Monaco was announced as a sports car race once more but the event did not take place.

The Commission Sportive Internationale introduced a new safety committee to approve all circuits with Colonel F. Stanley Barnes, competitions manager of the Royal Automobile Club, as chairman, supported by Piero Taruffi and Albert Divo. Also new was the requirement for drivers to pass a medical examination before each GP.

Ferrari trio: Farina (left), Ascari (second from right) and Villoresi (right)

Alberto Ascari and Onofre Marimón walk back to the pits after their last-lap collision at Monza

Alberto Ascari, Ferrari 500 (Dutch GP)

Mike Hawthorn, Ferrari 500 (Belgian GP)

SCUDERIA FERRARI

Discharged from hospital following his Modena accident in October 1952, Mike Hawthorn signed for Ferrari within the month, the first Englishman since Richard Seaman to join a continental GP team. Alberto Ascari, Giuseppe Farina and Luigi Villoresi were retained in an expanded line-up.

Four Ferrari 500s were shipped to Buenos Aires for the opening championship race, the four-cylinder engine now developing 180bhp and visibly different with two long exhausts replacing its stub outlets. The inaugural Argentine GP was a disaster as the huge crowd lined the track with fatal consequences. After 30 laps, Farina lost control while trying to avoid a boy in the road and crashed into the crowd, killing at least nine spectators and injuring another 26. Ascari led from start to finish with Villoresi second and Hawthorn fourth.

All four retired at Syracuse due to faulty valves but Ascari led dominant non-championship displays in Pau and Bordeaux, Farina beat Juan Manuel Fangio's Maserati in Naples, and Hawthorn scored popular home victories in the International Trophy and at Dundrod. The championship resumed at Zandvoort, where the cars were fitted with wire-mesh screens to protect the drivers from stones as the track broke up; Ascari was never headed, supported by Farina and Hawthorn in second and fourth places respectively. Ascari assumed his customary place at the front in Belgium after the Maseratis of José Froilán González and Juan Manuel Fangio retired, and this time it was

Giuseppe Farina, Ferrari 500 (Italian GP)

Villoresi who competed Ferrari's 1–2; a fuel leak ruined Hawthorn's race after running second.

The championship circus moved to Reims for the sensational French GP, although Ferrari threatened to withdraw after Umberto Maglioli and Piero Carini were disqualified from the supporting 12-hour sports car race. 'Never before has such a desperate struggle been waged on a GP circuit,' enthused *Autosport* after Hawthorn and Fangio repeatedly swapped the lead from half distance. Fangio eventually lost first gear and Hawthorn accelerated out of the Thillois hairpin to score his first GP victory by one second. With González and Fangio both in contention, Ferrari did not impose team orders for once and Ascari finished fourth, 4.6sec behind Hawthorn, ending his winning streak of nine GPs.

Ascari returned to winning ways in the British GP, leading all the way. Farina passed González for third, Villoresi retired and Hawthorn finished fifth after a lurid spin at Woodcote entering lap three. In the German GP Ascari's front right wheel fell off so he took over Villoresi's car but overstressed its engine and retired, having broken the F2 lap record with it. Sensing a rare victory Farina passed both Hawthorn and Fangio on lap eight to win a GP for the final time. In Switzerland, Ascari dropped to fourth following an 87.5sec pitstop to change plugs before charging back to a victory that confirmed his second world title. Second-placed Farina was furious as Ascari had ignored orders to hold station, the champion claiming he had not

seen the signals due to bright sunshine. Hawthorn completed Ferrari's 1–2–3 but Villoresi was delayed by steering and radiator damage after hitting a fence.

At Monza, the four regulars were augmented by Maglioli and Carini in a pair of new low-line Ferrari 553s. The prototype 1954 Formula 1 car had a lightweight tubular chassis, making it the first Ferrari single-seater to have a spaceframe. There was a new 1,997cc straight-four monobloc engine with twin-plug ignition and wider valve angles; although fuel injection was assessed, two twin-choke Weber carburettors were preferred. Bulbous fuel tanks were

Luigi Villoresi, Ferrari 500 (Dutch GP)

Piero Carini, Ferrari 553 'Squalo' (Italian GP)

Umberto Maglioli, Ferrari 553 'Squalo' (Italian GP)

side-mounted, rising-rate independent front suspension featured wishbones and transverse leaf springs, the de Dion rear axle was suspended by radius rods ahead of the differential, and outboard brakes were retained. Dubbed the *Squalo* ('shark'), the car proved dangerously unstable at high speed and oil overheated during practice. Maglioli finished eighth, four laps down, while Carini's engine blew up following numerous pitstops. The regular Ferrari 500s of Ascari and Farina battled with Fangio for victory throughout another terrific race. Ascari spun on oil at the final corner of the race and was hit by Onofre Marimón's lapped Maserati. Farina lost momentum in the mêlée so Fangio inflicted Ferrari's first GP defeat

since 1951 with Farina, Villoresi and Hawthorn placed 2–3–4.

After the Italian GP Enzo Ferrari announced his withdrawal from single-seater racing amid rumours of ill health and financial problems. It would not be the last time that such an empty threat was issued.

ECURIE ROSIER

Now 47 years old and past his prime, Louis Rosier raced his Ferrari 500 in all European World Championship races during 1953. Reliable if slow, he finished his first five GPs in the top 10 with seventh in Holland his best result of that sequence. He crashed into Jacques

Louis Rosier, Ferrari 500 (German GP)

Jacques Swaters, Ferrari 500 (German GP)

Swaters's spinning car on the opening lap of the Swiss GP and was delayed in the pits during the final round at Monza. Outright success was confined to lesser events: he won the Albi GP with his F1 Ferrari 375 and beat the works Gordinis on aggregate at Les Sables d'Olonne despite not leading a lap of either heat.

ECURIE FRANCORCHAMPS

The Ecurie Francorchamps Ferrari 500 appeared sporadically during a tragic campaign. Roger Laurent finished second at Chimay but an incident on lap 18 marred the race: he did not see Johnny Claes's Connaught as it attempted to pass and they collided; Claes was launched into the crowd, injuring several spectators, one of whom died the following day. Charles de Tornaco and team boss Jacques Swaters entered the Belgian GP but Ecurie Francorchamps did not arrive. Swaters won the Avusrennen on Berlin's fast motorway circuit and came seventh in the German GP. After a clash with Louis Rosier's Ferrari on the opening lap in Switzerland his car came to rest on a barrier and Swaters was hospitalised as a precaution. Worse was to come at the Modena non-championship race as de Tornaco was killed when his car rolled during practice.

ECURIE ESPADON

Rudolf Schoeller's Ecurie Espadon normally competed in hillclimbs and lesser events but made a rare appearance in the Eifelrennen at the Nürburgring. Kurt Adolff qualified the team's Ferrari 500 on pole

Peter Hirt, Ferrari 500 (Swiss GP)

Kurt Adolff, Ferrari 166C (German GP)

Max de Terra, Ferrari 166C (Swiss GP)

OFFICINE ALFIERI MASERATI

Juan Manuel Fangio was sufficiently recovered from his injuries to spectate at the 1952 Italian GP but Maserati spent the winter worrying about his fitness. José Froilán González and Felice Bonetto were confirmed in December with Fangio finally given the all-clear by his doctors a couple of weeks before the Argentine GP, where four 1952-specification Maserati A6GCMs were entered. Fangio qualified and ran second on his return before the transmission failed. González and local star Oscar Gálvez finished third and fifth while Bonetto retired when his transmission failed.

Alberto Massimino had left at the end of 1952 so Vittorio Bellentani was promoted to chief engineer. Former Ferrari designer Giaocchino Colombo arrived as a consultant and they reworked the A6CGM in time for the European season; another engineer, Giulio Alfieri, joined the design department from Innocenti in September. Engine capacity was increased to 1,997cc with twin-plug ignition helping develop 180bhp, rising to 190bhp by the end of 1953. Independent front suspension was via coil springs and wishbones, while the car's old-fashioned live rear axle was mounted on quarter-elliptic leaf springs and fixed by an 'A' bracket. The wider rear bodywork accommodated a larger fuel tank and the chassis was stiffened by an auxiliary frame to improve handling. The 1953 A6GCM (also listed as the A6SSG) was as fast as the Ferrari 500 on the straights but handling was inferior.

The updated car made its début at Naples where Fangio finished second despite a puncture with González third. Both had terminal

position and ran second in the wet before slipping back to finish fourth. He crashed on the opening lap of the Avusrennen so it was with an elderly V12 Ferrari 166C that he raced in the German GP but its transmission failed after three laps. Peter Hirt retired the type 500 from the Swiss GP while Max de Terra drove the 166C into a distant eighth position. The team did not appear at Monza – or in another World Championship GP.

Juan Manuel Fangio, Maserati A6GCM (A6SSG) (British GP)

Felice Bonetto, Maserati A6GCM (A6SSG) (British GP)

problems in the Dutch GP but González took over Bonetto's car and, despite a spin at Tarzan, passed Mike Hawthorn's Ferrari for third with 11 laps to go. The Maseratis had wire mesh in front of their cockpits to protect the drivers from stones thrown up from the newly resurfaced track. Onofre Marimón drove a fourth car from the Belgian GP, sporting blue-and-yellow national colours due to backing from the Automóvil Club Argentina. González led pole winner Fangio and the Ferraris at Spa-Francorchamps but both leading Maseratis retired once more with third-placed Marimón the only works driver to finish. Replacing Bonetto as a one-off at Spa-Francorchamps, local amateur Johnny Claes was eighth when he handed the car to Fangio, who climbed back into the top three only to crash heavily on the last lap when his steering failed at Stavelot.

A fortnight later, the French GP was dubbed the 'Race of the Century' by most commentators. Alberto Ascari was beaten for once and Fangio battled with Hawthorn's Ferrari for victory, the pair repeatedly passing and repassing each other. Crucially, Fangio lost first gear, which compromised acceleration out of the Thillois hairpin, so Hawthorn won by a second. Starting with half-full tanks, González led the opening 29 laps before refuelling and just failed to snatch second from Fangio on the line. Bonetto's engine blew up and Marimón was delayed when a stone holed his radiator.

Ascari returned to form at Silverstone with Fangio and González second and fourth respectively. Second early on, González was black-flagged for spilling oil but ignored the instruction for several laps

José Froilán González, Maserati A6GCM (A6SSG) (British GP)

Onofre Marimón, Maserati A6GCM (A6SSG) (British GP)

Oscar Gálvez, Maserati A6GCM (A6SSG) (Argentine GP)

Johnny Claes/Juan Manuel Fangio, Maserati A6GCM (A6SSG) (Belgian GP)

Hermann Lang, Maserati A6GCM (A6SSG) (Swiss GP)

Sergio Mantovani/Luigi Musso, Maserati A6GCM (A6SSG) (Italian GP)

and an animated argument followed when he eventually stopped. *The Autocar* noted its disapproval: 'there is no room for anarchy at 100mph.' González's season was ended by back injuries when he crashed his Lancia into a course car while practising for the following week's Portuguese GP for sports cars.

Plans to replace him with pre-war ace Hermann Lang at the Nürburgring were delayed, so only three works cars started the German GP. The 1953 Maserati was not suited to the sinuous *Nordschleife* but Fangio finished second despite fumes from a broken exhaust pipe. The brakeless Bonetto was fourth, while Marimón stalled at the start and had chassis failure after 13 laps. Fangio again qualified on pole in Switzerland but lost third gear during the race so swapped cars with Bonetto after 11 laps. He pushed too hard while recovering from 10th to fifth and blew his engine. Bonetto continued in Fangio's original car to finish fourth. Marimón ran as high as second before spinning when his transmission failed, while Lang came home a distant fifth.

Maserati's barren run finally ended in spectacular style in Italy. Fangio and Marimón diced with the Ferraris of Ascari and Giuseppe Farina until the impressive newcomer lost six minutes in the pits. Four laps down when he rejoined, Marimón ran with the leaders to help Fangio. In the final corner of another momentous race, Ascari lost control on a patch of oil and was hit by Marimón, with both eliminated. Farina was also impeded and Fangio took advantage to score Maserati's first victory in a championship race. Bonetto lost sixth

when he ran out of fuel on the last lap. Débutants Sergio Mantovani and Luigi Musso shared the fourth works car and finished seventh.

Fangio clinched second place in the World Championship with that victory and, with Ferrari absent, he led an easy Maserati 1–2–3 in the non-championship race at Modena.

SCUDERIA ENRICO PLATÉ

Enrico Platé decided against switching to an OSCA so ordered a new Maserati A6GCM (A6SSG) for regular driver Emmanuel de Graffenried. The Maserati was not ready for the beginning of the European season so they borrowed the original prototype in which the Swiss baron excelled in the early non-championship races. He had victories on début at Syracuse when the Ferraris failed, in both the F2 and *Formule Libre* races during Goodwood's Easter Monday meeting, and in the Eifelrennen at the Nürburgring; he also won the first heat for the International Trophy only to be penalised for jumping the start of the final.

Once de Graffenried's new car was ready, he scored points first time out at Zandvoort (fifth) and Spa-Francorchamps (fourth). He was seventh in France but retired from the British GP after stalling at the start and stopping to change spark plugs. He finished fifth in Germany despite fading brakes but retired from the last two GPs of the season. The Swiss privateer then qualified and finished third at Modena at the end of a satisfying campaign.

Emmanuel de Graffenried, Maserati A6GCM (A6SSG) (British GP)

Chico Landi, Maserati A6GCM (Italian GP)

OTHER MASERATI PRIVATEERS

Francesco 'Chico' Landi acquired a 1952-specification Maserati A6GCM from Escuderia Bandeirantes that he fitted with a new twin-ignition engine and entered the Swiss GP, retiring with gearbox failure while lying eighth. The car was tended by Scuderia Milano for the Italian GP, where Landi's engine failed after 18 laps.

'B. Bira' bought an ex-works A6GCM and finished the International Trophy in fourth position. Having raced for Connaught in three GPs, 'Bira' wheeled the Maserati out again at the Italian GP, the car officially entered by Scuderia Milano as well, and finished 12th after being lapped eight times.

'B. Bira', Maserati A6GCM (*International Trophy, Silverstone*)

EQUIPE GORDINI

Gordini retained Robert Manzon, Jean Behra (recovered from his Carrera Panamericana injuries) and Maurice Trintignant as its three drivers in December 1952 and Jean Lucas joined as team manager. With F2 in its final year and finances as tight as ever, 'The Sorcerer' continued to field his six-cylinder type 16s with an older Simca-Gordini 15 pressed into use when required. Plans for a two-car entry for the Indianapolis 500 were abandoned.

Poor fuel plagued practice in Argentina but Manzon began 1953 by overtaking José Froilán González (Maserati) and Luigi Villoresi (Ferrari) to run second before fading; he was sixth when a wheel fell off as he passed the grandstands for the 67th time. Fifth in the *Formule Libre* Buenos Aires GP, Manzon suddenly quit Gordini in April to race sports cars for Lancia.

Trintignant was the only Gordini driver to start all eight GPs and he scored the team's only points when fifth in Belgium and Italy. His was the quickest non-Italian car in Argentina qualifying but he had to stop for a plug change after just five laps and eventually handed over to Harry Schell, who completed the race in seventh position. After a sixth in Holland, Trintignant retired from four consecutive GPs as Gordini's frailty proved all too evident. Further success was limited to victory in the minor Circuit de Cadours, where he led Schell and Behra in a Gordini 1–2–3.

Behra finished sixth in Argentina but punctured a tyre and crashed while chasing the Ferraris at Pau. That sidelined him for two months

Robert Manzon, Gordini 16 (Argentine GP)

Harry Schell, Gordini 16 (Italian GP)

Maurice Trintignant, Gordini 16 (Belgian GP)

Roberto Mières, Gordini 16 (Italian GP)

Jean Behra, Gordini 16 (German GP)

Pablo Birger, Simca-Gordini 15 (Argentine GP)

Fred Wacker, Gordini 16 (Belgian GP)

Carlos MendIt̀eguy, Gordini 16 (Argentine GP)

with back and arm injuries before he returned in the Belgian GP only to retire from four of the next five GPs. The exception was 10th place in France when delayed as mechanics tried to make his engine run on all six cylinders. Gordini entered four cars in the French GP and five in the supporting sports car race. All nine gave trouble and *Motor Sport* described Gordini's Reims showing as 'a dismal failure'. Winner of the opening heat at Aix-les-Bains and Les Sables d'Olonne, Behra lost the latter event when he crashed out of the lead of heat two. Schell replaced Manzon in the team and finished an outclassed third at Pau. He ran in the top 10 in Holland and finished seventh in Belgium. He retired in France, Britain and Germany, missed the Swiss GP to race in the Goodwood Nine Hours, and was ninth in Italy.

Originally Gordini's reserve driver, Roberto Mières raced in non-championship events and replaced Behra for the Dutch GP when a misfire was followed by transmission failure. He drove a fourth car in France but lasted just four laps. For the Italian GP he again replaced Behra, who was competing in the Tour de France Automobile, and the Gordinis proved fast and reliable for once, Mières occupying sixth place at the finish.

Fred Wacker Jr, President of the Sports Car Club of America, drove a Gordini 16 in selected non-championship races, including third place at Chimay, and entered three World Championship GPs. He did not start the Dutch and Swiss GPs, having given his engine to a team-mate at Zandvoort and crashed at Bremgarten, but did finish at Spa-Francorchamps, in ninth place.

Carlos Mendit̀eguy drove a fourth Gordini 16 in Argentina and Pablo Birger's old 1.5-litre Simca-Gordini 15 completed the team's

Georges Berger, Simca-Gordini 15 (Belgian GP)

five-car line-up for that opening race of the season. Menditéguy ran fifth during the early stages but both locals retired before one-third distance. With his updated Maserati not yet ready, Juan Manuel Fangio raced a Gordini 16 in the Bordeaux non-championship event, finishing third behind Alberto Ascari and Luigi Villoresi.

VICOMTESSE DE WALCKIERS

Vicomtesse de Walckiers entered her ex-Johnny Claes Simca-Gordini 15 for Georges Berger in a couple of Belgian races. He was a late retirement at Chimay and slowest qualifier for the following month's GP at Spa-Francorchamps, his World Championship début, where he was running last when his engine expired after three laps.

HERSHAM & WALTON MOTORS (HWM)

HWM updated three of its 1952 cars with a new rear axle, Jaguar C-type synchromesh gearbox and shortened chassis. The oil tank was moved beside the driver so that the car was a couple of inches lower. The exhaust system was revised and the nose received a new radiator grille, but most work was directed at the Alta-based engine that *Autosport* noted now had 'only a superficial resemblance to the twin-ohc Alta'. Harry Weslake designed a new gear-driven cylinder head and the 1,996cc unit featured larger con rods. Weber carburettors were standard although Solex units were tried but not raced in Belgium. Although 160bhp was claimed, the revised engine proved disappointing. Fuel capacity was increased to 36 gallons. Lance

Lance Macklin, HWM 53-Alta (Belgian GP)

Peter Collins, HWM 53-Alta (Dutch GP)

Peter Collins, HWM 51/52-Alta (British GP)

Paul Frère, HWM 53-Alta (Swiss GP)

Macklin and Peter Collins were retained and a succession of local drivers or part-timers filled a third car. The fourth chassis was sold.

Duncan Hamilton won a qualifying heat for the Ulster Trophy and Paul Frère was a close second with Collins third in the Eifelrennen at a damp Nürburgring. Macklin was the first to retire from the Dutch GP, where Collins finished a distant eighth. Frère returned for the Belgian GP and outqualified his regular team-mates, who both retired from the race, while the Belgian journalist's car was second from last at the chequered flag after losing four laps in the pits. Yves Giraud-Cabantous drove the third car in the French GP both he and Collins finishing outside the top 10.

HWM entered four 'rather tired-looking cars', said *Autosport*, for the British GP with Macklin and Collins (who was forced to drive an old 1951 chassis) joined by Hamilton and Jack Fairman; three suffered clutch failures and Collins was lying 10th when he crashed at Chapel Curve after 56 laps of his last GP appearance for HWM. Macklin was third at Aix-les-Bains but the German GP organisers refused HWM's entry despite the team's 2–3 finish at the Nürburgring in May. Macklin and Frère retired from the Swiss GP, where local amateur Albert Scherrer handled the third car; Scherrer ran at the back before the magneto failed, whereupon he pushed the car back to the pits and rejoined once the fault had been remedied, finishing eighth and last, having been lapped 17 times. Heath made a rare start at Cadours but all three HWMs retired once again, Giraud-Cabantous when crashing heavily following a puncture. The Frenchman was 15th in the Italian GP, where débutant John Fitch and Macklin both blew engines. That maintained Macklin's dismal 100 per cent GP failure rate during 1953.

Jack Fairman, HWM 52/53-Alta (British GP)

Albert Scherrer, HWM 53-Alta (Swiss GP)

Duncan Hamilton, HWM 53-Alta (*International Trophy, Silverstone*)

Yves Giraud-Cabantous, HWM 53-Alta (French GP)

John Fitch, HWM 52/53-Alta (Italian GP)

John Barber, Cooper T23-Bristol (Argentine GP)

Adolfo Schwelm Cruz, Cooper T20-Bristol (Argentine GP)

COOPER CAR COMPANY

Cooper's successful 1952 Formula 3 car was built around a simple and cost-effective tubular frame and Owen Maddock followed this principle for his MkII F2 chassis. The prototype was displayed at the Earls Court Motor Show in October 1952 with larger brakes and lower and more streamlined bodywork facilitated by inclining the engine slightly. The driver was more reclined, allowing reduced frontal area. Transverse leaf springs/wishbone suspension was retained. The new radiator had water on either side of the engine air intake, which ran above the oil cooler. Hot air exited via stub exhausts on either side while increased use of magnesium helped save 100lbs. The car was powered by Bristol or Alta engines, with designations of T23 or T24 respectively.

Three Cooper-Bristols entered the Argentine GP, ostensibly as works cars. These were the prototype T23 for John Barber, this car having been acquired by the Fraser-Hartwell Syndicate, and T20s for Alan Brown and local Adolfo Schwelm Cruz, with Jesús Iglesias as reserve. John Cooper accompanied the cars by sea while Charles flew to Buenos Aires. Both Barber and a much-delayed Brown finished at the rear of the field of this tragic affair at which crowd control was non-existent, Brown's car having hit and killed a young boy who had strayed onto the track. Schwelm Cruz's wheel fell off after he hit a kerb. Barber was the only Cooper to finish the subsequent *Formule Libre* Buenos Aires GP, in 11th place.

Having turned down Ferrari's advances so that he could continue to race sports cars for Jaguar, Stirling Moss made an unorthodox

Alan Brown, Cooper T20-Bristol (Argentine GP)

Stirling Moss, Cooper-Alta Special (French GP)

choice for his World Championship campaign. Keen to drive a British car, he heeded the suggestion of *The Autocar*'s sports editor, John Cooper (no relation), to approach London-based Kieft F3 designer Ray Martin to create a one-off 'special'. HWM's Alf Francis was hired as chief mechanic and Tony Robinson assisted in extensively modifying a Cooper MkII frame with coil spring/double wishbone front and de Dion rear suspension, disc brakes and a dry-sump Alta engine. Although this creation, called the Cooper-Alta Special, was much modified, it was officially entered by the works team for Goodwood's Easter meeting. It was immediately obvious that the chassis lacked rigidity, suffered brake imbalance and handled poorly. Modified steering for Moss's first championship race with the car, at Reims, marginally improved matters but the clutch exploded, cutting Moss's leg.

Martin had already left the team by this time and Moss did not drive the Cooper-Alta Special again. Working around the clock, a standard T24 was built up in just 11 days, with Moss meanwhile having to miss the British GP. Plans to use a Jaguar XK engine were abandoned so Francis arranged for Barwell Engineering to tune the Alta engine, with four SU carburettors preferred to the same company's fuel injection, and it drove through an ENV pre-selector gearbox. Moss's new T24 was the quickest British car around the Nürburgring and he finished sixth despite gear-selection problems. For the Italian GP, Francis fitted fuel injection and converted the set-up to run on nitromethane additive, which resulted in blistering

straight-line speed but high fuel consumption; Moss was fifth at the start and proved fast in between four stops for fuel and tyres, eventually finishing 13th. After taking second place in the Madgwick Cup at Goodwood, Moss's frustrating campaign ended at Castle Combe with a broken shoulder after he crashed with Tony Rolt and rolled.

Ken Wharton was another whose Cooper was officially entered

Stirling Moss, Cooper T24-Alta (Italian GP)

Ken Wharton, Cooper T23-Bristol (Italian GP)

as a works car despite being run by Bernard Blyth from Wharton's garage in Smethwick. Wharton used backing from Shell to acquire a dark green Cooper T23-Bristol, complete with ENV pre-selector gearbox and yellow nose and wheels. Solex carburettors were preferred to SU units after problems on the dyno. Wharton qualified on pole for his heat at the International Trophy and won national races at Snetterton and Charterhall but was outclassed on five GP appearances. He retired in Holland and France before finishing a distant eighth at Silverstone. Absent from the German GP, he was seventh in Switzerland despite refuelling and was unclassified in Italy after pushing the car to the finish following fan-belt breakage on the far side of the circuit.

EQUIPE ANGLAISE

Alan Brown left Ecurie Richmond to join forces with Bob Chase to form Equipe Anglaise. Bernie Rodger of RJC Motors modified a MkII Cooper on their behalf with bodywork that resembled a Ferrari, de Dion rear suspension and a double-overhead-camshaft four-cylinder Alfa Romeo engine that proved an unreliable mistake. After his unhappy works outing in Argentina, Brown acquired the ex-Bobby Baird Cooper T23-Bristol with which he finished second in the Snetterton Coronation Trophy and crashed out of the lead at Avus. It was repaired for the following week's British GP, where he retired without making an impression. After a delay with

suspension problems in Germany, the six-cylinder Bristol engine broke on the last lap of the Nürburgring. For this race, the team's original T23, now painted silver and with a Bristol engine and gearbox instead of the disappointing Alfa unit, was rented to Helm Glöckler but he did not start after a con rod failed during practice. Brown's misfiring Cooper-Bristol was a regular in the pits during the Italian GP and he was lapped 10 times before finishing 12th.

ATLANTIC STABLE

British wool merchant Peter Whitehead and American Tom Cole acquired a pair of MkII Coopers, a T23 and a T24, which they intended to enter as Atlantic Stable. The T24 was given the twin-plug Alta engine (with Weber carburettors) from Whitehead's 1952 Alta, the chassis being completed by his mechanics at Cooper's Surbiton works. His only championship appearance of 1953 was the British GP, in which he was delayed by braking problems, leaving him lapped 11 times on the way to ninth place. The car was generally reliable in non-championship races and Whitehead was placed at Syracuse, Dundrod, Crystal Palace, Albi, Oulton Park and Snetterton.

Cole's blue-and-white Bristol-powered T23 was all-but destroyed by fire when he hit a wall and rolled on début at Syracuse. A replacement chassis was driven in subsequent minor races by both Cole and Graham Whitehead but Cole was killed during that year's Le Mans 24 Hours.

Alan Brown, Cooper T23-Bristol (Italian GP)

Peter Whitehead, Cooper T24-Alta (British GP)

OTHER COOPER PRIVATEERS

Winner of a couple of Scandinavian F3 races during his début season in 1952, Rodney Nuckey tested an F2 Connaught at Goodwood in January before ordering a Cooper T23-Bristol to compete at similarly far-flung racing outposts. He was third in a race of attrition at Syracuse, beat local Finnish fields in Helsinki and Tampere, then led the opening lap at Avus only to fade to fifth when a wishbone broke. Nuckey's championship début followed at the Nürburgring, where he came 11th after a long pitstop to check his suspension. After taking fourth place in the London Trophy at Crystal Palace, Nuckey crashed during practice for the final F2 race

of the year at Snetterton, severely damaging the car.

Bob Gerard prepared his own T23 at his workshops in Leicester. It was the second F2 car to take the chequered flag in the F1 Rouen GP, finished 11th in the following week's French GP at Reims, and retired early from the British GP. Gerard won the final two national races of the season at Castle Combe and Snetterton.

Tony Crook campaigned a Cooper T24-Alta during 1953. He dominated a 10-mile race at Silverstone in June but there was an altogether higher level of competition when he returned to the circuit for the following month's British GP, where he qualified on the penultimate row and retired at the start with a fuel-system problem.

Tony Crook, Cooper T24-Alta (*Coronation Trophy, Crystal Palace*)

Rodney Nuckey, Cooper T23-Bristol (German GP)

Bob Gerard, Cooper T23-Bristol (French GP)

Roy Salvadori, Connaught A-Lea-Francis (British GP)

CONNAUGHT ENGINEERING

Connaught Engineering announced plans to field a three-car team in British and selected European races with Kenneth McAlpine, Dennis Poore and motorcycle star Geoff Duke named as drivers, but Duke decided to concentrate on two-wheel sport and Poore soon ended his association with the marque. Instead, Roy Salvadori signed to lead the team after testing at Goodwood and various other drivers stepped in from time to time.

Two new long-chassis A-types were introduced during 1953. Rodney Clarke investigated alternative engines but judged it more cost-effective to continue with the Lea-Francis-based straight-four, with modification to run on up to 30 per cent nitromethane. Fuel injection by American specialist Hilborn-Travers was initially fitted to one car and normally used for the team's World Championship entries. Connaught took part in five of the season's eight GPs: the team decided against the long trip to Argentina, missed the Belgian GP 'through a contretemps over travelling expenses' (*The Autocar*) and withdrew its singleton entry from the Swiss GP.

Fuel injection transformed acceleration and Salvadori finished second in the Lavant Cup at Goodwood and in the International Trophy at Silverstone. In the championship races that followed, however, he retired from all five, despite reverting to more reliable carburettors for the Italian GP. He scored further second places at Crystal Palace and Charterhall and won Goodwood's final F2 race of the year, the Madgwick Cup.

McAlpine won a minor F2 race at Snetterton in June before making four GP starts, his only finish a lowly 13th in the German GP after a couple of stops to repair his car's rear suspension. He was lucky to escape injury when he rolled during the final non-championship race of the year at a wet Castle Combe.

Disappointed with his Cooper-Alta Special, Stirling Moss joined Connaught for the Ulster Trophy and Dutch GP. He was second in

Kenneth McAlpine, Connaught A-Lea-Francis (German GP)

'B. Bira', Connaught A-Lea-Francis (German GP)

Stirling Moss, Connaught A-Lea-Francis (Dutch GP)

Jack Fairman, Connaught A-Lea-Francis (Italian GP)

his heat in Ireland despite only having two workable gears and he scratched from the final. He made a great start at Zandvoort before losing a possible top-six finish when a stone damaged a fuel pipe, ending up ninth after a long pitstop.

'B. Bira' started three mid-season GPs for Connaught. A broken differential ended a strong performance in France, he finished seventh at Silverstone despite spinning twice, and retired from the midfield in Germany. Jack Fairman drove the third car in Italy but was not classified after pitting to fix a smoking engine.

ECURIE BELGE

Johnny Claes decided that a Connaught A-type best suited his privateer needs and took delivery before Easter, the car naturally finished in Belgian racing yellow. Steady rather than spectacular during four championship races with the car, Claes was unclassified after a troubled run in Holland, retired in Germany and Italy, and finished a distant 12th in the French GP. His best non-championship results were sixth at Bordeaux, Avus and Modena. Claes hired a works Maserati for his home race so André Pilette drove the Connaught at Spa-Francorchamps, qualifying on the penultimate row and finishing 11th and last.

In October the Guild of Motoring Writers awarded Claes its inaugural 'Driver of the Year' award in recognition of winning the Liège–Rome–Liège rally despite getting no respite at the wheel after his co-driver fell ill. In contrast there was tragedy in May when he crashed into the crowd at Chimay, killing a spectator.

Johnny Claes, Connaught A-Lea-Francis (Dutch GP)

André Pilette, Connaught A-Lea-Francis (Belgian GP)

Jimmy Stewart, Cooper T20-Bristol (British GP)

Ian Stewart, Connaught A-Lea-Francis (British GP)

Tony Rolt, Connaught A-Lea-Francis (British GP)

ECURIE ECOSSE

A new Connaught A-type ordered by Ecurie Ecosse in February was delivered to Merchiston Motors in April. The car was originally driven in non-championship events by Sir James Scott-Douglas but Ian Stewart was behind the wheel when it appeared at Silverstone for the British GP. A persistent misfire ruined his day and he did not appear in the World Championship again.

The unrelated Jimmy Stewart, whose younger brother, Jackie, would become a triple World Champion in years to come, drove the team's old Cooper T20-Bristol. He was the last-lap winner of an Easter handicap race at Goodwood and finished third in an F2 event at Charterhall, but shed a wheel when a stub axle sheared at Snetterton. He made a favourable impression on his GP début at Silverstone by running sixth before crashing through a *Daily Express* hording at Copse with 10 laps to go. This World Championship outing also proved to be a one-off.

ROB WALKER RACING

The most successful Connaught A-type on the British scene was Rob Walker's navy blue and white example. The Dorking-based team only entered one GP – the British – where Tony Rolt qualified 10th and lay a noteworthy sixth, and leading British car, when a half shaft fractured after 71 laps. Third in the International Trophy at Silverstone, Rolt won F2 races at Crystal Palace, Snetterton (both twice), Thruxton and Oulton Park. His last race of the year, the Joe Fry Memorial Trophy at Castle Combe, ended after contact with Stirling Moss on the second lap, Moss breaking his shoulder when thrown clear. Eric Thompson also steered the car to a couple of minor victories at Snetterton during 1953.

OFFICINE SPECIALIZZATE COSTRUZIONE AUTOMOBILI (OSCA)

A second OSCA 20 was built for Louis Chiron's return after the burns he suffered at Syracuse in March 1952. The large rear brakes were now outboard and Elie Bayol's original car was similarly modified. Both cars were privately entered. Twelve months on, Chiron finished second at Syracuse after all four Ferraris retired but both OSCA drivers were lapped repeatedly at Pau and Bordeaux. Chiron was fifth in the Ulster Trophy at Dundrod and Bayol qualified on pole at Albi, finishing second in his heat but spinning out of the final following clutch failure. Bayol inherited OSCA's first victory against a limited field at Aix-les-Bains and Chiron was second at Les Sables d'Olonne.

However, they struggled when points were on offer. Both cars broke during the French GP only for Chiron to push his across the line to the cheers of the crowd, making him the last classified finisher in 15th place. He was a non-starter in Britain and neither car started in Switzerland. Chiron finished 10th in the Italian GP but Bayol started from the pitlane and retired. That was OSCA's final World Championship appearance as the Maserati brothers concentrated on sports cars thereafter.

Louis Chiron, OSCA 20 (Italian GP)

Elie Bayol, OSCA 20 (Italian GP)

Hans Herrmann, Veritas Meteor (German GP)

Willi Heeks, Veritas Meteor (German GP)

VERITAS

The 1953 German GP at the Nürburgring attracted a record 34 starters, of which seven were an assortment of privately entered Veritas cars.

Hans Herrmann drove Hans Klenk's Meteor into an impressive ninth position when lapped just once while the similar cars of Willi Heeks and Veritas founder Ernst Loof retired. The other four cars were Veritas RS chassis: Theo Helfrich, in a BMW-powered version, and Wolfgang Seidel finished outside the top 10 while Erwin Bauer and Oswald Karch retired.

Arthur Legat again entered his Veritas Meteor in the Belgian GP, qualifying on the last row and breaking his transmission before completing a lap.

Ernst Loof, Veritas Meteor (German GP)

Theo Helfrich, Veritas RS-BMW (German GP)

Wolfgang Seidel, Veritas RS (German GP)

Oswald Karch, Veritas RS (*Eifelrennen, Nürburgring, 1952*)

Arthur Legat, Veritas Meteor (Belgian GP, 1952)

Erwin Bauer, Veritas RS (German GP)

Theo Fitzau, AFM 7-BMW (German GP)

Günther Bechem, AFM 2-BMW (German GP)

ALEX VON FALKENHAUSEN MOTORENBAU (AFM)

Hans Stuck initially persevered with his unreliable AFM-Küchen, which he took to Silverstone for the International Trophy. He qualified in the midfield only for the engine to fail in his heat. He acquired a Bristol unit to replace the V8 and finished fourth in the GP des Frontières at Chimay. Second at Dessau (with the Küchen) and Halle-Saale (Bristol), he used the latter engine for the German and Italian GPs. It blew up during the opening lap of his home GP but he finished 14th at Monza, albeit lapped 13 times. Stuck quit single-seaters at the end of the year but continued to compete with distinction in touring cars for another decade.

Having entered the 1952 German GP as 'Bernhard Nacke', Günther Bechem now raced under his true identity. Bechem and Theo Fitzau drove AFM-BMWs in the 1953 German GP, Fitzau entered by Helmut Niedermayr, but, like Stuck, both suffered early engine failures.

RENNKOLLEKTIV EMW

Deutsches Amt für Material und Warenprufung (DAMW) was a state-funded East German manufacturer that built sports-racing and F2 cars using BMW's six-cylinder engine from the 328. These were taken on by, and renamed after, Eisenacher Motoren Werke

Hans Stuck, AFM 4-Bristol (Italian GP)

Edgar Barth, EMW-BMW (German GP)

(EMW), which had been BMW in the Russian-controlled Eastern sector of post-war Germany.

Edgar Barth drove an F2 EMW-BMW with great success, winning back-to-back East German titles in 1952 and 1953. This offset single-seater had a ladder frame, double-wishbone front suspension and de Dion rear axle with torsion bars all round, and twin-plug ignition. Barth was less successful on occasional forays into the West: although fifth in the 1953 Eifelrennen, he retired from the German GP after 12 laps towards the back of the field.

A second DAMW/EMW F2 car was based on the still-born Auto Union E-type that would have raced from 1941. The rear-engine design had a 1,995cc V12 engine fitted in a ladder frame.

Suspension was via trailing links and torsion bars at the front a de Dion rear axle with torsion bars and lower wishbones.

BMW SPECIALS

Paul Greifzu's widow Dora entered his front-engine BMW *Eigenbau* (Special) in the German GP with Rudolf Krause once again driving. Winner of the opening East German F2 race at Chemnitz after Edgar Barth had retired, Krause finished the GP in 14th position with Ernst Klodwig's rear-engine Heck-BMW 15th. Krause and Klodwig finished second and fourth in the East German F2 Championship respectively.

Rudolf Krause, Greifzu-BMW (German GP)

Ernst Klodwig, Heck-BMW (German GP)

1953 RESULTS

DRIVER PERFORMANCE (EXCLUDING INDIANAPOLIS 500)

DRIVER	CAR-ENGINE	RA	NL	B	F	GB	D	CH	I
Kurt Adolff	Ferrari 166C	–	–	–	–	–	27 R	–	–
Alberto Ascari	Ferrari 500	1 1 FL	1 1	2 1	1 4 FL*	1 1 FL	1 8 FL	2 1 FL	1 R
John Barber	Cooper T23-Bristol	16 8	–	–	–	–	–	–	–
Edgar Barth	EMW-BMW	–	–	–	–	–	24 R	–	–
Erwin Bauer	Veritas RS	–	–	–	–	–	33 R	–	–
Elie Bayol	OSCA 20	–	–	–	15 R	–	–	NT DNS	13 R
Günther Bechem	AFM 2-BMW	–	–	–	–	–	30 R	–	–
Jean Behra	Gordini 16	11 6	–	14 R	22 10	22 R	9 R	12 R	–
Georges Berger	Simca-Gordini 15	–	–	20 R	–	–	–	–	–
'B.Bira'	Connaught A-Lea-Francis	–	–	–	11 R	19 7	15 R	–	–
	Maserati A6GCM	–	–	–	–	–	–	–	23 11
Pablo Birger	Simca-Gordini 15	14 R	–	–	–	–	–	–	–
Felice Bonetto	Maserati A6GCM (A6SSG)	15 R	13 3	–	2 R	16 6	7 4	10 4	7 R
Alan Brown	Cooper T20-Bristol	12 9	–	–	–	–	–	–	–
	Cooper T23-Bristol	–	–	–	–	21 R	17 R	–	24 12
Piero Carini	Ferrari 553 Squalo	–	–	–	–	–	–	–	20 R
Louis Chiron	OSCA 20	–	–	–	25 NC	29 DNS	–	NT DNS	25 10
Johnny Claes	Connaught A-Lea-Francis	–	17 NC	–	21 12	–	25 R	–	30 R
	Maserati A6GCM (A6SSG)	–	–	10 R	–	–	–	–	–
Peter Collins	HWM 53-Alta	–	16 8	16 R	17 13	–	–	–	–
	HWM 51/52-Alta	–	–	–	–	23 R	–	–	–
Tony Crook	Cooper T24-Alta	–	–	–	–	25 R	–	–	–
Emmanuel de Graffenried	Maserati A6GCM (A6SSG)	–	7 5	9 4	9 7	26 R	11 5	8 R	9 R
Max de Terra	Ferrari 166C	–	–	–	–	–	–	19 9	–
Jack Fairman	HWM 52/53-Alta	–	–	–	–	27 R	–	–	–
	Connaught A-Lea-Francis	–	–	–	–	–	–	–	22 NC
Juan Manuel Fangio	Maserati A6GCM (A6SSG)	2 R	2 R	1 R	4 2 FL*	4 2	2 2	1 4	2 1 FL
Giuseppe Farina	Ferrari 500	4 R	3 2	4 R	6 5	5 3	3 1	3 2	3 2
John Fitch	HWM 52/53-Alta	–	–	–	–	–	–	–	26 R
Theo Fitzau	AFM 7-BMW	–	–	–	–	–	21 R	–	–
Paul Frère	HWM 53-Alta	–	–	11 10	–	–	–	16 R	–
Oscar Gálvez	Maserati A6GCM (A6SSG)	9 5	–	–	–	–	–	–	–
Bob Gerard	Cooper T23-Bristol	–	–	–	12 11	18 R	–	–	–
Yves Giraud-Cabantous	HWM 53-Alta	–	–	–	18 14	–	–	–	28 15
Helm Glöckler	Cooper T23-Bristol	–	–	–	–	–	35 DNS	–	–
José Froilán González	Maserati A6GCM (A6SSG)	5 3	5 3	3 R FL	5 3	2 4 FL	–	–	–
Duncan Hamilton	HWM 53-Alta	–	–	–	–	17 R	–	–	–
Mike Hawthorn	Ferrari 500	6 4	6 4	7 6	7 1	3 5	4 3	7 3	6 4
Willi Heeks	Veritas Meteor	–	–	–	–	–	18 R	–	–
Theo Helfrich	Veritas RS-BMW	–	–	–	–	–	28 12	–	–
Hans Herrmann	Veritas Meteor	–	–	–	–	–	14 9	–	–
Peter Hirt	Ferrari 500	–	–	–	–	–	–	17 R	–
Oswald Karch	Veritas RS	–	–	–	–	–	34 R	–	–
Ernst Klodwig	Heck-BMW	–	–	–	–	–	32 15	–	–
Rudolf Krause	Greifzu-BMW	–	–	–	–	–	26 14	–	–
Chico Landi	Maserati A6GCM	–	–	–	–	–	–	20 R	21 R
Hermann Lang	Maserati A6GCM (A6SSG)	–	–	–	–	–	–	11 5	–
Arthur Legat	Veritas Meteor	–	–	19 R	–	–	–	–	–
Ernst Loof	Veritas Meteor	–	–	–	–	–	31 R	–	–
Lance Macklin	HWM 53-Alta	–	15 R	17 R	16 R	12 R	–	15 R	27 R
Umberto Maglioli	Ferrari 553 Squalo	–	–	–	–	–	–	–	11 8
Sergio Mantovani	Maserati A6GCM (A6SSG)	–	–	–	–	–	–	–	12 7
Robert Manzon	Gordini 16	8 R	–	–	–	–	–	–	–
Onofre Marimón	Maserati A6GCM (A6SSG)	–	–	6 3	8 9	7 R	8 R	5 R	4 R
Kenneth McAlpine	Connaught A-Lea-Francis	–	14 R	–	–	13 R	16 13	–	18 NC
Carlos Menditéguy	Gordini 16	10 R	–	–	–	–	–	–	–
Roberto Mières	Gordini 16	–	19 R	–	24 R	–	–	–	16 6
Stirling Moss	Connaught A-Lea-Francis	–	9 9	–	–	–	–	–	–
	Cooper-Alta Special	–	–	–	13 R	–	–	–	–
	Cooper T24-Alta	–	–	–	–	–	–	12 6	10 13
Luigi Musso	Maserati A6GCM (A6SSG)	–	–	–	–	–	–	–	NT 7
Rodney Nuckey	Cooper T23-Bristol	–	–	–	–	–	20 11	–	–

DRIVER PERFORMANCE CONTINUED

DRIVER	CAR-ENGINE	RA	NL	B	F	GB	D	CH	I
André Pilette	Connaught A-Lea-Francis	–	–	[18] 11	–	–	–	–	–
Tony Rolt	Connaught A-Lea-Francis	–	–	–	–	[10] R	–	–	–
Louis Rosier	Ferrari 500	–	[8] 7	[13] 8	[10] 8	[24] 10	[22] 10	[14] R	[17] 16
Roy Salvadori	Connaught A-Lea-Francis	–	[11] R	–	[19] R	[28] R	[13] R	–	[14] R
Harry Schell	Gordini 16	[NT] 7	[10] R	[12] 7	[20] R	[9] R	[10] R	–	[15] 9
Albert Scherrer	HWM 53-Alta	–	–	–	–	–	–	[18] 8	–
Adolfo Schwelm Cruz	Cooper T20-Bristol	[13] R	–	–	–	–	–	–	–
Wolfgang Seidel	Veritas RS	–	–	–	–	–	[29] 16	–	–
Ian Stewart	Connaught A-Lea-Francis	–	–	–	–	[20] R	–	–	–
Jimmy Stewart	Cooper T20-Bristol	–	–	–	–	[15] R	–	–	–
Hans Stuck	AFM 4-Bristol	–	–	–	–	–	[23] R	–	[29] 14
Jacques Swaters	Ferrari 500	–	–	–	–	–	[19] 7	[13] R	–
Maurice Trintignant	Gordini 16	[7] 7	[12] 6	[8] 5	[23] R	[8] R	[5] R	[4] R	[8] 5
Luigi Villoresi	Ferrari 500	[3] 2	[4] R FL	[5] 2	[3] 6	[6] R	[6] 8	[6] 6	[5] 3
Fred Wacker	Gordini 16	–	[20] DNS	[15] 9	–	–	–	[NT] DNS	–
Ken Wharton	Cooper T23-Bristol	–	[18] R	–	[14] R	[11] 8	–	[9] 7	[19] NC
Peter Whitehead	Cooper T24-Alta	–	–	[14] 9	–	–	–	–	–

*Some sources credit Fangio alone with the fastest lap during the French GP. **SHARED DRIVES** Argentine GP: Maurice Trintignant/Harry Schell (Gordini 16) 7. Dutch GP: Felice Bonetto/José Froilán González (Maserati A6GCM) 3. Belgian GP: Johnny Claes/Juan Manuel Fangio (Maserati A6GCM) R. German GP: Alberto Ascari/Luigi Villoresi (Ferrari 500) 8; Luigi Villoresi/Alberto Ascari (Ferrari 500) R. Swiss GP: Juan Manuel Fangio/Felice Bonetto (Maserati A6GCM) 4; Felice Bonetto/Juan Manuel Fangio (Maserati A6GCM) R. Italian GP: Sergio Mantovani/Luigi Musso (Maserati A6GCM) 7.

FORMULA 2 RACE WINNERS

ROUND	RACE (CIRCUIT)	DATE	WINNER
1	Gran Premio de la República Argentina (Buenos Aires)	Jan 18	Alberto Ascari (Ferrari 500)
–*	Gran Premio de la Ciudad de Buenos Aires (Buenos Aires)	Feb 1	Giuseppe Farina (Ferrari 625)
–	Gran Premio di Siracusa (Syracuse)	Mar 22	Emmanuel de Graffenried (Maserati A6GCM)
–	Grand Prix de Pau (Pau)	Apr 6	Alberto Ascari (Ferrari 500)
–	Lavant Cup (Goodwood)	Apr 6	Emmanuel de Graffenried (Maserati A6GCM)
–	Aston Martin Owners Club Formula 2 Race (Snetterton)	Apr 18	Eric Thompson (Connaught A-Lea-Francis)
–	Grand Prix de Bordeaux (Bordeaux)	May 3	Alberto Ascari (Ferrari 500)
–	Strassen-Rennen Chemnitz (Chemnitz)	May 3	Rudolf Krause (Greifzu-BMW)
–	Daily Express International Trophy (Silverstone)	May 9	Mike Hawthorn (Ferrari 500)
–	Gran Premio di Napoli (Posillipo)	May 10	Giuseppe Farina (Ferrari 500)
–	News of the World Ulster Trophy (Dundrod)	May 16	Mike Hawthorn (Ferrari 500)
–	Winfield J.C. Formula 2 Race (Charterhall)	May 23	Ken Wharton (Cooper T23-Bristol)
–	Grand Prix des Frontières (Chimay)	May 24	Maurice Trintignant (Gordini 16)
–	Coronation Trophy (Crystal Palace)	May 25	Tony Rolt (Connaught A-Lea-Francis)
–	Coronation Trophy (Snetterton)	May 30	Tony Rolt (Connaught A-Lea-Francis)
2**	Indianapolis 500 (Indianapolis)	May 30	Bill Vukovich (Kurtis KK500A-Offenhauser)
–	Coupe de Printemps (Montlhéry)	May 31	Marcel Balsa (BMW Special)
–	Eifelrennen (Nürburgring)	May 31	Emmanuel de Graffenried (Maserati A6GCM)
3	Grote Prijs van Nederland (Zandvoort)	Jun 7	Alberto Ascari (Ferrari 500)
–	Paul Greifzu Gedachnitsrennen (Dessau)	Jun 7	Edgar Barth (EMW-BMW)
4	Grand Prix de Belgique (Spa-Francorchamps)	Jun 21	Alberto Ascari (Ferrari 500)
–	Midland Motoring Enthusiasts' Formula 2 Race (Silverstone)	Jun 27	Tony Crook (Cooper T24-Alta)
–	West Essex Car Club Formula 2 Race (Snetterton)	Jun 27	Kenneth McAlpine (Connaught A-Lea-Francis)
–	Strassen-Rennen Halle-Saale (Halle-Saale)	Jul 5	Edgar Barth (EMW-BMW)
5	Grand Prix de l'Automobile Club de France (Reims)	Jul 5	Mike Hawthorn (Ferrari 500)
–	Crystal Palace Trophy (Crystal Palace)	Jul 11	Tony Rolt (Connaught A-Lea-Francis)
–	Avusrennen (Avus)	Jul 12	Jacques Swaters (Ferrari 500)
6	British Grand Prix (Silverstone)	Jul 18	Alberto Ascari (Ferrari 500)
–	United States Air Force Trophy (Snetterton)	Jul 25	Tony Rolt (Connaught A-Lea-Francis)
–	Circuit du Lac (Aix-les-Bains)	Jul 26	Elie Bayol (OSCA 20)
–	Dresden Autobahn-Spinne (Dresden)	Jul 26	Edgar Barth (EMW-BMW)
7	Grosser Preis von Deutschland (Nürburgring)	Aug 2	Giuseppe Farina (Ferrari 500)
–	Bristol Motor Club Formula 2 Race (Thruxton)	Aug 3	Tony Rolt (Connaught A-Lea-Francis)
–	Mid-Cheshire Motor Club Formula 2 Race (Oulton Park)	Aug 8	Tony Rolt (Connaught A-Lea-Francis)
–	Grand Prix des Sables d'Olonne (Les Sables d'Olonne)	Aug 9	Louis Rosier (Ferrari 500)
–	Newcastle Journal Trophy (Charterhall)	Aug 15	Ken Wharton (Cooper T23-Bristol)
8	Grand Prix de Suisse (Bremgarten)	Aug 23	Alberto Ascari (Ferrari 500)
–	Sachsenring-Rennen (Sachsenring)	Aug 23	Edgar Barth (EMW-BMW)
–	Circuit de Cadours (Cadours)	Aug 30	Maurice Trintignant (Gordini 16)
–	Redex Trophy (Snetterton)	Sep 12	Eric Thompson (Connaught A-Lea-Francis)
9	Gran Premio d'Italia (Monza)	Sep 13	Juan Manuel Fangio (Maserati A6SSG)
–	London Trophy (Crystal Palace)	Sep 19	Stirling Moss (Cooper T24-Alta)
–	Gran Premio di Modena (Modena Aerautodromo)	Sep 20	Juan Manuel Fangio (Maserati A6GCM)
–	Madgwick Cup (Goodwood)	Sep 26	Roy Salvadori (Connaught A-Lea-Francis)
–	Bernau Autobahn-Schleife (Bernau)	Sep 27	Arthur Rosenhammer (EMW-BMW)
–	Joe Fry Memorial Trophy (Castle Combe)	Oct 3	Bob Gerard (Cooper T23-Bristol)
–	Curtis Trophy (Snetterton)	Oct 17	Bob Gerard (Cooper T23-Bristol)

*Formule Libre **Run to AAA National Championship rules

DRIVERS' CHAMPIONSHIP

	DRIVERS	POINTS	
1	Alberto Ascari	34.5	(47)*
2	Juan Manuel Fangio	27.5	(29)*
3	Giuseppe Farina	26	(32)*
4	Mike Hawthorn	19	(27)*
5	Luigi Villoresi	17	
6	José Froilán González	13.5	(14.5)*
7	Bill Vukovich	9	
8	Emmanuel de Graffenried	7	
9	Felice Bonetto	6.5	
10	Art Cross	6	
11=	Onofre Marimón	4	
	Maurice Trintignant	4	
13=	Duane Carter	2	
	Oscar Gálvez	2	
	Sam Hanks	2	
	Hermann Lang	2	
	Jack McGrath	2	
18=	Fred Agabashian	1.5	
	Paul Russo	1.5	

*Best four results count

The streamlined Mercedes-Benz W196s of Juan Manuel Fangio and Karl Kling dominated the French GP at Reims

1954

TRIUMPHANT GP RETURN FOR MERCEDES-BENZ

Argentina's José Froilán González (Maserati) and Juan Manuel Fangio (Mercedes-Benz) lead the opening lap at the Nürburgring

Stirling Moss pushes his car after being denied victory at Monza

New rules for 1954–57 were ratified at an FIA meeting in Brussels on 17 February 1952, stipulating a 2,500cc maximum capacity for normally aspirated engines with 750cc allowed for forced-induction units. These regulations attracted two new manufacturers – Mercedes-Benz and Lancia – although neither was ready for the start of the season. Rumours of Alfa Romeo's return proved false. Barcelona-based Pegaso announced a lightweight V8 design from the pen of Wilfredo Ricart and entered the Spanish GP but the car never materialised. BMW, Porsche, Autoar (formerly Cisitalia), OSCA, Talbot and Tatra were all said to be entering F1. Cyril Kieft's Wolverhampton-based concern also looked to graduate and Gordon Bedson's design was built but unraced following the cancellation of the Coventry Climax 'Godiva' V8 engine.

The Automobilclub von Deutschland accepted the honour

Mercedes men (from left): Hermann Lang, team manager Alfred Neubauer, Juan Manuel Fangio, Karl Kling and Hans Herrmann at Monza

of hosting the Grosser Preis von Europa. Originally scheduled for 6 June, the Dutch GP was cancelled in March due to the cost of repairing Zandvoort and the absence of Mercedes-Benz and Lancia. The British Racing Drivers' Club and *Daily Express* delivered wine to each pit during the International Trophy meeting which was said to be appreciated by the visiting continental teams.

Mike Hawthorn was declared exempt from National Service in the UK on medical grounds, which prompted questions in the Houses of Parliament and uproar in the daily press. The young Ferrari star was suffering from a kidney complaint and required an operation after the season.

Forty years on from its famous victory in the 1914 GP de l'Automobile Club de France, Mercedes-Benz dominated on début at Reims and, stated *Autosport*, 'at one fell swoop, Italian supremacy was shattered'.

Mike Hawthorn wins the Spanish GP at Pedralbes

Juan Manuel Fangio, Mercedes-Benz W196 (Italian GP)

DAIMLER-BENZ (MERCEDES-BENZ)

The Mercedes (Daimler) and Benz marques amalgamated in 1926 and the Untertürkheim-based concern was pre-eminent in GP racing from 1934 to the outbreak of war in 1939. Mercedes-Benz made a tentative return to racing in the Argentine *Temporada* at the start of 1951 but a planned entry for the Italian GP did not happen. Driving 300SL sports cars the following year, Hermann Lang and Fritz Riess led a Mercedes 1–2 in the Le Mans 24 Hours and Karl Kling won the Carrera Panamericana.

The board of directors approved a new F1 car for 1954 and Lang, Kling and Riess accompanied legendary team manager Alfred Neubauer on a visit to the 1953 Italian GP as the company prepared

Karl Kling, Mercedes-Benz W196 (British GP)

for its much-anticipated return. Talented engineer Rudolf Uhlenhaut also remained from the pre-war 'Silver Arrows' racing department. Technical director Hans Scherenberg co-ordinated chief designers Ludwig Kraus (chassis) and Hans Gassmann (engines) in creating the Mercedes-Benz W196, which caused a stir when images were released in February due to its fully enclosed streamlined bodywork. The twin-overhead cam 2,496cc straight-eight engine had two plugs per cylinder, desmodromic valves and Bosch direct fuel injection, although Weber carburettors were also tried. The engine was mounted in the spaceframe chassis at an angle of 37 degrees, offset to the right to minimise frontal area, with the crankshaft to the left, and it drove through a five-speed synchromesh gearbox. Fuel tanks were between the wheels while suspension was by wishbones and torsion bars at the front with an old-fashioned swing axle at the rear. Large drum brakes were mounted inboard.

An all-German driver line-up was originally envisaged with Kling, Lang and 26-year-old Hans Herrmann all engaged. Juan Manuel Fangio, who ran a Mercedes agency in Argentina but seemed committed to Maserati, was announced as team leader in March. The prototype was tested at Monza in October 1953 but the programme was interrupted when Herrmann crashed at Hockenheim on 12 May 1954 when an oil pipe split. That part of the old circuit skirted the town and Herrmann, whose legs and feet were burned, narrowly missed a couple of young girls on bicycles.

Tests continued at Reims on 15–16 June and three race cars plus a spare were unloaded in the French GP paddock as planned at the

Hans Herrmann, Mercedes-Benz W196 (Spanish GP)

start of July. Fangio and Kling qualified 1–2 with the championship leader receiving 50 bottles of champagne for topping 200kph around the reconfigured track. They lapped the field as the Italian cars imploded, Fangio winning by a tenth of a second in a formation finish. Only seventh on the grid, Herrmann had climbed into third when his engine failed in a cloud of smoke.

The British GP at Silverstone was in complete contrast and Neubauer's expression was, according to *Autosport*, 'as sombre as the weather'. Mercedes only entered two cars and Kling struggled on this track's tighter confines, especially when it rained. Fangio qualified on pole but even he had problems positioning his car, which finished with heavy dents on either side after hitting the marker drums. Second for much of the race, he slipped to fourth at the chequered flag having lost third gear. Kling finished seventh after spinning at Copse Corner.

The introduction of open-wheel bodywork for slower circuits was accelerated and Uhlenhaut tested the revised W196 in the week before the German GP. Three such cars were entered for Fangio, Kling (who started last after missing practice) and Lang while Herrmann retained a streamliner. Fangio took the lead on the opening lap and soon headed Lang, the light-fuelled Kling and Herrmann in a silver 1–2–3–5. But Lang spun and stalled at Flugplatz, Herrmann's fuel pipe sheared and Kling, who led for a couple of laps, dropped to fourth following an unscheduled second pitstop to fix a broken suspension mount. When the Mercedes pit was invaded by officials, photographers and marshals during that stop, an irate Neubauer,

brandishing his signal flag, chased them away.

On a drying track, Fangio led the Swiss GP from start to finish to clinch his second world title with Herrmann third despite smoke bellowing with every gearchange. Kling recovered from a spin to run third before his engine's fuel injection gave trouble. All three cars were open-wheeled in Switzerland but Fangio and Kling had streamliners for Monza. Fangio scored a lucky victory when Stirling Moss's Maserati failed with 10 laps to go. Having jumped the start and led, Kling survived a high-speed excursion at Curva Grande only to crash when his suspension failed at Lesmo. Herrmann drove an open-wheeler into fourth after losing a lap changing plugs, which were very inaccessible on the W196.

Hermann Lang, Mercedes-Benz W196 (German GP)

During 1954 Mercedes only attended one non-championship race, the Berlin GP at Avus, where Kling led Fangio and Herrmann in a streamlined 1–2–3. Fangio chose the open-wheel configuration during practice for the Spanish GP and finished third despite oil spraying from his engine during the closing stages. Kling was lapped in fifth while Herrmann's fuel injection packed up.

As well as his four Mercedes victories, Fangio won two GPs for Maserati and became the only driver to have won the World Championship title driving for two different marques.

OFFICINE ALFIERI MASERATI

Giaocchino Colombo arrived as technical consultant in the winter of 1952/53 to work on Maserati's new F1 contender – the classic 250F. This was a further development of the A6GCM with new multi-tubular chassis and the twin-overhead-cam straight-six engine bored out to 2,493cc. Dual ignition was retained and three twin-choke Weber carburettors were fitted. The works cars revved to 8,200rpm but privateers were advised not to exceed 7,400rpm and this caused some resentment. The four-speed gearbox was mounted transversely behind the final drive, there was a new de Dion rear axle, and familiar coil spring/double wishbone suspension was used at the front. The oil tank was mounted beneath the carburettors but got too hot in this location so was moved behind the 44-gallon rear fuel tank for the German GP. Colombo had left by the time the 250F first tested at

Modena on Boxing Day of 1953 and the exhaustive six-month build programme was completed under the watchful eye of chief engineer Vittorio Bellentani. Maserati did not intend to field a works team until Juan Manuel Fangio became available because he had to wait for Mercedes-Benz to be ready.

Ferrari dominated the Argentine GP in the dry but Fangio's 250F gained up to five seconds a lap when it rained, 'driving at the outside limit of sanity' reported *The Autocar*, to score a controversial victory. Ferrari team manager Nello Ugolini protested that five Maserati mechanics, rather than the permitted three, had changed Fangio's tyres during a pitstop but an extraordinary meeting of the Automóvil Club Argentina confirmed Fangio's victory a few weeks later, on 11 February. Fangio retired from the subsequent *Formule Libre* Buenos Aires GP and did not race for five months before winning the Belgian GP on his return, the works cars now fitted with new cylinder heads and larger inlet ports and valves. That was Fangio's last race for Maserati in 1954 as the new Mercedes-Benz W196 made its début at the French GP.

Buoyed by Fangio's victory in Argentina, Maserati entered a factory team for the rest of the season. Onofre Marimón drove the second works entry from the start of 1954 and was assigned the only other true 250F to be shipped to Argentina, all other Maseratis being old F2 cars fitted with the new engine (and redesignated as 250Fs) or retaining their original 2-litre units. Marimón was forced to race one such *muletta*, which crashed when the clutch failed in

Juan Manuel Fangio, Maserati 250F (Belgian GP)

Stirling Moss, Maserati 250F (Italian GP)

practice. His 250F was second in the closing stages at Syracuse when he crashed again. He beat a national field at Rome's new Castel Fusano circuit to the south-west of the city – the biggest win of his brief career to date – but he retired from the subsequent Belgian and French GPs. Maserati missed qualifying for the British GP after arriving at the wrong channel port and Marimón started the race from the penultimate row of the grid; by the end of lap one he was a remarkable sixth but on lap three he spun at Abbey, then eventually passed Fangio's Mercedes to finish third. However, Marimón's promise was cruelly cut short while practising for the German GP when he crashed down a slope and into a tree, dying instantly.

Alfred Moss and Ken Gregory visited Mercedes-Benz in the hope of securing a drive for Stirling Moss but Alfred Neubauer thought the young British star needed a season driving a competitive F1 car to judge his talent. On Neubauer's suggestion, Equipe Moss bought a Maserati 250F that Alf Francis helped complete at the Modena factory. Francis moved the front bulkhead forward to accommodate Moss's preferred straight-arm driving style and the accelerator was repositioned to the right of the pedals rather than centrally, as was usual for Italian designs at the time. With his car finished in pale green with red stripes and delivered on 5 May, Moss initially raced as a privateer but ended the year leading the works team. During Moss's début at Bordeaux, a switch from Dunlop to Pirelli tyres transformed the 250F's handling and he finished fourth. He followed up with third in the opening heat for Silverstone's International Trophy and won the Aintree 200. Despite an unscheduled pitstop, he finished third at Spa-Francorchamps to score his first World Championship points.

Having lent the car to the works team in France, Moss equalled the fastest lap on five consecutive laps of the British GP before retiring when second with 10 laps to go. Second at Caen after a great dice with Maurice Trintignant's Ferrari, Moss was entered by the works team from the German GP with his 250F repainted red with green nose. The event was overshadowed by Marimón's death and Moss's engine failed after a lap. Winner of the Oulton Park Gold Cup from the back of the grid, he retired from the lead of the non-championship Pescara GP (having qualified on pole by a margin of 21.3sec) and in Switzerland. He dominated the Italian GP before the oil pressure plummeted to deny his breakthrough GP victory. Dominant winner of lesser races at Goodwood and Aintree, Moss crashed the spare works car during practice for the Spanish GP

Onofre Marimón, Maserati 250F (French GP)

Alberto Ascari, Maserati 250F (British GP)

Luigi Musso, Maserati 250F (Spanish GP)

when he pressed the central throttle by mistake, and in the race he retired his own car in a downbeat conclusion to what had been a promising campaign.

With Lancia almost four months from being ready, Gianni Lancia released Alberto Ascari and Luigi Villoresi to race works 250Fs at Reims and Silverstone. Ascari retired from both races and refused further opportunities with Maserati. Villoresi was fifth (of just six finishers) in the French GP after changing plugs. He handed his car to Ascari in Britain but the double World Champion suffered his second engine failure of the race. Villoresi withdrew from the German GP following Marimón's death, missed the Swiss GP, and briefly ran second in Italy (going to 8,800rpm to do so) before clutch

failure ended his final appearance for Maserati.

Luigi Musso re-signed with Maserati for a limited F1 schedule alongside sports car duties. A non-starter in Argentina, he inherited victory at Pescara when both Moss and Robert Manzon (Ferrari) retired. Musso started the last two championship races in Italy and Spain: at Monza he was sidelined by transmission failure and on the wide boulevards of Barcelona's Pedralbes district he passed Fangio's ailing Mercedes-Benz to snatch second.

Roberto Mières ordered a 250F and drove an updated A6GCM/250F while his new car was being built. Although initially a private entry, his car was prepared and run by the factory team. He retired from the opening round in Argentina before

Luigi Villoresi, Maserati 250F (Italian GP)

Roberto Mières, Maserati 250F (Spanish GP)

Sergio Mantovani, Maserati 250F (German GP)

finishing second in the Buenos Aires GP. Placed at Pau and in the International Trophy, his car caught fire of the opening lap of the Belgian GP after the fuel cap had not been secured and then was written off when its transporter crashed on the way to Rouen for a non-championship event. Sixth at Silverstone in a 250F borrowed from Jorge Daponte, his new chassis was ready for the German GP, where a stone holed the fuel tank. Mières was officially part of the works line-up for the last three championship rounds, which brought fourth places in Switzerland and Spain.

Sergio Mantovani was a steady and reliable works driver during the European season. Third in non-championship races at Syracuse and Rome, he finished seventh in Belgium despite three stops for plugs and did not start the French GP. Overlooked for the British GP when Maserati entered just three cars, he finished the German and Swiss GPs in fifth position to score the only championship points of his career. That latter race included hitting Ken Wharton's privately entered Maserati as they disputed seventh, an incident for which Mantovani apologised after the race. He was set to finish the Italian GP in a fine fourth before limping to the finish when the de Dion tube broke. Fourth in a minor race at Aintree, he ran in that position during the Spanish GP but lost a possible podium when he crashed while trying to pass Musso's sister car. Local Francesco 'Chico' Godia Sales drove a fifth works 250F into an unobtrusive sixth-place finish in Spain.

Chico Godia, Maserati 250F (Spanish GP)

'B. Bira', Maserati 250F (Spanish GP)

'B. BIRA'

Prince 'Bira' was a late replacement for Emilio Giletti in Argentina where he drove a 1953-specification Maserati A6GCM, powered by a new 250F engine, into seventh in the GP and *Formule Libre* races. An excellent second in his qualifying heat for the International Trophy, he won the GP des Frontières at Chimay before taking delivery of a *pukka* 250F before the Belgian GP. Reinvigorated by contemporary machinery, 'Bira' ran non-stop into sixth place at Spa-Francorchamps. The French GP, one of his finest races, saw him run out of fuel on the last lap while lying third but he was able to coast across the line to claim fourth place. After finishing second at Rouen-les-Essarts, he suffered from a bout of malaria over the British GP weekend and during the race handed his car to Ron Flockhart, who promptly rolled

'B. Bira'/Ron Flockhart, Maserati 250F (British GP)

it at Copse, thankfully without injury. 'Bira' retired in Germany and missed the next two championship races. Second at Pescara after repairing his exhaust out on the circuit, he returned to finish the Spanish GP ninth after pitting to fix a holed radiator. This was the Siamese prince's final GP as he retired from racing early in 1955.

HARRY SCHELL

Harry Schell left Gordini to run his own Maserati during 1954. In the Argentine GP he finished sixth with an ex-Juan Manuel Fangio 2-litre Maserati A6GCM (A6SSG) but for the European season he used a sister chassis fitted with a 250F engine. Fifth in Bari, he inherited second at Castel Fusano when Stirling Moss retired. Without an entry for the Belgian GP (the organisers as ever preferring works entries and local privateers), he retired from the midfield in France and was delayed by gear-selection difficulties at Silverstone. He was the leading privateer when seventh in Germany and took a distant third in the non-championship Pescara GP. For the Swiss GP, from which he retired, Schell had a new Maserati 250F that was officially entered by the works team. Like Moss, Schell had the throttle pedal moved to the right. He reverted to the A6GCM/250F to win a heat at Cadours before driving a true 250F once more in Spain, where he shocked the establishment. The quickest Maserati driver in practice, Schell started from the outside of the four-car front row with his blue-and-white 250F's tanks half full. He led the opening couple of laps, spun, then battled for the lead after Alberto Ascari's Lancia retired, only for his hour of glory to end with rear-axle failure after 29 laps.

Harry Schell, Maserati A6GCM (A6SSG) (Argentine GP)

Harry Schell, Maserati 250F (French GP)

Emmanuel de Graffenried/Ottorino Volonterio, Maserati 250F (Spanish GP)

SCUDERIA ENRICO PLATÉ/
BARON EMMANUEL DE GRAFFENRIED

Emmanuel de Graffenried endured a tragic and truncated campaign with Hollywood central to his plans. His old Maserati A6GCM was fitted with the new 2.5-litre engine when it was shipped to Argentina for the early-season races, with friend and long-term mechanic Enrico Platé in charge as ever. Eighth in the Argentine GP, de Graffenried retired from the Buenos Aires GP, where Platé was the victim of a freak accident; he was standing in the unguarded pitlane when Jorge Daponte lost control at the final corner and hit him, causing serious head injuries from which Platé died two days later.

The 1954 F1 season formed the backdrop for the movie *The Racers* (renamed *Such Men Are Dangerous* for British and European release), which was based on 1936 Donington GP winner Hans Rüesch's novel and starred Kirk Douglas as Italian racing driver Gino Borgesa. Hired as a consultant, de Graffenried completed 10 laps of the Belgian GP while filming action sequences, his A6GCM/250F having been modified to represent the fictitious Burano racing car. His next race was the final round in Spain where he pitted three times, lost an exhaust, briefly handed over to Ottorino Volonterio – his car's prospective new owner – and retired when the engine failed.

OWEN RACING ORGANISATION

British Racing Motors was offered for sale as a going concern in September 1952 and acquired by former BRM Trust chairman Sir Alfred Owen of Rubery, Owen & Co. The new 2.5-litre BRM under construction at Bourne would not be ready until late 1955, so a Maserati 250F was ordered for Ken Wharton. Turned out in British Racing Green, the 250F was delivered in June and entered for five of the remaining six championship rounds.

A bad vibration blighted the French GP, where Wharton retired when last. Eighth in his home GP at Silverstone after a plug change, he withdrew from the German GP without setting a practice time and returned at Bremgarten with the 250F – now repainted now olive green – much changed. It had disc brakes, alloy wheels and shortened exhausts while the oil tank had been moved to the left of the driver. Seventh in the early laps, he spun down to 12th when nudged by Sergio Mantovani as the Italian attempted to pass, and recovered to finish sixth. Owen did not enter Monza and Wharton lost another sixth place in the final GP in Barcelona when forced to pit with a misfire.

GILBY ENGINEERING

Roy Salvadori joined Sid Greene's South Norwood-based Gilby Engineering in November 1953 and negotiations to buy a Maserati 250F were concluded a month later. Salvadori tested the car at Modena in March and scored a couple of second places on début at Goodwood's Easter Monday meeting. He challenged Ken Wharton's BRM for the lead of that day's main event – the *Formule Libre* Glover Trophy – until they touched and spun. Wharton restarted and won while Salvadori's protest was unsuccessful. Salvadori won the minor

Ken Wharton, Maserati 250F (Spanish GP)

Roy Salvadori, Maserati 250F (British GP)

Curtis Trophy at Snetterton two days before finishing second at Goodwood once more. He qualified 10th for the French GP but retired, then a week later at Rouen-les-Essarts he finished a distant third after being black-flagged twice. During the British GP Salvadori had to stop to reattach a loose fuel tank only for the gearbox to fail. Gilby Engineering concentrated on national races for the rest of the summer, with a best result of second place at Crystal Palace. During the Oulton Park Gold Cup, Salvadori crashed heavily when the throttle stuck open, without injury.

OTHER MASERATI PRIVATEERS

Jorge Daponte's 2-litre Maserati A6GCM (A6SSG) was slowest in qualifying for the Argentine GP and his gearbox failed after 19 slow laps of the race. Worse was to come in the *Formule Libre* Buenos Aires GP for Daponte spun into the pitlane and hit Swiss entrant Enrico Platé, who died two days later. Daporte upgraded to a 250F engine to be placed in non-championship races at Rouen-les-Essarts and Pescara. He qualified the blue-and-yellow car on the last row for the Italian GP and ran at the back to finish 11th, 10 laps down.

Carlos Menditéguy was due to drive Onofre Marimón's 2-litre Maserati A6GCM in the Argentine GP but blew the engine in practice. Sardinian amateur Giovanni de Riu acquired an ex-works 2-litre Maserati A6GCM (A6SSG) from 'B. Bira' and entered a couple of F1 races during 1954. He was an early retirement at Castel Fusano and did not qualify for the Italian GP after completing a few slow laps during practice.

Jorge Daponte, Maserati 250F (Italian GP)

Jorge Daponte, Maserati A6GCM (A6SSG) (Argentine GP)

SCUDERIA FERRARI

Enzo Ferrari confirmed his U-turn by announcing the *Scuderia*'s entry for the 1954 World Championship at a celebratory dinner in Modena on 12 December 1953. Money was tight, so Ferrari refused to match Alberto Ascari's offer from Lancia and the World Champion's shock departure was confirmed on 29 December with Luigi Villoresi also on the move. Giuseppe Farina and Mike Hawthorn had already signed by then and José Froilán González's arrival from Maserati was confirmed in early January. The Ferrari 553 'Squalo' had disappointed on début in the 1953 Italian GP, so Ferrari fitted its successful type 500 chassis with an enlarged 2,498cc version of its four-cylinder engine that initially produced 230bhp at 7,000rpm. The car was renamed the Ferrari 625.

Ferrari dominated when dry in Argentina but Juan Manuel Fangio's Maserati took the lead in the rain. When Fangio stopped for a tyre change, Ferrari team manager Nello Ugolini claimed that five Maserati mechanics were involved rather than the permitted three, so protested. Believing Fangio would be disqualified, Ugolini ordered Farina to ease off and he duly finished second with González third, but several weeks later, on 11 February, the Automóvil Club Argentina refused Ugolini's protest, perhaps predictably. Hawthorn excelled in the wet but spun twice and was disqualified when pushed by enthusiastic spectators. An off-form Umberto Maglioli drove a fourth car and finished last. Hawthorn then lost the *Formule Libre* Buenos Aires GP when his engine failed on the last lap.

González drove a new version of the troublesome 553 'Squalo' in the opening European race at Syracuse. The engine was bored

Mike Hawthorn, Ferrari 625 (Italian GP)

Maurice Trintignant, Ferrari 625 (German GP)

José Froilán González, Ferrari 625 (British GP)

Giuseppe Farina, Ferrari 625 (Argentine GP)

Umberto Maglioli/José Froilán González, Ferrari 625 (Italian GP)

out to 2,497cc and fitted with two twin-choke Weber carburettors, the wheelbase was extended by 2½in to improve road-holding and the left-hand pannier tank was replaced by a rear-mounted tank within taller bodywork. Early race leader Hawthorn crashed his standard 625 and the car caught fire, prompting González to stop and help, unaware that Hawthorn had escaped, albeit with second-degree burns; meanwhile the Argentine driver's empty car rolled into Hawthorn's and fire engulfed the 'Squalo' too. Ferrari nevertheless won the race, Farina recovering from a spin to take victory, while Maurice Trintignant brought his 625 home in second place on his first drive for the works team.

Piero Taruffi, Ferrari 625 (German GP)

Trintignant's 625 finished second in Pau and González's won in Bordeaux. Back in the 553 'Squalo', González won his heat for the International Trophy but his engine would not start before the final, so he requisitioned Trintignant's 625 and eased to victory, and won the supporting sports car race as well. At Bari, González made it three non-championship F1 wins on successive weekends.

Ferrari sent modified 553s to Spa-Francorchamps for Farina (with his right arm in a cast after breaking it during the Mille Miglia) and González. Weight had been redistributed by moving the engine forward but handling remained unpredictable. All the same, they qualified on the front row and González led away only for an oil pipe to break on the opening lap. Farina assumed the lead but he had ignition failure before half distance. Trintignant and Hawthorn drove 625s: the Frenchman finished second while Hawthorn, having his first race since Syracuse and grieving for his father following his death in a road accident on Whit Monday, was overcome by fumes after an exhaust guard broke away and had to be lifted from the cockpit when he pitted; González took over to finish fourth after two lengthy pitstops for repairs. Ferrari's troubled campaign continued with the Supercortemaggiore sports car race at Monza, where Farina was badly burned in a practice crash, ending his season.

In France, González and Hawthorn in the 553s and Trintignant's old 625 were outclassed by the new Mercedes-Benz W196s and all three retired on a crushing day. Trintignant beat a non-championship field at Rouen-les-Essarts where Hawthorn drove a 625 fitted with the newer engine from the 553 'Squalo'. This configuration was chosen for all three Ferraris at Silverstone, where Mercedes-Benz struggled. González qualified second and led from start to finish to maintain his 100 per cent record at Silverstone that year. 'He finished as unruffled as if he had been down to Brackley and back,' Bill Boddy wrote in *Motor Sport*'s leader. Hawthorn completed a surprise 1–2 with Trintignant fifth.

Trintignant beat Stirling Moss at Caen and the engine experiments continued at the Nürburgring. Four 625s were entered with González's and Hawthorn's engines now using the bottom end of the Ferrari 735 'Monza' sports car and cylinder heads from the 553 F1 unit with twin magnetos mounted vertically at the front. Trintignant and Piero Taruffi, returning to the GP team as a one-off, handled standard 625s. González led at the start but Fangio soon dominated

Alberto Ascari, Ferrari 625 (Italian GP)

Mike Hawthorn, Ferrari 553 'Squalo' (Spanish GP)

José Froilán González, Ferrari 553 'Squalo' (Italian GP)

Giuseppe Farina, Ferrari 553 'Squalo' (Belgian GP)

in the new open-wheel Mercedes-Benz. Hawthorn retired but drove brilliantly after relieving González, who was devastated to have lost compatriot Onofre Marimón in practice. Hawthorn eventually finished 1min 36.5sec behind Fangio with Trintignant third and Taruffi sixth after puncturing a tyre.

Maglioli practised a singleton 553 'Squalo' at Pescara but withdrew when he was told that his mother was gravely ill. Robert Manzon was originally entered for the Swiss GP but injured his ribs when he crashed in the wet Friday practice session. Maglioli replaced him in the unloved car and finished seventh after a plug change. González, Hawthorn and Trintignant all drove the latest 625/sports/ F1 engine mash-up and the Argentinian starred again by finishing second in the rain despite a rough-sounding engine.

Monza has always been especially important to Ferrari and the team arrived with a confusing array of machinery and a returning superstar. With his own F1 car still not ready, Gianni Lancia released Ascari, who drove the 625 with the engine from the 553 'Squalo'. He almost stalled at the start but delighted the *tifosi* by challenging Fangio and Stirling Moss (Maserati) for the lead before the engine expired after 48 laps. Hawthorn and Trintignant, who stopped to repair his exhaust, drove similar cars into second and fifth places respectively. González's 553 retired early so he temporarily took over Maglioli's standard 625: despite stopping for a cushion as the driving position was tailored to his taller team-mate, he hauled it into the points before handing back to Maglioli, who took third place.

González was injured during practice for the Tourist Trophy and returned to Argentina having announced his retirement from racing.

Umberto Maglioli, Ferrari 553 'Squalo' (Swiss GP)

Just two works Ferraris were entered for the championship finale in Spain, a 625/553 for Trintignant and Hawthorn's much-modified 553. Following extensive testing, the 553's front transverse leaf springs were replaced by coil springs and rubber blocks, a first for Ferrari. A front anti-roll bar was also fitted to improve its handling and a 3sec improvement around Monza was reported. The quick new Lancia D50s retired and Mercedes-Benz's cars were delayed so Trintignant led before his gearbox failed. After crashing in the first practice session, Hawthorn survived a spin during the race to win a GP for the second time.

It had been an unsatisfactory season for Ferrari but González, Hawthorn and Trintignant finished the championship 2–3–4 behind the dominant Fangio.

ECURIE ROSIER

Louis Rosier announced in November 1953 that he would be entering two F1 Ferraris in the 1954 World Championship, with Maurice Trintignant chosen as his team-mate for Argentina. With a 625 engine installed in his old F2 car, Rosier had brake failure on the second lap of the GP and crashed into a gate, suffering cuts to his face. Driving a new Ferrari 625, Trintignant was fourth in the GP and inherited victory in the *Formule Libre* Buenos Aires GP after Mike Hawthorn retired on the last lap.

Trintignant joined Scuderia Ferrari for the European season so was replaced by Robert Manzon. Manzon's second place in Bordeaux was followed by third in the French GP when lapped by

Louis Rosier, Ferrari 625 (French GP)

Robert Manzon, Ferrari 625 (German GP)

Louis Rosier, Maserati 250F (Spanish GP)

the new streamlined Mercedes-Benz W196s. Both light blue Ferraris retired from the British GP without making an impression. Rosier was eighth in Germany but Manzon lost a sixth-place finish when his engine lost power.

Having missed the Swiss GP, Rosier replaced his two-year-old Ferrari with a new Maserati 250F, which was finished in dark blue. The engine failed during practice for the Italian GP so for the race he borrowed a red works 250F with which he finished eighth. He followed that with third in a minor race at Cadours and seventh in Spain. Manzon suffered a series of engines failures that caused early retirements at Monza and Barcelona.

ECURIE FRANCORCHAMPS

Jacques Swaters's Ecurie Francorchamps acquired a 2.5-litre Ferrari 625 engine for installation in the team's existing Ferrari 500 chassis. Roger Laurent began the season by finishing fourth at Syracuse but it was Swaters himself who started three championship GPs during 1954. He retired at the end of the opening lap at Spa-Francorchamps with a broken engine, which forced him to miss the French and British GPs. A replacement was finally fitted for Pescara's non-championship race, where the yellow Ferrari failed after just two laps. In the Swiss GP, Swaters ran at the back for most of the race and was classified eighth. He finished fifth at Avus before making his final GP appearance in Spain, where the engine failed once again.

Jacques Swaters, Ferrari 625 (Belgian GP)

Reg Parnell, Ferrari 625 (British GP)

Alberto Ascari, Lancia D50 (Spanish GP)

SCUDERIA AMBROSIANA

Continuing his arrangement with Count 'Johnny' Lurani to enter races as Scuderia Ambrosiana, Reg Parnell bought the ex-Bobby Baird Ferrari 500 in March and sent it to Modena to have a 2.5-litre type 625 engine installed. Winner of non-championship races at Goodwood and Crystal Palace, he started the British GP from 14th and retired from the midfield after 25 laps. It was Parnell's final championship GP appearance.

SCUDERIA LANCIA

In 1906 Fiat racing driver Vincenzo Lancia formed his own Turin-based marque that concentrated on road car production until his death on 15 February 1937. Vincenzo believed that the costs of racing as a means to promote his company were prohibitive but his son, Giovanni (Gianni), was seduced by the sport's attractions. He assumed control of the company in 1948, poached Vittorio Jano from Alfa Romeo and went racing, achieving a landmark victory in the 1953 Carrera Panamericana. Rumours of F1 abounded and were confirmed when World Champion Alberto Ascari and his mentor Luigi Villoresi signed lucrative contracts on 21 January 1954.

Ascari tested the prototype Lancia D50 by the start of March although it was not ready to race until the final GP of 1954. The innovative Jano used the engine as a stressed member in the lightweight spaceframe chassis, mounted at an angle to lower the driving position. Ettore Zaccone was responsible for the 2,489cc 90-degree V8 engine, which was fitted with four twin-choke Solex

carburettors, developed 260bhp and drove through a five-speed gearbox. Large pannier fuel tanks were placed on either side of the cockpit, the one on the left also containing the oil tank. Brakes were mounted outboard while front suspension was via transverse leaf springs and double wishbones with de Dion rear axle.

Two dark red Lancia D50s entered the end-of-season Spanish GP with a spare car also available. Ascari qualified on pole position and was extending his lead when the clutch broke after 10 laps. Villoresi, who had recovered from injuries sustained while practising for the Mille Miglia, started fifth but lasted just two laps before the brakes failed. It had been a promising if brief début.

Luigi Villoresi, Lancia D50 (Spanish GP)

Jean Behra, Gordini 16 (Belgian GP)

Elie Bayol, Gordini 16 (Argentine GP)

Roger Loyer, Gordini 16 (Argentine GP)

EQUIPE GORDINI

Amédée Gordini's perennially under-funded operation announced in December 1953 that it was entering three cars in the Argentine GP with Jean Behra confirmed as team leader. The Gordini 16 was retained for a third season with the straight-six's engine capacity increased to 2,473cc. The size of the torsion bars was reduced and a front anti-roll bar added, along with raised cockpit sides with a curved windscreen. At 580kg, the revised type 16 was the lightest car in the F1 field although the engine's 220bhp was not enough to challenge. Jean Lucas left before the start of the season after just a year as team manager.

Behra beat the works Ferrari and Maserati teams at Pau (when just 0.2sec ahead of Maurice Trintignant) but suffered a frustrating final campaign with Gordini. He was disqualified for a push start after a spin in Argentina and followed that surprise Pau victory by finishing the International Trophy in second place, with André Simon third. Third at Bari despite another spin, he took over Simon's sick-sounding car to finish fourth in Rome. His rear suspension mounting failed when running fifth in Belgium and the Gordinis were forced to start the French GP from the back of the grid after missing practice. Behra drove a fine race and was disputing fourth with Trintignant and 'B. Bira' when he ran into his countryman's Ferrari at Thillois. Behra dropped to the back of the field as the damage was assessed and finished sixth (and last). He would have been third at Silverstone but for another suspension failure and was last in Germany following repeated plug changes. Winner of the minor race at Cadours, he was an early retirement from the last two GPs.

André Pilette, Gordini 16 (Belgian GP)

Paul Frère, Gordini 16 (German GP)

Georges Berger, Gordini 16 (French GP)

Jacques Pollet, Gordini 16 (French GP)

Clemar Bucci, Gordini 16 (German GP)

Fred Wacker, Gordini 16 (Italian GP)

Elie Bayol began 1954 by finishing fifth after running non-stop in Argentina but he crashed into the crowd on the opening lap of the *Formule Libre* Buenos Aires GP after losing a wheel, with the consequence that a spectator was killed and a policeman seriously injured. Placed at both Pau and Bordeaux, Bayol ignored signals to hand over to Behra at that latter race and was promptly sacked.

Roger Loyer drove the third car in Argentina but it sprung a terminal oil leak after 19 laps. André Pilette survived a spin to finish second at Chimay but team-mate Jacques Pollet crashed into the crowd with two laps to go, killing two spectators. Pilette finished the Belgian GP fifth after a race of attrition, claimed ninth place in Britain and retired on the opening lap in Germany. He was second at Cadours to complete a Gordini 1–2 and fourth at Avus. Pollet's engine failed on both of his 1954 GP appearances in France and Spain. He handed his car to Behra at Caen who completed the race in third place.

Paul Frère also started three GPs for Gordini during 1954. He retired in Belgium and lost fifth after a fine race in France when his rear axle broke in the closing stages. Frère then qualified sixth in Germany only for a wheel to fall off when on course for a points finish. Driving a fourth car, Georges Berger retired from the French GP after just nine laps and finished the non-championship Rouen GP in fourth position.

Clemar Bucci joined Gordini from the Rouen GP but was only classified once in seven outings. He crashed at Silverstone's Copse Corner on his championship début and a wheel fell off in

Peter Collins, Vanwall Special (Italian GP)

Germany. He crashed at Pescara but managed to limp across the line to claim sixth at the finish. His was the quickest Gordini in practice at Bremgarten only for the fuel pump to fail on the grid, while in Italy his transmission broke after 13 laps.

Fred Wacker Jr returned to the team for the Swiss GP, which was a disastrous race as all three Gordinis were eliminated by the end of lap 10. The American finished a distant sixth at Monza after stopping for new goggles.

VANWALL

Having entered an F1 Ferrari 375 as the Thinwall Special since 1951, uncompromising industrialist Guy Anthony (Tony) Vandervell commissioned Cooper to design and build a new British contender for 1954. Originally intended for F2 but delayed, the Vanwall Special had a Ferrari-style ladder chassis and running gear penned by Cooper's Owen Maddock. Leo Kusmicki's Norton-based straight-four engine was launched with 1,998cc capacity, four Amal carburettors and an ugly surface-mounted tubular radiator on the bonnet. The front suspension was via double wishbones and transverse leaf springs with a de Dion rear axle. The car had Goodyear disc brakes and a four-speed gearbox. Having initially been refused, Vandervell used his considerable influence in the Italian automotive industry to secure a supply of Pirelli tyres. David Yorke joined as team manager and a base was established at the Vandervell Bearings factory in the west London suburb of Acton.

Engines were maintained in a plant in Maidenhead.

Ambitious negotiations with Alberto Ascari fell through so Alan Brown was chosen for Vanwall's low-key début in the very wet International Trophy on 15 May. He ran as high as fifth in the final before an oil pipe fractured. The team returned to Silverstone for the British GP with Peter Collins behind the wheel, the engine enlarged to 2,236cc and the radiator enclosed by a cowling. The young Englishman qualified 11th and passed Karl Kling's Mercedes-Benz to run eighth before retiring when the cylinder head blew.

After Vandervell hired Frank Costin, a redesigned version of the Vanwall appeared at the Italian GP with conventional radiator, wrap-around windscreen and engine further 'stretched' to 2,490cc, although Collins was forced to use the old 2,236cc engine following valve trouble in practice. The Vanwall was unstable in Monza's fast corners but Collins did well to run fifth when an oil pipe split, covering the driver and cockpit; after a lengthy pitstop he finished seventh. Second places followed in the Goodwood Trophy, when Collins used the 2.5-litre engine, and in Aintree's *Daily Telegraph* Trophy with Mike Hawthorn now at the wheel. During Thursday practice for the Spanish GP, Collins crashed into a tree without hurting himself but the car could not be repaired for the race.

There had been enough promise for Vandervell to be presented with the Ferodo Trophy for 'fostering the belief that a serious effort was being made to build a British GP car'.

HERSHAM & WALTON MOTORS (HWM)

John Heath was among the British team owners to approach Coventry Climax's Leonard Lee in 1952 in the hope that the company would build a 2.5-litre engine for the new formula. Technical Director Walter Hassan persuaded former BRM engineer Harry Mundy to join and they chose a 90-degree V8 configuration for the 2,477cc Climax FPE, colloquially known as the 'Godiva'. A mock-up was displayed at the 1953 Earls Court Motor Show but initial dyno testing was plagued by teething trouble, particularly with the valve springs. Wrongly believing the 260bhp it developed would be no match for the forthcoming Mercedes-Benz or existing Italian designs, the company cancelled the project, leaving HWM without an adequate power source for the new season.

As a stop-gap, the old 2-litre Alta engine was bored out to 2,448cc, fitted with SU fuel injection and installed into a 1953 chassis, with large side tanks and an air intake on top of the bonnet. Lance Macklin finished fourth at Goodwood but was an early retirement from the International Trophy. For the French GP, the block was reduced to 2.3 litres to improve reliability, but to no avail as Macklin, who qualified 15th, was running last when the big end blew a hole in the engine. That was HWM's final GP appearance as a works team for the company announced that it would henceforth concentrate on sports car racing.

After Heath's death during the 1956 Mille Miglia, business partner George Abecassis concentrated on HWM's car dealership.

CONNAUGHT PRIVATEERS

Rodney Clarke spent 1954 designing and building a new F1 car but it was not ready until after the season had finished. Connaught Engineering decided not to run a works team on financial grounds, although a three-car entry was made for the British GP only to be withdrawn three weeks before the event. The old Connaught A-type was a mainstay of the British national scene and five privateers started the British GP, their 2-litre Lea-Francis-derived engines all fitted with Amal carburettors rather than fuel injection.

Don Beauman drove Sir Jeremy Boles's long-chassis version, which was prepared by Leslie Hawthorn. Winner of a couple of British *Formule Libre* races, he scored podium finishes in minor F1 races at Chimay, Crystal Palace and Snetterton. The quickest Connaught driver in practice for the British GP, Beauman finished 11th. Boles hoped to acquire Louis Rosier's Ferrari 625 but negotiations fell through. Also regulars on the national scene, Leslie Marr (self-entered) and Leslie Thorne (Ecurie Ecosse) finished the GP 13th and 14th respectively.

Bill Whitehouse and John Riseley-Prichard both retired from the British GP. Whitehouse acquired his long-chassis A-type from the factory in May and scored a couple of second places in national races. In the GP he was delayed while a fuel-system blockage was cleared and his engine broke when he resumed. After winning at Davidstow in Cornwall, Riseley-Prichard spun his Rob Walker-entered car at Becketts on lap 41 of the GP; Riseley-Prichard subsequently bought the car and raced in national *Formule Libre* races into 1955.

Lance Macklin, HWM 54-Alta (French GP)

Don Beauman, Connaught A-Lea-Francis (British GP)

Leslie Marr, Connaught A-Lea-Francis (*Oulton Park Gold Cup*)

Leslie Thorne, Connaught A-Lea-Francis (British GP)

John Riseley-Prichard, Connaught A-Lea-Francis (British GP)

Bill Whitehouse, Connaught A-Lea-Francis (British GP)

Bob Gerard, Cooper T23-Bristol (British GP)

'Horace Gould', Cooper T23-Bristol (British GP)

COOPER PRIVATEERS

Cooper was busy building the new Vanwall in 1954 so it was left to old private MkIIs to represent the marque in the British GP.

Bob Gerard's Cooper T23-Bristol beat Don Beauman's Connaught into 10th spot to become both the highest-placed 2-litre car and British car in the British GP. After finishing third in the Oulton Park Gold Cup, Gerard dominated the *Formule Libre* London Trophy at Crystal Palace. 'Horace Gould' (real name Horace Twigg) was classified 15th in the British GP despite his Cooper T23-Bristol failing to reach half distance following numerous plug changes and a seized front wheel. The Bristolian had the satisfaction of winning his local F1 race at Castle Combe in August.

Ecurie Richmond entered a T23 for Eric Brandon, with Rodney Nuckey listed as reserve driver. Brandon started the race but lasted just two laps before the Bristol engine expired. Alan Brown

had hoped to drive the still-born Kieft-Climax V8 but sporadic appearances in Bob Chase's Equipe Anglaise T23-Bristol included the British GP, where he did not start. The only Cooper in the British GP to have a higher engine capacity was Peter Whitehead's T24, which used the new 2,470cc Alta engine and Bristol gearbox. He qualified 24th and was another early casualty in the race.

HANS KLENK

Hans Klenk modified the Veritas that Hans Herrmann had driven in the 1953 German GP sufficiently to rename the 2-litre BMW-powered open-wheel car as the Klenk Meteor. Klenk's own racing career was ended by injuries sustained while testing a Mercedes-Benz 300SL, so Theo Helfrich drove in the 1954 German GP. Slowest in qualifying when 1min 28.2sec off pole position, Helfrich lasted eight laps of the Nürburgring until halted by engine failure.

Peter Whitehead, Cooper T24-Alta (*Lavant Cup, Goodwood*)

Eric Brandon, Cooper T24-Alta (*Lavant Cup, Goodwood*)

Theo Helfrich, Klenk Meteor-BMW (German GP)

1954 RESULTS

DRIVER PERFORMANCE (EXCLUDING INDIANAPOLIS 500)

DRIVER	CAR-ENGINE	RA	B	F	GB	D	CH	I	E
Alberto Ascari	Maserati 250F	–	–	³ R	³⁰ R FL	–	–	–	–
	Ferrari 625	–	–	–	–	–	–	² **R**	–
	Lancia D50	–	–	–	–	–	–	–	¹ **R** FL
Elie Bayol	Gordini 16	¹⁵ 5	–	–	–	–	–	–	–
Don Beauman	Connaught A-Lea-Francis	–	–	–	¹⁷ 11	–	–	–	–
Jean Behra	Gordini 16	¹⁷ R	⁷ R	¹⁷ 6	⁵ R FL	⁹ 10	¹⁴ R	¹² R	¹⁸ R
Georges Berger	Gordini 16	–	–	²⁰ R	–	–	–	–	–
'B. Bira'	Maserati 250F	¹⁰ 7	¹³ 6	⁶ 4	¹⁰ R	¹⁹ R	–	–	¹⁵ 9
Eric Brandon	Cooper T23-Bristol	–	–	–	²⁵ R	–	–	–	–
Alan Brown	Cooper T23-Bristol	–	–	–	²⁶ DNS	–	–	–	–
Clemar Bucci	Gordini 16	–	–	–	¹³ R	¹⁶ R	¹⁰ R	¹⁷ R	–
Peter Collins	Vanwall Special	–	–	–	11 R	–	–	¹⁶ 7	NT DNS
Jorge Daponte	Maserati A6GCM (A6SSG)	¹⁸ R	–	–	–	–	–	–	–
	Maserati 250F	–	–	–	–	–	–	¹⁹ 11	–
Emmanuel de Graffenried	Maserati 250F	¹³ 8	NT R *	–	–	–	–	–	²¹ R
Giovanni de Riu	Maserati A6GCM (A6SSG)	–	–	–	–	–	–	²¹ DNQ	–
Juan Manuel Fangio	Maserati 250F	³ 1	¹ **1** FL	–	–	–	–	–	–
	Mercedes-Benz W196	–	–	¹ **1**	¹ 4 FL	¹ **1**	² 1 FL	¹ **1**	² 3
Giuseppe Farina	Ferrari 625	¹ 2	–	–	–	–	–	–	–
	Ferrari 553 'Squalo'	–	³ **R**	–	–	–	–	–	–
Ron Flockhart	Maserati 250F	–	–	–	NT R	–	–	–	–
Paul Frère	Gordini 16	–	¹⁰ R	¹⁹ 7	–	⁶ R	–	–	–
Bob Gerard	Cooper T23-Bristol	–	–	–	¹⁸ 10	–	–	–	–
Chico Godia	Maserati 250F	–	–	–	–	–	–	–	¹³ 6
José Froilán González	Ferrari 625	² **3** FL	NT 4	–	² **1** FL	⁵ 2	¹ 2	NT 3 FL	–
	Ferrari 553 'Squalo'	–	² R	⁴ R	–	–	–	⁵ R	–
'Horace Gould'	Cooper T23-Bristol	–	–	–	²⁰ 15	–	–	–	–
Mike Hawthorn	Ferrari 625	⁴ **DSQ**	⁵ 4	–	³ 2 FL	² 2	⁶ R	⁷ 2	–
	Ferrari 553 'Squalo'	–	–	⁸ R	–	–	–	–	³ **1**
Theo Helfrich	Klenk Meteor-BMW	–	–	–	–	²¹ R	–	–	–
Hans Herrmann	Mercedes-Benz W196	–	–	⁷ R FL	–	⁴ R	⁷ 3	⁸ 4	⁹ R
Karl Kling	Mercedes-Benz W196	–	–	² **2**	⁶ 7	²³ 4 FL	⁵ R	⁴ **R**	¹² 5
Hermann Lang	Mercedes-Benz W196	–	–	–	–	¹¹ R	–	–	–
Roger Loyer	Gordini 16	¹⁶ R	–	–	–	–	–	–	–
Lance Macklin	HWM 54-Alta	–	–	¹⁵ R	–	–	–	–	–
Umberto Maglioli	Ferrari 625	¹² 9	–	–	–	–	–	¹³ 3	–
	Ferrari 553 'Squalo'	–	–	–	–	–	¹¹ 7	–	–
Sergio Mantovani	Maserati 250F	–	¹¹ 7	NT DNS	–	¹⁵ 5	⁹ 5	⁹ 9	¹⁰ R
Robert Manzon	Ferrari 625	–	–	¹² 3	¹⁵ R	¹² 9	–	¹⁵ R	¹⁷ R
	Ferrari 553 'Squalo'	–	–	–	–	–	²² DNS	–	–
Onofre Marimón	Maserati 250F	⁶ R	⁴ R	⁵ R	²⁸ 3 FL	⁸ DNS	–	–	–
Leslie Marr	Connaught A-Lea-Francis	–	–	–	22 13	–	–	–	–
Carlos Menditéguy	Maserati A6GCM (A6SSG)	⁹ DNS	–	–	–	–	–	–	–
Roberto Mières	Maserati 250F	⁸ R	¹² R	¹¹ R	³² 6	¹⁷ R	¹² 4	¹⁰ R	¹¹ 4
Stirling Moss	Maserati 250F	–	⁹ 3	–	⁴ R FL	³ R	³ R	³ **10**	⁶ R
Luigi Musso	Maserati 250F	⁷ DNS	–	–	–	–	–	14 R	7 2
Rodney Nuckey	Cooper T23-Bristol	–	–	–	²⁹ DNS	–	–	–	–
Reg Parnell	Ferrari 625	–	–	–	¹⁴ R	–	–	–	–
André Pilette	Gordini 16	–	⁸ 5	–	¹² 9	²⁰ R	–	–	–
Jacques Pollet	Gordini 16	–	–	¹⁸ R	–	–	–	–	¹⁶ R
John Riseley-Prichard	Connaught A-Lea-Francis	–	–	–	²¹ R	–	–	–	–
Louis Rosier	Ferrari 625	¹⁴ R	–	¹³ R	³¹ R	¹⁸ 8	–	–	–
	Maserati 250F	–	–	–	–	–	–	²⁰ 8	²⁰ 7
Roy Salvadori	Maserati 250F	–	–	¹⁰ R	⁷ R	–	–	–	–

DRIVER PERFORMANCE CONTINUED

DRIVER	CAR-ENGINE	RA	B	F	GB	D	CH	I	E
Harry Schell	Maserati A6GCM (A6SSG)	[11] 6	–	–	–	–	–	–	–
	Maserati 250F	–	–	[21] R	[16] 12	[14] 7	[13] R	–	[4] **R**
Jacques Swaters	Ferrari 625	–	[14] R	–	–	–	[16] 8	–	[19] R
Piero Taruffi	Ferrari 625	–	–	–	–	[13] 6	–	–	–
Leslie Thorne	Connaught A-Lea-Francis	–	–	–	[23] 14	–	–	–	–
Maurice Trintignant	Ferrari 625	[5] 4	[6] 2	[9] R	[8] 5	[7] 3	[4] R	[11] 5	[8] **R**
Luigi Villoresi	Maserati 250F	–	–	[14] 5	[27] R	[10] DNS	–	[6] R	–
	Lancia D50	–	–	–	–	–	–	–	[5] R
Ottorino Volonterio	Maserati 250F	–	–	–	–	–	–	–	[NT] R
Fred Wacker	Gordini 16	–	–	–	–	–	[15] R	[18] 6	–
Ken Wharton	Maserati 250F	–	–	[16] R	[9] 8	[22] DNS	[8] 6	–	[14] 8
Peter Whitehead	Cooper T24-Alta	–	–	–	[24] R	–	–	–	–
Bill Whitehouse	Connaught A-Lea-Francis	–	–	–	[19] R	–	–	–	–

*Camera car for *The Racers*, not competing in Grand Prix. **SHARED DRIVES** Belgian GP: Mike Hawthorn/José Froilán González (Ferrari 625) 4. British GP: 'B.Bira'/Ron Flockhart (Maserati 250F) R; Luigi Villoresi/Alberto Ascari (Maserati 250F) R. German GP: José Froilán González/Mike Hawthorn (Ferrari 625) 2. Italian GP: Umberto Maglioli/José Froilán González (Ferrari 625) 3. Spanish GP: Emmanuel de Graffenried/Ottorino Volonterio (Maserati 250F) R

FORMULA 1 RACE WINNERS

ROUND	RACE (CIRCUIT)	DATE	WINNER
1	**Gran Premio de la República Argentina (Buenos Aires)**	**Jan 17**	**Juan Manuel Fangio (Maserati 250F)**
–*	Gran Premio de la Ciudad de Buenos Aires (Buenos Aires)	Jan 31	Maurice Trintignant (Ferrari 625)
–	Gran Premio di Siracusa (Syracuse)	Apr 11	Giuseppe Farina (Ferrari 625)
–	Lavant Cup (Goodwood)	Apr 19	Reg Parnell (Ferrari 625)
–	Grand Prix de Pau (Pau)	Apr 19	Jean Behra (Gordini 16)
–	Grand Prix de Bordeaux (Bordeaux)	May 9	José Froilán González (Ferrari 625)
–	Daily Express International Trophy (Silverstone)	May 15	José Froilán González (Ferrari 553 'Squalo')
–	Gran Premio di Bari (Bari)	May 22	José Froilán González (Ferrari 625)
2**	**Indianapolis 500 (Indianapolis)**	**May 31**	**Bill Vukovich (Kurtis KK500A-Offenhauser)**
–	Curtis Trophy (Snetterton)	Jun 5	Roy Salvadori (Maserati 250F)
–	Gran Premio di Roma (Castel Fusano)	Jun 6	Onofre Marimón (Maserati 250F)
–	Grand Prix des Frontières (Chimay)	Jun 6	'B. Bira' (Maserati 250F)
–	Cornwall MRC Formula 1 Race (Davidstow)	Jun 7	John Riseley-Prichard (Connaught A-Lea-Francis)
–	BARC Formula 1 Race (Goodwood)	Jun 7	Reg Parnell (Ferrari 625)
–	Crystal Palace Trophy (Crystal Palace)	Jun 19	Reg Parnell (Ferrari 625)
3	**Grand Prix de Belgique (Spa-Francorchamps)**	**Jun 20**	**Juan Manuel Fangio (Maserati 250F)**
4	**Grand Prix de l'Automobile Club de France (Reims)**	**Jul 4**	**Juan Manuel Fangio (Mercedes-Benz W196)**
–	Grand Prix de Rouen-les-Essarts (Rouen-les-Essarts)	Jul 11	Maurice Trintignant (Ferrari 625)
5	**British Grand Prix (Silverstone)**	**Jul 17**	**José Froilán González (Ferrari 625)**
–	Grand Prix de Caen (Caen)	Jul 25	Maurice Trintignant (Ferrari 625)
6	**Grosser Preis von Deutschland und Europa (Nürburgring)**	**Aug 1**	**Juan Manuel Fangio (Mercedes-Benz W196)**
–	Cornwall MRC Formula 1 Race (Davidstow)	Aug 2	John Coombs (Lotus 8-Lea-Francis)
–	August Trophy (Crystal Palace)	Aug 2	Reg Parnell (Ferrari 625)
–	International Gold Cup (Oulton Park)	Aug 7	Stirling Moss (Maserati 250F)
–	Redex Trophy (Snetterton)	Aug 14	Reg Parnell (Ferrari 625)
–	Gran Premio di Pescara (Pescara)	Aug 15	Luigi Musso (Maserati 250F)
7	**Grand Prix de Suisse (Bremgarten)**	**Aug 22**	**Juan Manuel Fangio (Mercedes-Benz W196)**
–	Joe Fry Memorial Trophy (Castle Combe)	Aug 28	'Horace Gould' (Cooper T23-Bristol)
8	**Gran Premio d'Italia (Monza)**	**Sep 5**	**Juan Manuel Fangio (Mercedes-Benz W196)**
–	Circuit de Cadours (Cadours)	Sep 12	Jean Behra (Gordini 16)
–	Grosser Preis von Berlin (Avus)	Sep 19	Karl Kling (Mercedes-Benz W196)
–	Goodwood Trophy (Goodwood)	Sep 25	Stirling Moss (Maserati 250F)
–	Daily Telegraph Trophy (Aintree)	Oct 2	Stirling Moss (Maserati 250F)
9	**Gran Premio de España (Pedralbes)**	**Oct 24**	**Mike Hawthorn (Ferrari 553 'Squalo')**

*Formule Libre **Run to AAA National Championship rules

DRIVERS' CHAMPIONSHIP

DRIVERS		POINTS
1	Juan Manuel Fangio	42 (57.14)*
2	José Froilán González	25.14 (26.64)*
3	Mike Hawthorn	24.64
4	Maurice Trintignant	17
5	Karl Kling	12
6=	Hans Herrmann	8
	Bill Vukovich	8
8=	Jimmy Bryan	6
	Giuseppe Farina	6
	Roberto Mières	6
	Luigi Musso	6
12	Jack McGrath	5
13=	Onofre Marimón	4.14
	Stirling Moss	4.14
15=	Sergio Mantovani	4
	Robert Manzon	4
17	'B. Bira'	3
18=	Elie Bayol	2
	Umberto Maglioli	2
	Mike Nazaruk	2
	André Pilette	2
	Luigi Villoresi	2
23=	Duane Carter	1.5
	Troy Ruttman	1.5
25	Alberto Ascari	1.14
26	Jean Behra	0.14

*Best five results count

Reigning champion Juan Manuel Fangio led from start to finish to win the Belgian GP in his Mercedes-Benz W196

1955

FANGIO PREVAILS IN RACING'S DARKEST HOUR

Mercedes-Benz versus Lancia at Monaco: Fangio, Moss, Castellotti and Ascari race past the station during the early laps

Alberto Ascari's Lancia D50 is retrieved from Monaco's harbour

The 1955 season brought a terrible catalogue of tragedies that threatened the very existence of the sport. In the third hour of the Le Mans 24 Hours, and completing his 34th lap, the Mercedes-Benz 300SLR of 'Pierre Levegh' was launched into the crowd opposite the pits. 'Levegh' and over 80 spectators were killed in the worst accident in motor racing history. It had already been a bleak summer with double World Champion Alberto Ascari and defending Indianapolis 500 winner Bill Vukovich both killed in May. Racing was temporarily outlawed in France, Italy and Germany while Switzerland only lifted its ban for Zürich's Formula E race in 2018.

The original F1 calendar had been ratified by the Fédération Internationale de l'Automobile in Paris on 6 October 1954 with the Monaco and Dutch GPs both restored. The best five scores would decide the World Champion. But the French GP was postponed and German, Swiss and

Spanish GPs all cancelled following the Le Mans disaster. No alternative date for the French GP could be found so only seven championship rounds (including Indy) were held. The Royal Automobile Club switched the British GP to the new circuit at Aintree with the British Automobile Racing Club responsible for organisation and the *Daily Telegraph* providing publicity. In the wake of the race cancellations, Ken Gregory of the British Racing & Sports Car Club offered to organise a second GP in Britain but the RAC did not accept.

Monza was rebuilt with new 45-degree concrete banking that proved excessively bumpy, shaking the drivers mercilessly and testing suspension and tyres to the limit. The race organiser considered a compulsory mid-race tyre change when the Lancia-Ferraris suffered delamination during practice. New facilities such as the paddock tunnel, shops and restaurants proved less controversial.

Moss and Fangio after the Englishman's victory at Aintree

Eventual winner Maurice Trintignant (44) and Roberto Mières prepare to lap Giuseppe Farina as they go through Monaco's Casino Square

Juan Manuel Fangio, Mercedes-Benz W196 (Monaco GP)

DAIMLER-BENZ (MERCEDES-BENZ)

Mercedes-Benz management realised it needed a top-line team-mate to support World Champion Juan Manuel Fangio, who re-signed as number one driver in December. Maserati hoped Stirling Moss would remain but he tested for Mercedes at Hockenheim on 4 December 1954 and signed in London five days later. Hermann Lang was released while Hans Herrmann and Karl Kling were both retained. The Mercedes-Benz W196 was modified with lighter chassis and power increased from 260bhp to 290bhp. Three different wheelbase variations were produced for slow, medium and fast circuits.

The Argentine GP was among the hottest races in history and almost every driver needed relief during the course of it. The 'superhuman' Fangio drove a medium-wheelbase chassis unaided for three hours, including a three-minute pitstop for fuel and refreshments on lap 34, and won by 1min 29.6sec. Moss was second when a vapour lock in a fuel line forced his 1954-specification (long) W196 to retire. He persuaded over-eager medical staff that he did not have sunstroke before taking over Herrmann's car (which Kling had also driven) to finish fourth. Kling crashed his own 1955 medium-length chassis during the early stages. With 3-litre sports car

Stirling Moss, Mercedes-Benz W196 (British GP)

Karl Kling, Mercedes-Benz W196 (British GP)

André Simon, Mercedes-Benz W196 (Monaco GP)

engines fitted for the *Formule Libre* Buenos Aires GP, Fangio won on aggregate with Moss second.

Moss's greatest win so far followed in the Mille Miglia with *Motor Sport*'s continental correspondent Denis Jenkinson navigating. Kling broke three ribs during that race when he crashed into a tree near Rome so Herrmann drove the third W196 in Monaco. Fangio and Moss handled ultra-short-wheelbase versions with front brakes mounted outboard. Practice began badly when Herrmann crashed through a palisade on the ascent to Casino Square and broke his hip. Searching for a replacement driver, team manager Alfred Neubauer found Ecurie Rosier's André Simon in the Hotel Mirabeau and the

Frenchman accepted the spare Mercedes for the race. Having beaten Rudolf Caracciola's 18-year qualifying record (with the great pre-war champion in attendance), Fangio retired from the lead. Taking over at the front, Moss had almost lapped the field when he coasted to a halt not far from the finish line, so he waited for winner Maurice Trintignant to complete the race before pushing his crippled car home to claim ninth place. Simon's engine refused to run cleanly and he was 12th when an oil pipe broke.

Fangio and Moss ran 1–2 throughout the Belgian GP while Kling, fit again, retired from fourth place. Mercedes-Benz's withdrawal had already been mooted in the pages of *The Autocar* before the Le Mans

Hans Herrmann/Karl Kling/Stirling Moss, Mercedes-Benz W196 (Argentine GP)

Piero Taruffi, Mercedes-Benz W196 (British GP)

and Moss in medium-length streamliners and Kling and Taruffi in open-wheelers. The old long streamliner, only one of which had been sent to Monza, handled better than its shorter successor, so Fangio chose it for practice and the race. A new long streamliner was built up at Untertürkheim with 1954 bodywork and transported to Monza on Saturday for Moss. Fangio led all but one lap and Taruffi followed him home in another formation 1–2. Running second behind Fangio, Moss's windscreen was shattered by a stone and he dropped to eighth during a 1min 40sec stop to replace it. He lapped at record pace as he recovered before a piston failed after 27 laps. The often-unlucky Kling was second when his gearbox seized after 32 laps.

With 'ace commentator' Luis Elías Sojit reporting his every power slide and followed by a boisterous band of Argentine fans, Fangio was crowned World Champion for the third time with Moss runner-up.

SCUDERIA LANCIA

Lancia began 1955 with a three-car team comprising Alberto Ascari, Luigi Villoresi and young charger Eugenio Castellotti. Four lighter D50s were flown to Argentina aboard a Douglas aircraft where Ascari qualified third but spun out of the lead. Having already crashed when the fuel pump failed on lap two, Villoresi relieved Castellotti, who was suffering from sunstroke, in the third car and hit a wall head-on. With two cars badly damaged, Lancia abandoned the *Temporada* and returned to Turin.

Denied victory at Pau by a split fuel pipe, Ascari beat the works Maseratis and Ferraris in Turin's Valentino Park (not far from the team's

disaster on 11 June and the company's decision to quit GP racing at the end of the season was confirmed by the end of the month.

The Dutch GP followed a week after Le Mans and Fangio, Moss and Kling lined up on an all-silver front row. Fangio and Moss scored another dominant 1–2 but Kling spun out at the back of the circuit while defending his fifth position from Roberto Mières. A fourth entry was added for veteran Piero Taruffi at the British GP with all four drivers in short-specification W196s. Fangio and Moss juggled the lead but it was Moss who won by 0.2sec in a 1–2–3–4 finish for the team. Whether or not Fangio handed Moss his breakthrough victory or was genuinely beaten has been a matter of conjecture ever since.

Ten weeks passed before the next championship race – the final round at Monza. Mercedes entered the same quartet with Fangio

Eugenio Castellotti, Lancia D50 (Monaco GP)

Alberto Ascari, Lancia D50 (Monaco GP)

Luigi Villoresi, Lancia D50 (Monaco GP)

factory in Via Caraglio) and also in Naples. The D50 had a new oil cooler with the radiators repositioned between the cockpit and pannier tanks for Monaco, where a fourth car was entered for 55-year-old local favourite Louis Chiron. Second on the grid after equalling Juan Manuel Fangio's pole time, Ascari entered lap 80 in that position, albeit almost a lap behind Stirling Moss. In the dramatic next two miles, Moss retired and Ascari misjudged the chicane and flew into the harbour in a great cloud of steam. Having changed a punctured tyre, Castellotti, challenged Maurice Trintignant for victory before sliding wide at the Gasworks hairpin as his brakes faded, but he still claimed second place. Villoresi was fifth after spinning twice and an exhausted Chiron sixth.

Just four days after surviving his dip in the Mediterranean with little more than a cut nose, Ascari was killed while practising a Ferrari sports car before the Supercortemaggiore at Monza. Financially challenged, Lancia withdrew from the sport but was persuaded to enter one car for Castellotti in the Belgian GP. He proved the D50's single-lap pace with pole position on his first appearance at Spa-Francorchamps. It handled badly on full tanks and Castellotti was running third when the gearbox failed.

Lancia confirmed its withdrawal and reached agreement to hand its cars, equipment and technical data to Ferrari in July. The six Lancia D50s (including streamlined bodywork developed for the cancelled French GP) were officially transferred in a simple ceremony on 26 July outside Lancia's Turin base with designer Vittorio Jano, team manager Attilio Pasquarelli, Fiat press supremo Dr Gino Pestelli and veteran Ferrari engineer Luigi Bazzi present.

Louis Chiron, Lancia D50 (Monaco GP)

Eugenio Castellotti, Ferrari 625 (British GP)

SCUDERIA FERRARI

Despite winning the last GP of 1954 with a modified Ferrari 553, old-type 625s were sent to Argentina. These were still powered by the outdated four-cylinder engine from the 'Squalo' but drove through a new five-speed gearbox. The coil spring suspension introduced at the 1954 Spanish GP was retained, with the rear leaf springs moved above the differential. Still limping from his Monza burns, Giuseppe Farina tested at Modena in December and he was joined at the opening championship race by Maurice Trintignant and José Froilán González, the latter reversing his decision to retire for a one-off outing. Enzo Ferrari announced in December 1954 that

Mike Hawthorn would continue with the team but the Englishman moved to Vanwall instead.

The oppressive heat experienced during the 1955 Argentine GP turned the race into a confusing muddle as drivers constantly swapped cars to get some respite. González took a surprise pole position and fought with Juan Manuel Fangio and Alberto Ascari for the lead before the Italian crashed. Overcome by fumes and exhaustion, but leading once more, González handed over to Trintignant, whose 625 had retired with a bent valve, and then Farina to finish second. Needing painkillers to drive, Farina qualified fifth and that car finished third following stints at the wheel by both reserve driver Umberto Magioli and Trintignant. Thus, both Farina and Trintignant finished second and third – a unique occurrence.

Farina used a 3-litre sports car engine to win the opening heat of the *Formule Libre* Buenos Aires GP but spun while avoiding Pablo Birger's Gordini in the second race. Trintignant's F1 Ferrari 625 finished third overall.

The 'Squalo' was updated as the Ferrari 555 (or 'Supersqualo') for the European season, featuring a new frame with two large main tubes and redesigned rear suspension. The front bodywork was lower and side-mounted pannier tanks were augmented by a larger one at the tail. *Motor Sport* was not impressed and described the new car as 'ungainly', 'very abbreviated and fat' with a 'rather ugly tail'. The four-cylinder engine lacked the power of newer rivals and Farina did not like it when he practised for the opening European

Maurice Trintignant, Ferrari 625 (British GP)

Giuseppe Farina, Ferrari 625 (Monaco GP, practice)

José Froilán González/Maurice Trintignant/Giuseppe Farina, Ferrari 625 (Argentine GP)

Giuseppe Farina/Umberto Maglioli/Maurice Trintignant, Ferrari 625 (Argentine GP)

race in Turin; the car was withdrawn when an oil line broke.

A four-car team was sent to Monaco with Farina and Trintignant driving 625s. Harry Schell made a one-off GP appearance and Piero Taruffi returned, although neither was particularly keen on the 555. Qualifying was a disaster with ninth-placed Trintignant the quickest Ferrari driver but the Frenchman inherited a shock victory when Fangio, Stirling Moss and Ascari all retired and Eugenio Castellotti was delayed. Farina's 625 recovered from a first-lap bump to finish fourth and Taruffi's 'Supersqualo' was delayed in eighth, Paul Frère having driven as relief. Schell lost a points finish when his engine came to a smoky end after 68 laps.

For its three-car entry in Belgium, Ferrari concentrated on the 555s, which now featured a longer nose and smaller air intake.

Mike Hawthorn/Eugenio Castellotti, Ferrari 625 (British GP)

Maurice Trintignant, Ferrari 555 'Supersqualo' (Belgian GP)

Harry Schell, Ferrari 555 'Supersqualo' (Monaco GP)

Piero Taruffi/Paul Frère, Ferrari 555 'Supersqualo' (Monaco GP)

Giuseppe Farina, Ferrari 555 'Supersqualo' (Belgian GP)

Paul Frère, Ferrari 555 'Supersqualo' (Belgian GP)

Farina qualified fourth, passed Karl Kling's Mercedes-Benz after two laps and inherited a third-place finish when Castellotti retired. Preferred to Schell, Frère delighted the locals by claiming fourth and Trintignant, battered and bruised following a crash during the previous weekend's sports car race at Monza, was sixth after an early plug change.

There were wholesale driver changes for the Dutch GP at Zandvoort as Farina, still in pain from his legs and mindful of the recent Le Mans tragedy, considered retirement. Only Trintignant remained from the original line-up, joined by Hawthorn following his departure from Vanwall and Castellotti from Lancia. Any optimism generated at Spa-Francorchamps evaporated as understeer beset the Ferraris in Holland with fifth-placed Castellotti three laps off the pace. Ferrari thought the type 625 best suited Aintree's slow corners but the British GP was even more disappointing with only one car circulating at the finish, Castellotti sixth having taken over from an unwell Hawthorn.

With Ferrari in a state of technical disarray and, stated *The Autocar*, 'feeling the pinch for a second time recently', FIAT agreed to sponsor the company's racing activities for the next five years to the tune of £28,500 per annum. FIAT also brokered the deal to take over Lancia's racing programme, including its six D50s, as announced in Turin on 26 July. Vittorio Jano, veteran engineer and designer of the D50, replaced FIAT-bound Aurelio Lampredi in August, with young engineer Andrea Fraschetti also arriving from Lancia.

Eugenio Castellotti, Ferrari 555 'Supersqualo' (Dutch GP)

Six cars were entered for the Italian GP: Farina, Castellotti and Luigi Villoresi were in rebadged Lancia-Ferrari D50s; Hawthorn, Trintignant and Maglioli drove 'Supersqualos' that now featured a five-speed gearbox. The excessive strain generated by the cornering speeds on the bumpy new banking took its toll on the D50s' Englebert tyres: Farina twice threw a tread during practice, crashing heavily on Thursday, so all three were withdrawn on safety grounds. Farina and Villoresi did not start but Castellotti starred in the spare 'Supersqualo', the first Italian car to finish, in third place following a tense dice with Luigi Musso. 'Hero of the day was undoubtedly Castellotti,' *Motor Sport* reported, 'who had proved himself Italy's

Mike Hawthorn, Ferrari 555 'Supersqualo' (Italian GP)

Umberto Maglioli, Ferrari 555 'Supersqualo' (Italian GP)

Jean Behra, Maserati 250F (Dutch GP)

real hope.' Hawthorn retired while Maglioli (sixth) and Trintignant (eighth) finished outside the points.

The final race of this disjointed campaign followed a fortnight later when two Lancia-Ferraris were sent to Oulton Park for the International Gold Cup. Hawthorn qualified on pole position despite tonsillitis and finished second behind Moss's Maserati 250F, with Castellotti an unhappy seventh.

Castellotti was third in the World Championship with Trintignant and Farina fourth and fifth respectively.

OFFICINE ALFIERI MASERATI

Maserati failed to persuade Stirling Moss to remain so Jean Behra joined as team leader. No fewer than seven works 250Fs were sent to Buenos Aires for the Argentine GP at the beginning of a disappointing season for the Modena-based team. The 250F's original louvres were removed from the now-smooth bodywork. A five-speed gearbox was introduced at the Italian GP featuring a low bottom gear to improve starts. Giulio Alfieri was promoted to technical director in May.

Behra qualified fourth in Argentina as four different marques filled the front row. Both Behra and Carlos Menditéguy, who hit Pablo Birger's spinning Gordini, crashed on the chaotic opening lap. Harry Schell started seventh in his blue-and-white 250F, briefly led when Juan Manuel Fangio refuelled, then handed over at his own stop on lap 36 to Behra, who brought the car home sixth. Sergio Mantovani and Clemar Bucci also needed relief drivers before retiring. Mantovani and Schell took turns behind the wheel of Luigi Musso's 250F, which

Roberto Mières, Maserati 250F (British GP)

Luigi Musso, Maserati 250F (British GP)

Harry Schell/Jean Behra, Maserati 250F (Argentine GP)

Carlos Menditéguy, Maserati 250F (Italian GP)

Clemar Bucci/Harry Schell/Carlos Menditéguy, Maserati 250F (Argentine GP)

finished seventh and last. Roberto Mières also led and was one of only two drivers to complete the gruelling three hours single-handedly; he could have won but lost eight minutes in the pits having the fuel pump changed.

Mantovani then crashed during practice in Turin and broke his left leg so badly that it had to be amputated above the knee, ending his racing career, although he continued to work in the sport as an administrator. Musso spun out of the lead of that non-championship event but Mières finished second. Behra won at Pau and Bordeaux with Musso second in France's wine capital and Mières third on both occasions. Stirling Moss's privately entered 250F was fourth in Bordeaux as Maseratis finished 1–2–3–4. Behra's car featured revised cylinder heads and three large Weber carburettors for that race and this engine configuration became standard.

GP débutant Cesare Perdisa drove a fourth works entry in Monaco and he swapped cars with Behra on lap 44, the Frenchman having lost a couple of laps in the pits. Behra lay third when he spun out of the race in Casino Square, handing that position to Perdisa in his original car. Musso's transmission failed after seven laps while Mières's rear axle broke just after he had taken third place from eventual winner Maurice Trintignant.

After three laps of the Belgian GP, Behra had a substantial crash on the approach to La Source so he walked back the pits, took over from Mières (who had twisted his ankle in the paddock) and finished a subdued fifth. Both Musso, who was slow away from the

André Simon, Maserati 250F (British GP)

Cesare Perdisa, Maserati 250F (Belgian GP)

behind the four Mercedes. Perdisa had 'a minor difference of opinion with his employers', according to *The Autocar*, so André Simon made a one-off with the works team but retired early.

Menditéguy returned at the Italian GP with Peter Collins drafted into the works line-up for the first time. Behra drove a streamlined version of the 250F that finished fourth, crossing the line with its engine billowing smoke due to a broken piston, with Menditéguy fifth and Mières seventh after several plug changes. Musso climbed into the top four after a poor start but overstressed his gearbox duelling with Eugenio Castellotti while Collins's suspension failed.

Maserati hoped Moss would return in 1956 now that Mercedes-Benz's withdrawal had been confirmed, so lent him a works 250F to win the Oulton Park Gold Cup. Musso's sister car was second when his gearbox failed with five laps to go. The final race of the year was the postponed Syracuse GP where Musso and Luigi Villoresi qualified 1–2 but were famously beaten by Tony Brooks's Connaught. With Behra in a Belfast hospital having crashed during the Tourist Trophy, Harry Schell (driving the streamliner), Carroll Shelby and Luigi Piotti also drove works 250Fs in Sicily and finished 5–6–7.

STIRLING MOSS LTD

Stirling Moss retained his green-painted Maserati 250F, fitted with magnesium Dunlop wheels and disc brakes, to use when his Mercedes-Benz commitments allowed. SU fuel injection fitted for

grid and had a couple of unscheduled pitstops, and Perdisa finished outside the points. Musso starred in the Dutch GP as the fastest non-Mercedes participant throughout qualifying and the race: fourth on the grid, he was second into the first corner and third from lap two to the finish despite a quick spin at Hunzerug. Mières was fourth and set the fastest race lap, while Behra, off form after being run over in the pitlane during practice for the previous week's Le Mans 24 Hours, finished sixth. The Frenchman recovered to split the Mercedes in qualifying for the British GP, where he was running third when an oil pipe broke. The excellent Mières also challenged only for a piston to fail so it was Musso who finished as the best-placed Maserati, fifth

Sergio Mantovani/Luigi Musso/Jean Behra, Maserati 250F (Argentine GP)

Lance Macklin, Maserati 250F (British GP)

Goodwood's Easter Monday meeting failed while he was leading the F1 Richmond Trophy but he finished third in the *Formule Libre* Chichester Cup that day. As the fuel injection brought no significant benefit, it was abandoned for Bordeaux, where Moss finished fourth after being delayed when the fuel tank worked loose. The Redex Trophy at Snetterton yielded third place but his engine failed during the International Trophy at Silverstone and in Aintree's *Daily Telegraph* Trophy, while he was running second in the latter. He dominated the Oulton Park Gold Cup with a borrowed works car.

Mike Hawthorn and Bob Gerard used Moss's Alf Francis-prepared 250F to win at Crystal Palace and Charterhall respectively in mid-summer. Moss had the car repainted for the British GP as he feared it was jinxed. 'Celluloid in a grey dual colour scheme, and very pretty too,' according to *The Autocar* but *Motor Sport* described it as 'grey with a sickly green bonnet top'.

Moss's Maserati was also entered in all five European GPs for a succession of clients. Lance Macklin did not qualify in Monaco and finished a distant eighth at Aintree after spinning on oil at Tatt's Corner and having to return to the pits on foot to request a push start from Francis and a couple of mechanics; Macklin also did the non-championship race at Albi and was lying second when a loose water hose ended his day. Johnny Claes rented the car for the Belgian GP but did not set a practice time or start due to a lack of big-end bearings for a necessary engine overhaul. Peter Walker lasted two laps at Zandvoort before a wheel bearing failed and tall American John Fitch was ninth in the Italian GP after a long pitstop tending to its sick-sounding engine.

Peter Walker, Maserati 250F (Dutch GP)

John Fitch, Maserati 250F (Italian GP)

Louis Rosier, Maserati 250F (Monaco GP)

ECURIE ROSIER

Louis Rosier and André Simon formed a loose partnership to enter their Maserati 250Fs in Europe. Simon passed Rosier during the International Trophy and they finished fourth and fifth respectively. Both entered the Monaco GP but Simon was the surprise last-minute choice to replace the injured Hans Herrmann in the Mercedes-Benz team; Rosier retired before quarter distance after damaging his fuel tank against the Tabac wall on the opening lap. Back in his ex-Harry Schell Maserati once more, Simon beat Rosier by a lap to win an under-supported race at Albi. After his ninth places in the Belgian and Dutch GPs, Rosier's remaining F1 outings during 1955 were confined to non-championship races. Simon raced a works car at Aintree in his final F1 race of the year.

OWEN RACING ORGANISATION

Peter Collins signed for the Owen Racing Organisation on the eve of the European season even though the new BRM was far from ready. That project was further delayed when designer Peter Berthon was seriously injured in a road accident in February. The team's old disc-brake Maserati 250F was pressed into action for the International Trophy at Silverstone, where Collins initially diced with Roy Salvadori before easing to victory. Owen entered the French, British and Swiss GPs but Collins only started once as race after race was cancelled. On the back row at Aintree having missed

second qualifying, Collins passed eight cars on the opening lap and was challenging Piero Taruffi's sixth-placed Mercedes-Benz when his clutch failed.

The BRM P25 was eventually ready for the *Daily Telegraph* Trophy at Aintree in September but Collins crashed in practice so could not start. He then charged through the Gold Cup field to run third at Oulton Park before retiring after nine impressive laps. In contrast to the V16 BRM, Berthon and Stewart Tresilian opted for simplicity when designing the compact and attractive P25. Tresilian's four-cylinder 2,491cc engine had twin overhead camshafts and developed 250bhp at 9,000rpm. It had a spaceframe chassis and four-speed gearbox with unusual oleo-pneumatic struts in the front and rear suspension.

GILBY ENGINEERING

Roy Salvadori continued as a mainstay of British national events with Gilby Engineering's Maserati 250F. Winner of Goodwood's Richmond Trophy on Easter Monday despite spinning at the chicane, he was second in the International Trophy at Silverstone. Victory at Snetterton in June was rewarded with a crate of Curtis gin. Third at Crystal Palace, he inherited victory in Aintree's *Daily Telegraph* Trophy when Reg Parnell slowed with two laps to go. Salvadori's only championship race was the British GP, where his gearbox seized after 23 laps.

Peter Collins, Maserati 250F (Italian GP)

Roy Salvadori, Maserati 250F (British GP)

'Horace Gould', Maserati 250F (Dutch GP)

OTHER MASERATI PRIVATEERS

Uruguayan amateur Alberto Uría acquired a Maserati A6GCM and 250F engine for the *Temporada* races in Argentina at the start of 1955. The slowest car in qualifying for the GP, Uría lasted 22 laps before fuel starvation proved terminal and he was a distant 14th in the *Formule Libre* Buenos Aires GP.

Prince 'Bira' retired from motor racing in the spring and sold his Maserati 250F to garage owner 'Horace Gould' who finished third at Albi on his first appearance in the car, which remained in its previous owner's blue-and-yellow colours. 'Gould' crashed at Hunzerug during the Dutch GP but the car was repaired – and painted dark green – for his home GP at Aintree, where fading

Alberto Uría, Maserati 250F (Argentine GP)

brakes and understeer caused another retirement. Second at Charterhall, he borrowed a newer works car to finish Aintree's *Daily Telegraph* Trophy in third place. This car was officially entered by the works team for the Italian GP, where it bottomed on the banking so badly that a hole was worn into the sump. Based at Maserati's Modena factory for much of the year, the intrepid 'Gould' was second in the Avon Trophy at Castle Combe and fourth at Syracuse.

VANWALL

It was a coup when Tony Vandervell announced Mike Hawthorn as his lead driver on 5 January. Already named as part of Ferrari's line-up, the two-time GP winner wanted to be based in England so he could manage the TT Garage in Farnham following the death of his father. Vandervell originally intended to re-sign Peter Collins but Hawthorn's 'Mon Ami Mate' joined the Owen Racing Organisation instead. Three new 1955 chassis were based on the existing ladder frame, with fuel injection and new suspension that featured coil springs/double wishbones at the front and an improved de Dion rear end. A recently acquired Maserati 250F was analysed before the frame was refined.

Vanwall was not ready for the start of the season and entries for Goodwood's Easter Monday meeting were withdrawn. Hawthorn lapped Silverstone at record pace when he tested in April and two cars appeared at the International Trophy, where Hawthorn

Mike Hawthorn, Vanwall VW1 (Monaco GP)

qualified second but retired, while Ken Wharton crashed after hitting a marker barrel at Copse and suffered second-degree burns as his car burned to a cinder. Hawthorn's singleton entry for the Monaco GP arrived late due to storms in the English Channel and he retired without making an impression. Problems during practice at Spa-Francorchamps included a pigeon in the radiator, split header tank, clutch failure, gear-selection difficulties and wayward handling. After nine laps of the race the gearbox broke – and Hawthorn quit the team by mutual consent.

Vanwall missed the Dutch GP but returned to a two-car line-up for the British GP at Aintree with Wharton fit again and Harry Schell recruited. The American qualified an excellent eighth and

after stalling at the start climbed through the field to ninth only for his accelerator pedal to break. In the sister car, Wharton lost 16 laps in the pits and Schell took over when the car rejoined, lapping impressively at Ferrari's race pace and ending the race classified ninth. Schell was second at Crystal Palace and led Wharton in a 1–2 in the Redex Trophy at Snetterton, beating the Maserati 250Fs of Stirling Moss and Roy Salvadori. That excellent result suggested real progress but the Italian GP was a disaster, with both cars out by lap eight. Schell won the final race of the domestic season, the Avon Trophy at Castle Combe.

The Vanwall's Norton-based engine had potential but an improved chassis was required.

Harry Schell, Vanwall VW2 (British GP)

Ken Wharton, Vanwall VW4 (Italian GP)

Kenneth McAlpine, Connaught B-Alta (British GP)

CONNAUGHT ENGINEERING

Connaught Engineering reached an exclusive agreement to use Alta's new F1 engine from 1954 and it was modified by Mike Oliver with 240bhp at 6,400rpm claimed. Rodney Clarke began designing the Connaught B-type in July 1953 with conventional ladder-frame chassis, double wishbone/coil spring front suspension and de Dion axle, torsion bars and radius arms to the rear. The 2,470cc four-cylinder unit had twin overhead camshafts and drove through a four-speed pre-selector gearbox. SU fuel injection was replaced by a proprietary system although twin-choke Weber carburettors were also tried. Dunlop disc brakes were mounted outboard. Clarke used a newly installed wind tunnel (a novelty for the 1950s) to shape the enclosed streamlined bodywork and first tested the prototype at Goodwood on 12 August 1954 after production delays with the engine.

Clarke and Tony Rolt completed more than 1,000 testing miles before the latter finished fourth in the *Formule Libre* Chichester Cup at Goodwood on Easter Monday. Jack Fairman and Kenneth McAlpine ran third and fifth in Silverstone's International Trophy before retiring and Connaught entered the French and British GPs only for the former to be cancelled. Fairman did not start at Aintree due to a misfire in practice, a problem that plagued McAlpine's race before his oil pressure disappeared. Reg Parnell joined Fairman for the Oulton Park Gold Cup and finished fourth despite a faulty magneto in the rebodied open-wheel B-type.

'None too well for funds,' according to *Motor Sport*, Connaught sent two cars to Sicily for the final non-championship race of the season at Syracuse. Parnell was unavailable due to business commitments at the London Motor Show so the inexperienced Tony Brooks and 'Les Leston' (real name Alfred Fingleston) were chosen. Brooks qualified the open-wheel car on the outside of the three-car front row and, recovering from a poor start, took the lead after 15 laps and pulled away from the Maseratis to win by 50.5sec – the first continental victory for a British driver in a British car since 1923. 'Leston' was ninth in the streamlined version following a spin. Connaught's achievement was rewarded with the Ferodo Trophy in February 1956.

ROB WALKER RACING

Rob Walker took delivery of a new Connaught B-type on 20 June, choosing open-wheel bodywork after back-to-back tests with the enclosed version, and entered the British GP at Aintree. When Tony Rolt pitted after 11 laps after his throttle stuck open, Peter Walker took over the repaired car but retired eight laps later.

LESLIE MARR

Leslie Marr won a minor race at Davidstow on his début in his newly acquired Connaught B-type. He stalled at the start of the British GP and spun, fracturing a brake pipe as he rejoined the track. He finished fifth at Charterhall and crashed out of the Oulton Park Gold Cup after 16 laps.

Tony Rolt/Peter Walker, Connaught B-Alta (British GP)

Leslie Marr, Connaught B-Alta (British GP)

EQUIPE GORDINI

Financial constraints delayed Gordini's new eight-cylinder engine so the team began 1955 with four-year-old Gordini 16 'sixes'. Messier disc brakes were fitted on one car from Monaco and were standard by the end of the season. Jean Behra joined Maserati so Elie Bayol was forgiven for his Bordeaux disobedience and retained as team leader. Bayol retired from all five F1 races he started in 1955, including championship rounds in Argentina and Monaco, before suffering serious head injuries during practice for the Le Mans 24 Hours. Pablo Birger and Jesús Iglesias also retired from the Argentine GP; Birger was the quickest Gordini driver in practice (ninth) but spun and was hit by Carlos Menditéguy on the second lap. In the Buenos Aires GP, Birger crashed into Giuseppe Farina during the second heat.

Robert Manzon returned to Gordini for Pau and finished fifth in Bordeaux. The Monaco, Dutch and British GPs all ended with all-too-predictable mechanical failures. Jacques Pollet qualified the third car last at Monaco and finished seventh when nine laps adrift. Fourth in the non-championship race at Albi and 10th after an unscheduled pitstop in Holland, engine failure ended Pollet's Italian GP. Hermano da Silva Ramos finished eighth on his GP début at Zandvoort but retired from the British GP (engine) and Italian GP (fuel pump). French sports car driver 'Mike Sparken' (real name Michel Poberejsky) made the only GP appearance of his career at Aintree and finished seventh after pitting on lap 59.

Gordini missed the Belgian GP to complete the new Gordini 32, which was finally unveiled at Montlhéry in July, with Juan Manuel

Pablo Birger, Gordini 16 (Argentine GP)

Jesús Iglesias, Gordini 16 (Argentine GP)

Elie Bayol, Gordini 16 (Monaco GP)

Robert Manzon, Gordini 16 (Dutch GP)

Jacques Pollet, Gordini 16 (Dutch GP)

Hermano da Silva Ramos, Gordini 16 (British GP)

'Mike Sparken', Gordini 16 (British GP)

Jean Lucas, Gordini 32 (Italian GP)

Fangio present to give moral support. Power came from a 2,474cc twin-overhead-camshaft straight-eight engine with four double-choke Weber carburettors and single-plug ignition. This unit was heavier than its six-cylinder predecessor but developed an extra 20bhp. The car had a five-speed gearbox, ladder-frame chassis, full-width nose, bulbous bodywork, Messier disc brakes, oil tank under the driver's seat and 35-gallon fuel tank over the rear axle. Independent suspension front and rear was via torsion bars and unconventional Watt's linkage.

Manzon tested the new Gordini on Monza's banked circuit on the Thursday before the Italian GP but turned down the opportunity to race, returning home on family business. So former team manager Jean Lucas raced the type 32, which proved hopelessly slow, partly because of its excess weight. Unable to qualify within 10 seconds of anyone else, Lucas ran at the back for seven laps before the engine failed.

COOPER CAR COMPANY

Australian 'comingman' Jack Brabham travelled to England to race Peter Whitehead's old Cooper T24-Alta in the spring and he was soon a fixture at Cooper's Surbiton factory. While there, he modified a 'bob-tail' Cooper T39 sports car with central driving seat, rear-mounted 1,971cc Bristol six-cylinder engine and streamlined

Jack Brabham, Cooper T40-Bristol (British GP)

bodywork. The chassis was extended by two inches, wheels and brakes enlarged, and Citroën final drive and gearbox fitted.

Brabham's Cooper T40 'special' was completed during British GP week and passed scrutineering at Aintree despite the minimum engine capacity of 2 litres. Officially listed as a '2.2', it weighed just 483kg but only developed 140bhp and Brabham was further hindered by clutch trouble during practice. The Cooper was outclassed by the top F1 machinery and Brabham was six laps down when an overheating engine forced him to retire after 33 laps. He sorted the car during the summer, returning for the wet Redex Trophy at Snetterton, where he diced with Stirling Moss's Maserati 250F and finished fourth after spinning at the Norwich hairpin. Brabham took the car to Australia at the end of the season and won the *Formule Libre* Australian GP at Port Wakefield.

EQUIPE NATIONALE BELGE

The Royal Automobile Club of Belgium hosted a cocktail party at its Brussels headquarters in January where Jacques Swaters and Johnny Claes announced the merger of their privateer Ecurie Francorchamps and Ecurie Belge as the Equipe Nationale Belge (ENB). A stand was booked for the Brussels Motor Show where Swaters's yellow Ferrari 625 was displayed. The team was not ready for its home Belgian GP but finished the tragic Le Mans 24 Hours

in third place with a works-prepared Jaguar D-type. Claes drove the Ferrari in the Dutch GP, qualifying and finishing last. This turned out to be the enthusiastic amateur's last GP as he died from tuberculosis on 3 February 1956.

TED WHITEAWAY

West London export merchant Ted Whiteaway acquired an HWM-Alta in 1954 and continued to race it on the continent during 1955. Between two non-championship outings, he went to Monaco – the only championship appearance of his career – but was a non-qualifier, 16.1sec adrift of pole position. He retired at Naples following a troubled run at the back and his engine failed at Albi.

ARZANI-VOLPINI

Egidio Arzani and Giampaolo Volpini took the unraced Milano 02 from 1950 and bored out its twin-overhead-cam four-cylinder engine to 2,492cc, with unhappy consequences. The car first appeared at Pau for little-known Mario Alborghetti, who had pitted three times by lap 20 when he crashed head-on at the Virage de la Gare and was killed instantly, with 11 spectators injured in the incident. The car was entered in the Italian GP for gentleman driver Luigi Piotti but he failed to set a qualifying time and did not start.

Johnny Claes, Ferrari 625 (Dutch GP)

1955 RESULTS

DRIVER PERFORMANCE (EXCLUDING INDIANAPOLIS 500)

DRIVER	CAR-ENGINE	RA	MC	B	NL	GB	I
Alberto Ascari	Lancia D50	2 R	2 R	–	–	–	–
Elie Bayol	Gordini 16	15 R	16 R	–	–	–	–
Jean Behra	Maserati 250F	4 6	5 3	5 5	6 6	3 R	6 4
Pablo Birger	Gordini 16	9 R	–	–	–	–	–
Jack Brabham	Cooper T40-Bristol	–	–	–	–	25 R	–
Clemar Bucci	Maserati 250F	20 R	–	–	–	–	–
Eugenio Castellotti	Lancia D50	12 R	4 2	1 R	–	–	–
	Ferrari 555 'Supersqualo'	–	–	–	9 5	–	4 3
	Ferrari 625	–	–	–	–	10 6	–
Louis Chiron	Lancia D50	–	19 6	–	–	–	–
Johnny Claes	Maserati 250F	–	–	NT DNS	–	–	–
	Ferrari 625	–	–	–	16 11	–	–
Peter Collins	Maserati 250F	–	–	–	–	24 R	11 R
Hermano da Silva Ramos	Gordini 16	–	–	–	14 8	18 R	18 R
Jack Fairman	Connaught B-Alta	–	–	–	–	21 DNS	–
Juan Manuel Fangio	Mercedes-Benz W196	3 1 FL	1 R FL	2 1 FL	1 **1**	2 2	1 **1**
Giuseppe Farina	Ferrari 625	5 3+2	14 4	–	–	–	–
	Ferrari 555 'Supersqualo'	–	–	4 3	–	–	–
	Lancia-Ferrari D50	–	–	–	–	–	5 DNS
John Fitch	Maserati 250F	–	–	–	–	–	20 9
Paul Frère	Ferrari 555 'Supersqualo'	–	NT 8	8 4	–	–	–
José Froilán González	Ferrari 625	1 **2**	–	–	–	–	–
'Horace Gould'	Maserati 250F	–	–	–	15 R	22 R	21 R
Mike Hawthorn	Vanwall VW1	–	12 R	9 R	–	–	–
	Ferrari 555 'Supersqualo'	–	–	–	5 7	–	14 R
	Ferrari 625	–	–	–	–	12 6	–
Hans Herrmann	Mercedes-Benz W196	10 4	NT DNP	–	–	–	–
Jesús Iglesias	Gordini 16	17 R	–	–	–	–	–
Karl Kling	Mercedes-Benz W196	6 4	–	6 R	3 R	4 3	3 R
Jean Lucas	Gordini 32	–	–	–	–	–	22 R
Lance Macklin	Maserati 250F	–	21 DNQ	–	–	16 8	–
Umberto Maglioli	Ferrari 625	NT 3	–	–	–	–	–
	Ferrari 555 'Supersqualo'	–	–	–	–	–	12 6
Sergio Mantovani	Maserati 250F	19 7	–	–	–	–	–
Robert Manzon	Gordini 16	–	13 R	–	11 R	11 R	–
Leslie Marr	Connaught B-Alta	–	–	–	–	19 R	–
Kenneth McAlpine	Connaught B-Alta	–	–	–	–	17 R	–
Carlos Menditéguy	Maserati 250F	13 R	–	–	–	–	16 5
Roberto Mières	Maserati 250F	16 **5**	6 R	13 5	7 4 FL	6 R	7 7
Stirling Moss	Mercedes-Benz W196	8 4	3 **9**	3 2	2 2	1 **1** FL	2 R FL
Luigi Musso	Maserati 250F	18 7	8 R	7 7	4 3	9 5	10 R
Cesare Perdisa	Maserati 250F	–	11 3	11 8	–	–	–
Luigi Piotti	Milano 02-Anzani	–	–	–	–	–	NT DNS
Jacques Pollet	Gordini 16	–	20 7	–	12 10	–	19 R
Tony Rolt	Connaught B-Alta	–	–	–	–	14 R	–
Louis Rosier	Maserati 250F	–	17 R	12 9	13 9	–	–
Roy Salvadori	Maserati 250F	–	–	–	–	20 R	–
Harry Schell	Maserati 250F	7 **6+7**	–	–	–	–	–
	Ferrari 555 'Supersqualo'	–	18 R	–	–	–	–
	Vanwall VW2	–	–	–	–	7 R	13 R
	Vanwall VW3	–	–	–	–	NT 9	–
André Simon	Mercedes-Benz W196	–	10 R	–	–	–	–
	Maserati 250F	–	NT DNS	–	–	8 R	–
'Mike Sparken'	Gordini 16	–	–	–	–	23 7	–

DRIVER PERFORMANCE CONTINUED

DRIVER	CAR-ENGINE	RA	MC	B	NL	GB	I
Piero Taruffi	Ferrari 555 'Supersqualo'	–	15 8	–	–	–	–
	Mercedes-Benz W196	–	–	–	–	5 4	9 2
Maurice Trintignant	Ferrari 625	14 2+3	9 1	–	–	13 R	–
	Ferrari 555 'Supersqualo'	–	–	10 6	8 R	–	15 8
Alberto Uría	Maserati 250F	21 R	–	–	–	–	–
Luigi Villoresi	Lancia D50	11 R	7 5	–	–	–	–
	Lancia-Ferrari D50	–	–	–	–	–	8 DNS
Peter Walker	Maserati 250F	–	–	–	10 R	–	–
	Connaught B-Alta	–	–	–	–	NT R	–
Ken Wharton	Vanwall VW3	–	–	–	–	15 9	–
	Vanwall VW4	–	–	–	–	–	17 R
Ted Whiteaway	HWM 54-Alta	–	22 DNQ	–	–	–	–

SHARED DRIVES Argentine GP: José Froilán González/Maurice Trintignant/Giuseppe Farina (Ferrari 625) 2; Giuseppe Farina/Umberto Maglioli/Maurice Trintignant (Ferrari 625) 3; Hans Herrmann/Karl Kling/Stirling Moss (Mercedes-Benz W196) 4; Harry Schell/Jean Behra (Maserati 250F) 6; Luigi Musso/Sergio Mantovani/Harry Schell (Maserati 250F) 7; Clemar Bucci/Harry Schell/Carlos Menditéguy (Maserati 250F) R; Sergio Mantovani/Luigi Musso/Jean Behra (Maserati 250F) R; Eugenio Castellotti/Luigi Villoresi (Lancia D50) R. Monaco GP: Jean Behra/Cesare Perdisa (Maserati 250F) 3; Piero Taruffi/Paul Frère (Ferrari 555 'Supersqualo') 8; Cesare Perdisa/Jean Behra (Maserati 250F) R. Belgian GP: Roberto Mières/Jean Behra (Maserati 250F) 5. British GP: Mike Hawthorn/Eugenio Castellotti (Ferrari 625) 6; Ken Wharton/Harry Schell (Vanwall VW3) 9; Tony Rolt/Peter Walker (Connaught B-Alta) R.

FORMULA 1 RACE WINNERS

ROUND	RACE (CIRCUIT)	DATE	WINNER
1	Gran Premio de la República Argentina (Buenos Aires)	Jan 16	Juan Manuel Fangio (Mercedes-Benz W196)
–*	Gran Premio de la Ciudad de Buenos Aires (Buenos Aires)	Jan 30	Juan Manuel Fangio (Mercedes-Benz W196/300SLR)
–	Gran Premio del Valentino (Valentino Park)	Mar 27	Alberto Ascari (Lancia D50)
–	Glover Trophy (Goodwood)	Apr 11	Roy Salvadori (Maserati 250F)
–	Grand Prix de Pau (Pau)	Apr 11	Jean Behra (Maserati 250F)
–	Grand Prix de Bordeaux (Bordeaux)	Apr 24	Jean Behra (Maserati 250F)
–	Daily Express International Trophy (Silverstone)	May 7	Peter Collins (Maserati 250F)
–	Gran Premio di Napoli (Posillipo)	May 8	Alberto Ascari (Lancia D50)
2	Grand Prix de Monaco et d'Europe (Monte Carlo)	May 22	Maurice Trintignant (Ferrari 625)
–	Curtis Trophy (Snetterton)	May 28	Roy Salvadori (Maserati 250F)
–	Grand Prix d'Albi (Albi)	May 29	André Simon (Maserati 250F)
3**	Indianapolis 500 (Indianapolis)	May 30	Bob Sweikert (Kurtis KK500D-Offenhauser)
–	Cornwall MRC Formula 1 Race (Davidstow)	May 30	Leslie Marr (Connaught B-Alta)
4	Grand Prix de Belgique (Spa-Francorchamps)	Jun 5	Juan Manuel Fangio (Mercedes-Benz W196)
5	Grote Prijs van Nederland (Zandvoort)	Jun 19	Juan Manuel Fangio (Mercedes-Benz W196)
6	British Grand Prix (Aintree)	Jul 16	Stirling Moss (Mercedes-Benz W196)
–	International Trophy (Crystal Palace)	Jul 30	Mike Hawthorn (Maserati 250F)
–	Daily Record Trophy (Charterhall)	Aug 6	Bob Gerard (Maserati 250F)
–	Redex Trophy (Snetterton)	Aug 13	Harry Schell (Vanwall VW2)
–	Daily Telegraph Trophy (Aintree)	Sep 3	Roy Salvadori (Maserati 250F)
7	Gran Premio d'Italia (Monza)	Sep 11	Juan Manuel Fangio (Mercedes-Benz W196)
–	Daily Dispatch Gold Cup (Oulton Park)	Sep 24	Stirling Moss (Maserati 250F)
–	Avon Trophy (Castle Combe)	Oct 1	Harry Schell (Vanwall VW2)
–	Gran Premio di Siracusa (Syracuse)	Oct 23	Tony Brooks (Connaught B-Alta)

*Formule Libre **Run to AAA National Championship rules

DRIVERS' CHAMPIONSHIP

	DRIVERS	POINTS
1	Juan Manuel Fangio	40 (41)*
2	Stirling Moss	23
3	Eugenio Castellotti	12
4	Maurice Trintignant	11.33
5	Giuseppe Farina	10.33
6	Piero Taruffi	9
7	Bob Sweikert	8
8	Roberto Mières	7
9=	Jean Behra	6
	Luigi Musso	6
11	Karl Kling	5
12	Jimmy Davies	4
13=	Tony Bettenhausen	3
	Paul Frère	3
	Paul Russo	3
	Johnny Thomson	3
17=	José Froilán González	2
	Carlos Menditéguy	2
	Cesare Perdisa	2
	Luigi Villoresi	2
21	Umberto Maglioli	1.33
22=	Walt Faulkner	1
	Hans Herrmann	1
	Bill Homeier	1
	Bill Vukovich	1

*Best five results count

At Monaco Stirling Moss's Maserati 250F leads the Lancia-Ferrari D50s of Eugenio Castellotti and Juan Manuel Fangio, and Harry Schell's Vanwall VW1

1956
COLLINS HANDS FANGIO TITLE AS MOSS STARS

Juan Manuel Fangio: World Champion for a fourth time

Although Juan Manuel Fangio won a fourth world title, he did not enjoy the political atmosphere at Ferrari and spent a single season with the *Scuderia*. He qualified on pole position for each GP except the British but only won three times, including taking over Luigi Musso's car in Argentina.

The 1956 Formula 1 calendar was ratified on 14 October 1955 with races in Holland (17 June), Switzerland (19 August) and Spain (28 October) included. However, Bern's local government maintained its ban on motor racing, the Dutch GP was cancelled on financial grounds and Spain due to the Suez crisis. Rumours that the Belgian and German GPs would switch to sports cars proved groundless. Prince Rainier III of Monaco married film star Grace Kelly on 19 April and the happy couple were still on honeymoon (a seven-week cruise aboard Aristotle Onassis's yacht *Deo Juvante II*) at the time of the Monaco GP. Political upheaval in Argentina threatened the opening race of the season and

Peter Collins celebrates victory in the French GP at Reims

The Lancia-Ferrari D50s in the paddock for the British GP at Silverstone

it was only confirmed on 19 December 1955, with the date postponed by a week until 22 January. A British Army vehicle depot since 1940, Donington Park was derequisitioned on 29 September 1956 but talk of it reopening proved premature.

The horrors of the 1955 Le Mans 24 Hours placed spectator safety at a premium. Reims was passed as 'safe' at the start of the year by Jean Briancourt of the French ministry of public works but Pau's non-championship race was cancelled as work was required in the pit area. In May, *The Autocar* reported that Kermit Pollock, president of the United States Automotive Testing Company, suggested that motor racing should become an Olympic sport but that did not meet with enthusiasm.

Pirelli announced its withdrawal from F1 at the end of 1956 on the grounds that racing had little relevance to road tyre technology, although Maserati and Vanwall persuaded the company to delay that decision for one final season.

Tony Brooks was injured when his BRM rolled and caught fire at Silverstone

Juan Manuel Fangio, Lancia-Ferrari D50 (Italian GP)

Peter Collins, Ferrari 555 'Supersqualo' (Argentine GP)

Olivier Gendebien, Ferrari 555 'Supersqualo'-Lancia (Argentine GP)

SCUDERIA FERRARI

Speculation regarding Juan Manuel Fangio's future was rife during the winter of 1955/56. He visited Maserati on 28 October but was announced by Ferrari by Christmas. Eugenio Castellotti re-signed while Luigi Musso and Peter Collins joined from Maserati and the Owen Racing Organisation respectively. Young Belgian Olivier Gendebien was announced as a reserve. Reports that Mike Hawthorn had re-signed were proved false when he opted for BRM in January. Former journalist Eraldo Sculati replaced Maserati-bound Nello Ugolini as team manager while Girolamo Amorotti was the technical director.

Armed with the disappointing 555 'Supersqualo' and the fast but unstable Lancia D50, Ferrari sent a confused array of machinery to Argentina for the start of the season. Fangio and Musso had modified D50s with the engine no longer stressed and a new fuel tank in the rear. The panniers included smaller tanks at the front and four megaphone exhausts at the back. The rear suspension now had transverse leaf springs. Castellotti's D50 was unmodified, Collins had a standard 'Supersqualo' while Gendebien's 'Supersqualo' was powered by a Lancia engine.

Inevitably, Fangio qualified on pole position (over two seconds quicker than Castellotti and Musso) but his car was not right from the start. He swapped cars with Musso on lap 23 and resumed in fifth place before passing Jean Behra only to spin. The complexion of the race changed from lap 40 for third-placed Castellotti's gearbox failed, Fangio repassed Behra and Carlos Menditéguy retired from the lead. The reigning champion then passed Stirling Moss's misfiring Maserati to win in Musso's car. A GP winner for the only time, Musso retired

Peter Collins, Lancia-Ferrari D50 (Monaco GP)

Fangio's original car. Collins crashed into the back of Luigi Piotti's Maserati when lapping the tardy Italian and Gendebien finished fifth. Ugolini protested the result of the Argentine GP for the second time in three years, this time claiming that Fangio had received a push start following his spin. Just as in 1954, this was rejected (on 25 June). The Buenos Aires GP moved 600 miles to Mendoza in the heart of Argentina's wine region, where Castellotti led from the start but Fangio prevailed once more.

The panniers on Fangio's D50 were 'blended' into the bodywork at Syracuse and he led Musso and Collins (both driving standard Lancia-Ferraris) in a formation 1–2–3. Ferrari split its attack at the beginning of May with Fangio and Collins at the International Trophy and Castellotti, who had just won the Mille Miglia, and Musso racing a day later in Naples, but all four retired.

Eugenio Castellotti, Lancia-Ferrari D50 (Monaco GP)

Ferrari took three of the Syracuse-specification cars to Monaco with only Castellotti's D50 still with exposed pannier tanks. Fangio had a ragged race and Cyril Posthumus noted in *Autosport* that 'the traditional polish of the Champion was certainly not in evidence last Sunday'. Having spun at Ste Dévote on lap two, causing Musso and Harry Schell (Vanwall) to crash, Fangio dented his nose cone in a separate incident and damaged a wheel against the wall at Tabac. He handed his battered machine to Castellotti, who had already retired and went on to finish fourth despite a slipping clutch. Fangio requisitioned Collins's second-placed D50 and finished in that position, setting the race's fastest lap on the final tour.

With Fangio's Syracuse bodywork now standard, Ferrari sent an extra D50 to Spa-Francorchamps for Hawthorn following BRM's

Luigi Musso, Lancia-Ferrari D50 (Italian GP)

Paul Frère, Lancia-Ferrari D50 (Belgian GP)

withdrawal. Hawthorn had also offered his services to Maserati and Enzo Ferrari threatened to report him to the FIA when he drove a 250F in practice, so the Englishman returned home rather than antagonise both Italian teams. As Musso had broken his arm during the previous week's Nürburgring 1,000Kms, local journalist Paul Frère deputised. A fifth D50 was hastily painted yellow and entered for André Pilette by Equipe Nationale Belge although it was run by Ferrari in all but name. Fangio was at Stavelot, far from the pits, when his transmission failed while leading so on this occasion he was unable to

take over Collins's car, allowing the Englishman to duly complete the remaining 13 laps and score his breakthrough victory. Frère delighted the locals by finishing second and the out-of-his-depth Pilette was sixth. Castellotti also retired with transmission failure.

Team personnel wore black armbands on race day at the French GP as Enzo's 24-year-old son, Dino, died on the Saturday after a long illness. Fangio won 100 bottles of champagne for qualifying on pole position with Castellotti and Collins alongside. Fangio led a Lancia-Ferrari 1–2–3–4 before Schell's Vanwall, which Ferrari

Olivier Gendebien, Lancia-Ferrari D50 (French GP)

Alfonso de Portago, Lancia-Ferrari D50 (French GP, practice)

André Pilette, Lancia-Ferrari D50 (Belgian GP)

believed to be a lap down, briefly challenged for the lead until the American over-stretched his engine. Fangio stopped to repair a split fuel pipe and finished fourth. That left Collins and Castellotti free to dispute the lead with Collins the winner once more. It was his third victory on successive weekends for he had also won the intervening Supercortemaggiore sports car race at Monza. Alfonso de Portago made his GP début for Ferrari in France but both he and Gendebien retired. One Lancia-Ferrari had streamlined bodywork at Reims but it handled badly and was not raced.

Collins now led the World Championship but Fangio won at Silverstone despite poor handling and a spin at Becketts. Collins retired before taking over de Portago's D50 to finish second. Having damaged a wheel when he spun at Club Corner, Castellotti gave his car to de Portago, who was black-flagged before pushing it over the line after the finish, without crash helmet and with a lit cigarette in hand.

Musso returned at the Nürburgring as part of a five-car line-up. Fangio, in the only Lancia-Ferrari to finish, led the German GP from the third mile (when he passed Collins) until the chequered flag. Still groggy from fuel vapours after a leak in his own car, Collins took over de Portago's but crashed into the trees, without injury. Castellotti's magneto failed so he took over from Musso, only to spin out of the race. The 17-year-old lap record was beaten six times by Fangio, Moss and Collins, with Fangio claiming the extra championship point.

Fangio entered the final round at Monza eight points ahead of Collins and the consistent Jean Behra, who could steal Fangio's title by winning and setting fastest lap if the championship leader failed to score. Ferrari's weekend began badly for Wolfgang von Trips, who, driving a sixth D50, rolled into the trees at the Curva Grande during practice. While he blamed mechanical failure, team personnel cited driver error but subsequent breakages suggested that the German was correct. Furthermore, the Englebert tyres fitted to the Lancia-Ferraris could not cope with the high forces generated on the banking.

Sharing the front row with Fangio, both Castellotti and Musso charged into the lead at the start. Each desperate to be recognised as Italy's new star, they drove too hard on cold rubber and full tanks and both punctured left rear tyres during lap five. De Portago crashed next time around when his tyre delaminated at 160mph. Monza's full oval and road course included two straights between the main grandstand and pits that were just separated by white cones and it was here that Castellotti suffered another blow-out four laps later while exiting the south banking and spun across the other straight and into a barrier, thankfully without hitting another car. Musso was back up to third when champion-elect Fangio's steering arm broke. Fangio's car was eventually repaired and Castellotti took it to the finish in eighth place.

Having refused to hand his car to Fangio, Musso took the lead when Moss ran out of fuel but his steering arm also broke with three laps to go, his out-of-control car only just missing the pit counter. Collins had suffered his own left-rear puncture on lap 11 and was third when he stopped 24 laps later for fresh rubber. He offered his car to Fangio, thereby helping to guarantee another world title for the great man, at the expense of his own lingering ambitions. Collins/Fangio finished second in the race with Collins third in the championship and widely praised for his sportsmanship.

Five days after the Italian GP, Ferrari test driver Sergio Sighinolfi was killed while testing a new sports car on the public roads near Ferrari's factory at Maranello.

OFFICINE ALFIERI MASERATI

Having spent a year learning from the master, Stirling Moss tested for Vanwall, BRM and Connaught before signing as Maserati team leader in December. Jean Behra remained and spent the winter recovering from the injuries sustained in the 1955 Tourist Trophy, including reconstructive plastic surgery on his ear. Roberto Mières could not agree terms so Cesare Perdisa signed as Maserati's third driver, although he missed the Argentine races due to appendicitis. Nello Ugolini moved from Ferrari as team manager, allegedly doubling his salary in the process.

The cars left Genoa for Buenos Aires aboard the *Julio Cesare* in December. In addition to Moss and Behra, works cars were entered for local stars José Froilán González and Carlos Menditéguy plus Brazil's Chico Landi. The Maserati 250F now had a second fuel pump, new exhausts and a five-speed gearbox as standard. Behra was the quickest Maserati man in qualifying for the GP and started from the outside of the four-car front row as Ferrari dominated. González jumped from fifth on the grid to lead the first three laps before halted by a valve breakage when placed fourth. The sensational Menditéguy assumed the lead and pulled away from Moss until a half shaft snapped on lap 43; he was lucky not to be decapitated as he crashed through a fence as a result. Moss, who was in pain after mechanics inadvertently ran his car over his foot before the start, lost the lead when his 250F developed a misfire and had faded to third when his engine blew up in smoke. He was taken to hospital after the race for

a precautionary x-ray of his foot. Behra survived a late spin to finish second. Landi handed over to Italian Gerino Gerini, who finished fourth, six laps behind the winning Lancia-Ferrari. Fangio's Lancia-Ferrari dominated in Mendoza with Moss, Behra and Menditéguy (following an unscheduled stop) 2–3–4 for Maserati. Winner of the Buenos Aires 1,000Kms with Moss, Menditéguy was injured during the Sebring 12 Hours and did not race again in 1956.

Using fuel injection for the first time, Moss won the Glover Trophy at Goodwood but much of 1956 was wasted trying to perfect the problematic system, which was inferior to carburettors at low revs and less fuel efficient. For Monaco all the race cars reverted to Weber carburettors after Moss carried out a back-to-back comparison. Using a four-speed gearbox, Moss led all the way from the middle of the front row to win an overseas GP for the first time despite contact with team-mate Perdisa on lap 86. Behra finished third while Perdisa limped home seventh with no brakes.

BRM missed the Belgian GP so Mike Hawthorn offered his services to both Maserati and Ferrari. When Hawthorn practised a 250F in the wet on Friday, Enzo Ferrari was incensed because he had also sent a car for him, so the Englishman decided it was better not to race for either team and withdrew. Moss tried fuel injection again on his new long-nose 250F during practice but had carburettors fitted for the race. He lost the lead to Fangio at Stavelot on lap five and then retired when his wheel and hub assembly broke away on the climb from Eau Rouge, from where he ran back to the pits and took over Perdisa's

Jean Behra, Maserati 250F (French GP)

Stirling Moss, Maserati 250F (Monaco GP)

Cesare Perdisa, Maserati 250F (Monaco GP)

Carlos Menditéguy, Maserati 250F (Argentine GP)

José Froilán González, Maserati 250F (Argentine GP)

Chico Landi/Gerino Gerini, Maserati 250F (Argentine GP)

Umberto Maglioli/Jean Behra, Maserati 250F (Italian GP)

Luigi Villoresi/Joakim Bonnier, Maserati 250F (Italian GP)

Chico Godia, Maserati 250F (French GP)

Piero Taruffi, Maserati 250F (French GP)

sixth-placed car, finishing third after breaking the lap record, having lapped 20sec faster than Perdisa. In case the team leader needed to requisition the car, Perdisa's 250F had been set up with Moss's preferred right accelerator pedal arrangement from the start of the season. Behra over-revved his engine when third and so pushed the broken 250F over the line to claim seventh.

The under-geared Maseratis lacked straight-line speed in France, where Behra qualified ahead of Moss for once. Fit again after a minor operation on his leg, Behra inherited third when Fangio made a lengthy pitstop. There had been chaos before the start when Moss's engine did not fire: with clerk of the course Charles Faroux ready to drop the flag, the Maserati mechanics push-started the car and Moss had to reverse back across the grass into his third-row grid position. Moss's gear lever soon broke so he again replaced Perdisa, who was running ninth in a fuel-injected car, and went on to finish fifth after stopping for fuel due to the engine's thirst. A streamlined 250F was taken to Reims but did not race.

Maserati concentrated on developing the carburettor engine from the British GP, where Moss took a surprise pole position. He recovered from a bad start to lead for 53 laps before making three stops to change ignition leads and for fuel after the tank split. He was still running second in the closing stages when his rear axle failed. Behra consequently inherited third with Perdisa seventh at the finish. Ferrari dominated at the Nürburgring, where Moss and Behra survived a race of attrition to finish second and third respectively. As

Perdisa was injured during the supporting sports car race, Scuderia Guastalla's Umberto Maglioli replaced him on race morning but dropped out after three laps with suspension failure.

Both Moss and Behra had brand-new 250Fs for the Italian GP, Moss's so new that it arrived unpainted on Friday evening. These cars were two inches longer, with enlarged cockpits. The engine was angled slightly in a new frame with the propeller shaft offset to the left so that the seating position and centre of gravity could be lowered.

Eight points behind Fangio before the Italian GP, Behra required maximum points without Fangio scoring to become World Champion. With Ferrari in tyre trouble, Moss assumed the lead early on and battled with Fangio and Harry Schell until the champion-elect's steering arm broke and the Vanwall's transmission failed. Unfortunately, Moss had another fuel leak and he ran dry at the Lesmos. Luigi Piotti's 250F was following and the privateer nudged Moss around the rest of the lap to the pits. Luigi Musso led by the time Moss refuelled but the young Italian's steering also failed, so Moss won again to finish as World Championship runner-up once more. Behra's magneto failed when fourth so he took over Maglioli's car, which also failed, leaving the Frenchman fourth in the final standings.

Chico Godia joined the three regulars from Belgium, where he used the spare car with Moss's pedal arrangement and, on the first lap of the race, hit the wrong pedal while trying to avoid Piero

Luigi Villoresi, Maserati 250F (Belgian GP)

Scotti's wayward Connaught and crashed. Godia finished outside the points in France and Britain (having spun at Becketts) and was fourth in the German (despite illness) and Italian GPs. Piero Taruffi drove a fifth works car in France without making an impression. He needed several stops for new plugs and was running last when the engine blew up after 40 laps. At Monza Luigi Villoresi raced this fifth car but handed it to reserve driver Joakim Bonnier during an early stop for new plugs, then the engine expired after just seven slow laps. Villoresi was injured during a sports car race at Castel Fusano in October and announced his racing retirement from his hospital bed.

LUIGI PIOTTI

Construction entrepreneur Luigi Piotti acquired a new works-prepared Maserati 250F that *Autosport* believed had 'far too much bhp for his own tranquillity'. Hopelessly slow and difficult to lap in Argentina, he jumped on the brakes when a blue flag was waved at him and fifth-placed Peter Collins's Ferrari hit the 250F, eliminating both cars. Last in the Buenos Aires GP and at Syracuse, Piotti invited Luigi Villoresi to race in the Belgian, French, British and German GPs, the veteran finishing fifth at Spa-Francorchamps and sixth at Silverstone. Piotti, who had practised at the Nürburgring before Villoresi's late arrival, returned to the cockpit for the Italian GP. He finished sixth having pushed Stirling Moss's out-of-fuel works car to the pits – a controversial manoeuvre that allowed Moss to win.

Luigi Piotti, Maserati 250F (Argentine GP)

Louis Rosier, Maserati 250F (German GP)

ECURIE ROSIER

Louis Rosier steadfastly refused to retire and drove his old blue
Maserati 250F at a leisurely pace around Europe. Fourth in the
Aintree 200 and sixth in the International Trophy, he retired from
the Monaco GP when the engine blew up after 70 laps while he
was running last but one. He was eighth (and last) in Belgium and

sixth in France after winning his midfield battle with Chico Godia's
works 250F. The first retirement from the British GP, Rosier scored
points in the German GP when elevated to fifth (of six finishers) by
Bruce Halford's disqualification. He crashed in the rain at Caen and
the car could not be repaired in time for Monza. It was equally wet
at Montlhéry the following month for the Coupe du Salon sports
car race: Rosier crashed his Ferrari 750 Monza on the first lap and
succumbed to his severe head injuries three weeks later in hospital
in Neuilly-sur-Seine.

GILBY ENGINEERING

Roy Salvadori's Gilby Engineering Maserati 250F finished second in
the Glover Trophy at Goodwood on Easter Monday and crashed
out of that position in Silverstone's International Trophy with three
laps to go. Sid Greene's team returned to Silverstone for the British
GP and enjoyed a highly competitive weekend: Salvadori qualified
seventh (on the second row) and the dark green 250F ran second
for 31 glorious laps before a fuel tank strap came loose, forcing
him to pit; now fourth, he stopped again to have an ignition lead
reattached before fuel starvation ended a splendid run. Winner
of the Vanwall Trophy at Snetterton, he retired from fifth after
a couple of laps of the German GP and finished third at Caen.
He broke his engine during practice for the Italian GP so Greene
borrowed a works unit for the race; numerous pitstops to change
plugs ruined Salvadori's race and he finished last.

Roy Salvadori, Maserati 250F (British GP)

Emmanuel de Graffenried, Maserati 250F (Italian GP)

Giorgio Scarlatti, Ferrari 500 (German GP)

SCUDERIA CENTRO SUD

Guglielmo Dei, Maserati dealer for central and southern Italy, formed Scuderia Centro Sud in 1956 with a factory and racing drivers' school in Modena. He acquired an ex-works Maserati 250F that Luigi Villoresi used to finish fourth at Syracuse. Veteran Louis Chiron was hired for Monaco: he blew the engine after over-revving to 8,600rpm during Thursday practice and a fuel-injected replacement borrowed from the works team failed as well so he was sadly a non-qualifier on his final championship appearance.

As Vanwall withdrew from the German GP, Harry Schell drove the 250F: he pitted for new plugs and the fuel injection proved temperamental but in this race of attrition he was still on course to finish fourth when a smoky engine forced him to pit, where water was replenished, but it evaporated in a jet of steam so Schell retired. The works Maserati team decided against racing at Caen so Centro Sud took over the entry for Schell, who survived a very wet race to win after 'Horace Gould' crashed and Roy Salvadori spun. Schell returned to Vanwall at the Italian GP so Emmanuel de Graffenried had a go in the 250F, driving a steady race to seventh place following a poor start.

Giorgio Scarlatti's old 2-litre Ferrari 500 was entered by Centro Sud during 1956. Fourth at Naples, he did not qualify in Monaco, where he was 17.4sec slower than anyone else. He started in Germany but retired at the end of the first lap.

Harry Schell, Maserati 250F (German GP)

Gerino Gerini, Maserati 250F (Italian GP)

SCUDERIA GUASTALLA

Milan-based Maserati agent Franco Cornacchia's Scuderia Guastalla acquired the works Maserati 250F that Chico Landi and Gerino Gerini shared in Argentina. The chain-smoking Gerini continued to drive in the early non-championship races, finishing fifth at Syracuse and third in Naples. The team graduated to the World Championship at Silverstone where sports car exponent Umberto Maglioli retired. Maglioli qualified seventh in Germany but Cornacchia was left without a driver when he was offered Cesare Perdisa's works car on the morning of the race. Gerini was back with Cornacchia in Italy, where he finished 10th.

OTHER MASERATI PRIVATEERS

Alberto Uría shared his elderly ex-Jorge Daponte Maserati A6GCM (with 250F engine) with fellow Uruguayan Oscar González in the Argentine GP. Neither set a qualifying time and they finished sixth and last when lapped 10 times. Uría did not start the Buenos Aires GP two weeks later.

'Horace Gould' continued to race his 250F across Europe, the car immaculate in red with a green stripe on the bonnet. Second in a thin field at Naples, he qualified and finished last (eighth) at Monaco following two lengthy stops. He also started from the back in Belgium but only lasted two laps before the gearbox seized. Winner of a national race at Aintree, 'Gould' enjoyed his best showing of 1956 at the British GP, where he qualified 14th and was rewarded for perseverance by finishing fifth to score his only championship

Alberto Uría/Oscar González, Maserati 250F (Argentine GP)

Bruce Halford, Maserati 250F (German GP)

Jack Brabham, Maserati 250F (British GP)

points. He retired from the German GP and crashed out of the non-championship race at Caen when second. The car could not be repaired in time for the Italian GP at Monza.

'Gould' sold his ex-'Bira' Maserati 250F to Bruce Halford, who hired Stirling Moss's former mechanic Tony Robinson and ran the car in the same colour scheme. Halford made a wild non-championship début at Aintree, spinning twice before crashing into a wall. Third on his return to Aintree in June, he entered the last three championship races at Silverstone (retired), Nürburgring (disqualified) and Monza (retired). He had a dramatic afternoon in the German race: after parts of his exhaust system fell off, he suffered from breathing in fumes

(although it was later claimed that he exaggerated the effects after the race) before stopping for remedial work; although exhaust parts scavenged from the retired 'Gould' car did not fit, Halford was able to resume and eventually finished fourth in a greatly depleted field, but along the way he repeatedly ignored black flags for a push start and was disqualified and fined.

Jack Brabham considered buying Stirling Moss's Maserati 250F before finalising a deal with the Owen Racing Organisation for the ex-Mike Hawthorn example. Third on début with the car in the Aintree 200, the Australian was black-flagged during the International Trophy for dropping oil. He qualified on the last row for the British GP and

'Horace Gould', Maserati 250F (Monaco GP)

André Simon, Maserati 250F (French GP)

retired after just four laps. The future champion was third a week later in the Vanwall Trophy at Snetterton.

André Simon's Maserati 250F was slowest in qualifying for a one-off appearance at the French GP and he retired the misfiring machine from last place on lap two.

Ottorino Volonterio drove his elderly Maserati A6GCM/250F in a couple of F1 races in 1956. Fifth in a poorly supported race at Naples (when lapped 11 times), he was described as 'very slow' in the German GP by more than one contemporary report. He ran at the back all day and made a comical pitstop, during which his mechanics fell over each other and spilt fuel into the cockpit. Work finally completed, he finished his drink of water before returning to the track. He was not classified.

Ottorino Volonterio, Maserati 250F (German GP)

BRITISH RACING MOTORS/ OWEN RACING ORGANISATION

Stirling Moss and Peter Collins tested the BRM P25 in November 1955 but both chose Italian teams for 1956. Mike Hawthorn moved in the opposite direction when he signed as the Owen Racing Organisation's number one driver on 11 January with Tony Brooks confirmed as his team-mate 10 days later. Ron Flockhart was retained as test driver.

The P25 was not ready at the start of the year so the team's dark green Maserati 250F, complete with the disc brakes, was a late entry for the *Temporada* races in Argentina. Hawthorn benefited from retirements to finish third in the Argentine GP but was delayed by a lengthy pitstop in the Buenos Aires GP. The car was sold to Jack Brabham in April.

Hawthorn and Brooks had a pair of P25s for Goodwood's Glover Trophy on Easter Monday. Both retired, Hawthorn having rolled out of second place without injury when a wheel fell off at Fordwater. Hawthorn led the Aintree 200 and the International Trophy at Silverstone but crashed when his brakes failed in the former and lost victory in the latter with a sheared magneto drive. Brooks was on course for victory at Aintree until his brakes faded, the promising youngster eventually finishing second behind Moss's privately entered Maserati.

Memories of the original BRM follies resurfaced at Monaco where both cars were over-geared and had engine valves on the point of failure so were withdrawn. Entries for the Belgian and French GPs were scratched but three cars arrived at Silverstone for

Mike Hawthorn, BRM P25 (British GP)

Mike Hawthorn, Maserati 250F (Argentine GP)

Tony Brooks, BRM P25 (British GP)

the British GP, with Ron Flockhart rewarded for his testing miles at Folkingham and elsewhere. Hawthorn qualified third (on a four-car front row) and led into Copse with championship débutant Brooks behind him after a great start from the third row. They sent the home crowd into delirium by running 1–2 for the opening six laps but it did not last. Hawthorn retired with oil seeping from a universal joint and Brooks, who had already had a lengthy pitstop, had a huge barrel roll when something failed approaching at Abbey; he broke his jaw when thrown clear as the car shattered and caught fire. Flockhart's engine failed after just two laps.

BRM withdrew from the last two GPs of the season and vowed not to return until it had successfully completed a three-hour GP distance in testing.

Ron Flockhart, BRM P25 (British GP)

Piero Scotti, Connaught B-Alta (Belgian GP)

Archie Scott Brown, Connaught B-Alta (British GP)

CONNAUGHT ENGINEERING

Tony Brooks's historic victory at Syracuse on 23 October 1955 brought wide recognition for Connaught but little much-needed financial assistance. In accepting the Ferodo Trophy on 15 February 1956, Rodney Clarke announced that Connaught could not afford a full GP campaign but intended to enter three examples of its B-type model (now forever known as the 'Syracuse' Connaught) in British races and up to three continental GPs.

Despite a deformed right hand, Archie Scott Brown had proved himself on the national scene with Brian Lister's sports cars and he signed following a successful test at Goodwood in March. Returning to the Sussex venue, his works B-type battled with Stirling Moss's Maserati for the lead of the Glover Trophy until a piston failed. 'Les Leston' finished third and Reg Parnell was fifth in Rob Walker's car. Two Connaughts were sent back to Syracuse a fortnight later with the newly married Desmond Titterington driving Brooks's winning car from 1955 and Italian amateur Piero Scotti having hired the second car with an option to buy, but there was no fairy-tale repeat as both cars retired.

Scott Brown qualified for the Aintree 200 on pole position and led the race until another piston failed while Titterington's streamlined car lined up third and also retired. At Silverstone for the International Trophy, Scott Brown and Titterington finished second and third respectively to provide, as Peter Garnier enthused in *The Autocar*, 'a much-needed boost to flagging British spirits'. Scotti was also at Silverstone with his red machine and finished a distant seventh. The Italian also went to Spa-Francorchamps for the Belgian GP, where he spent half an hour of the race in the pits tracing a misfire and finally

Desmond Titterington, Connaught B-Alta (British GP)

Jack Fairman, Connaught B-Alta (British GP)

resumed only for the gearbox oil pressure to plummet; far from happy, Scotti returned the car to Connaught and never raced in F1 again.

After Scott Brown retired from the lead of minor races at Aintree and Snetterton, three cars were entered for the British GP with test driver Jack Fairman joining the regulars. Both Scott Brown, who ran seventh in the early laps before losing a wheel at Becketts, and Titterington retired on their only GP appearances. *Autosport* noted that Fairman was 'a model of consistency and reliability' as he finished an excellent fourth.

Connaught did not enter the German GP but three cars were sent to the Italian GP. Pirelli refused to supply 16in tyres to suit the

Connaughts' wheels and the team did not have any 17in rims so appropriately sized Avons were flown out from England. There was controversy before the meeting even started because Scott Brown's entry was refused due to his disability, so Flockhart deputised. 'Leston' retired early but Flockhart and Fairman (despite puncturing his front left on lap 14) finished third and fifth respectively after a race of attrition. Fairman scored points in both GPs he started and was eighth in the 1956 World Championship.

Scott Brown finally scored his maiden F1 win by leading Stuart Lewis-Evans and 'Leston' in a Connaught 1–2–4 in the first F1 race to be held at Brands Hatch.

'Les Leston', Connaught B-Alta (Italian GP)

Ron Flockhart, Connaught B-Alta (Italian GP)

Harry Schell, Vanwall VW1 (Belgian GP)

Maurice Trintignant, Vanwall VW4 (Italian GP)

Piero Taruffi, Vanwall VW1 (Italian GP)

VANWALL

Colin Chapman was hired to design a lightweight new spaceframe chassis to replace the ladder frame, having been introduced to team manager David Yorke by Vanwall truck driver Derek Wootton, who was a friend from Chapman's early career modifying Austin Sevens. The Bosch fuel injection, brakes, front suspension and gearbox were retained from the 1955 cars while the revised de Dion rear axle featured Watt's links and transverse leaf springs. At Chapman's suggestion, de Havilland aerodynamicist Frank Costin designed the distinctive 'teardrop' body with high tail housing a 39-gallon fuel tank. Maurice Trintignant, who was contracted to Bugatti but agreed to drive until its new car was ready, complained about the car's high aerodynamic windscreen but Costin refused his request to have it trimmed down. Leo Kusmicki further developed the potent if tall four-cylinder engine with a handy 270bhp now available. Stirling Moss tested the old car at Silverstone and Oulton Park in November 1954 and agreed to drive when his Maserati commitments allowed. Harry Schell re-signed for the Acton-based team in December.

Two new Vanwalls were completed in April and, with Maserati absent, Moss and Schell were entered for the International Trophy at Silverstone. They qualified 1–2 with identical times but Moss was awarded pole position because he set his time first. Moss made a poor start but eased through the field and passed Juan Manuel Fangio's Lancia-Ferrari to score a famous victory, but Schell retired. Schell and Trintignant qualified 5–6 in Monaco although understandable optimism lasted just five laps. Schell was a victim of Fangio's lap-two spin at Ste Dévote while Trintignant's overheating

Mike Hawthorn/Harry Schell, Vanwall VW2 (French GP)

and dented car was soon pushed to the 'dead car park'.

Schell used the Vanwall's prodigious straight-line speed to finish fourth in Belgium while Trintignant retired after a succession of stops to trace a mysterious loss of power. Trintignant was committed to Bugatti in France, where Vanwall ran three cars for the first time, so Mike Hawthorn – available due to BRM's absence – had a seat and Chapman, surprisingly, was offered the third car. Thursday evening practice was a disaster as Chapman locked a rear brake at the Thillois hairpin and hit Hawthorn and then a concrete pylon, so he was a non-starter, although Schell had earlier set a time in Chapman's car that would have put it fifth on the grid, one place behind his own. Hawthorn won 100 bottles of champagne for becoming the first driver to lap Reims at over 200kph in practice. Rather ambitiously, Hawthorn drove for Jaguar in the 12-hour sports car race that preceded the GP, finishing at midday. Feeling tired and unwell in the early stages of the GP, he handed over to Schell, who had over-revved his engine and dropped out after just five laps. The American drove the 'race of his life': he caught the Ferraris and challenged Fangio for the lead but his glory was all too brief as the engine went off song, forcing a couple of lengthy pitstops and leaving Schell to finish 10th on three cylinders.

Trintignant returned for the British GP where a notably trim José Froilán González drove the third car. Both Schell and González lined up on the second row but González's long journey from Argentina was in vain due to transmission failure at the start. The two remaining Vanwalls retired when fuel dissolved the aluminium of their tanks and the detritus blocked the fuel lines.

All three British manufacturers missed the German GP but

José Froilán González, Vanwall VW1 (British GP)

Vanwall returned at Monza with Piero Taruffi in the third car. He qualified fourth but it was Schell who challenged Moss, Fangio and Collins for the lead. His green car even led across the line on lap 11 before pitting for fuel with Schell saturated in oil following a leak. Another promising showing ended when the transmission failed. Both Trintignant and Taruffi retired with suspension problems despite thicker de Dion rear axles to cope with the centrifugal forces generated on the banking.

Still lacking reliability, the Vanwall was now as quick as its Italian rivals in a straight line and promise would soon become reality.

Maurice Trintignant, Bugatti T251 (French GP)

USINES BUGATTI

Ettore Bugatti died on 21 August 1947 and control of his famous company passed to the younger son from his first marriage, Roland, his widow Geneviève's second husband, René Bolloré, and faithful works manager Pierre Marco. It was an uneasy alliance as Ettore Bugatti died intestate and tension reigned between Roland and Ettore's second wife. Heir to a cigarette paper fortune, Bolloré financed a new F1 car with work starting in the summer of 1953. Famed Alfa Romeo and Ferrari engineer Gioacchino Colombo had set up a consultancy in Milan and he was commissioned to design the Bugatti T251. Although Colombo delivered the design, he was little involved in its build and crucial alterations were made. Ferrari chief mechanic Stefano Meazza was hired on Colombo's recommendation. With Maurice Trintignant already mentioned as lead driver, Marco hoped the new car would be ready in September 1954.

However, the cessation of the Indochina war on 20 July 1954 and resulting loss of lucrative armaments contracts hit Bugatti hard and delayed the F1 project. It was 21 November 1954 when the prototype T251 was finally unveiled at Entzheim airfield, where Marco did a shakedown test. The car was notably short, stubby and unconventional, with a straight-eight engine mounted transversely behind the driver and a full-width nose. This 2,430cc unit had twin overhead camshafts, two valves per cylinder, twin-plug ignition and four twin-choke Weber carburettors. A five-speed Porsche synchromesh gearbox was fitted and suspension was by an old-fashioned rigid front axle (which *Autosport*

described as an 'anachronism in this day and age') and de Dion rear. Within the spaceframe chassis, bag fuel tanks were mounted on either side of the cockpit in bulbous flanks.

Testing began at Entzheim at the start of 1956 with a newer alloy engine and a longer-wheelbase second car was built with revised bodywork. Nevertheless, the cars remained unproven as Bugatti's scheduled début in the French GP approached and Bolloré did not heed his engineer's advice to withdraw. Trintignant opted to drive the prototype and found that it was overweight and under-powered, weaved dangerously on the straights and handled badly in the fast corners. He qualified on the penultimate row, 18.6sec slower than Juan Manuel Fangio's pole time, and retired after 18 laps when dust from the track fouled the carburettors and caused the throttle to stick. The car was pushed away and never raced again.

Roland Bugatti and René Bolloré both resigned and Pierre Marco left in 1958. The Bugatti family eventually sold the factory and all of its assets to Hispano-Suiza in July 1963.

EQUIPE GORDINI

Amédée Gordini struggled on into his final season as a GP constructor with two examples of the disappointing eight-cylinder type 32 (with five-speed gearbox) as well as the ancient six-cylinder type 16. Robert Manzon, Hermano da Silva Ramos and Jacques Pollet were expected to continue in a three-car team but Pollet did not appear and four different drivers filled the third seat in championship races.

Gordini avoided the expense of sending cars to Argentina and, with Pau cancelled, the Glover Trophy at Goodwood was the équipe's first F1 race of the season. Both Manzon (sixth in the type 32) and Bayol (eighth and last) were lapped at least twice in the 32-lap race. Da Silva Ramos retired a singleton type 16 at Syracuse without making an impression but finished fifth in the International Trophy at Silverstone with the same car, albeit five laps down. Manzon used the older car to score a surprise victory against a limited field in Naples.

Again in a type 16, Manzon challenged Eugenio Castellotti's ailing Lancia-Ferrari for fourth place at Monaco until he damaged his suspension by hitting both sides of the chicane and then lost his brakes and a fifth-place finish when he crashed at Le Portier. That elevated da Silva Ramos into fifth place to score championship points for the only time; the Franco-Brazilian was also in a type 16 as he had damaged the suspension of the original type 32 during practice by clouting a kerb at the chicane. Elie Bayol started the only available eight-cylinder car but handed it over to André Pilette, who brought it home sixth.

After missing the Belgian GP, Gordini went to its home race fielding Manzon and da Silva Ramos in the type 32s and Pilette in the type 16. Driving with restricted revs to aid reliability, all three finished – but outside the points – after battling with Maurice Trintignant's Bugatti for the glory of France! For the next two championship rounds Gordini concentrated on the eight-cylinder

Robert Manzon, Gordini 32 (French GP)

Elie Bayol/André Pilette, Gordini 32 (Monaco GP)

Hermano da Silva Ramos, Gordini 32 (French GP)

André Milhoux, Gordini 32 (German GP)

Robert Manzon, Gordini 16 (Monaco GP)

André Pilette, Gordini 16 (French GP)

André Simon, Gordini 16 (Italian GP)

cars and Manzon finished ninth at Silverstone. Pilette was due to partner Manzon at the Nürburgring but crashed in practice and injured his knee. His replacement, débutant André Milhoux, went into the race without so much as a practice lap but he had little chance to show his worth as his engine suffered a persistent misfire and he retired after two stops to change plugs failed to cure the problem. Manzon parked his car at the end of lap one with deranged front suspension.

Manzon crashed an eight-cylinder car in the wet at Caen, where André Simon and ex-motorcyclist Georges Burgraff finished 2–4 in the older model. At Monza Manzon and da Silva Ramos drove the newer cars, which retired within the first seven laps, while Simon in the type 16 ran non-stop to finish ninth.

The 1956 Italian GP turned out to be Gordini's last GP as he withdrew from F1 after appearances at Pau and Naples at the start of 1957. Always lacking adequate finance, the Gordini marque débuted at Monaco in 1950 and started 40 GPs, with two third-place finishes during 1952 its best World Championship results.

Amédée Gordini transferred his attention to road cars when he negotiated a deal with Renault to produce 10,000 modified versions of the new Dauphine, to be known as the Renault Dauphine Gordini.

Hermano da Silva Ramos, Gordini 16 (Monaco GP)

Paul Emery, Emeryson Mk1-Alta (British GP)

EMERYSON CARS

Paul Emery had been an apprentice at his father George's New Malden-based preparation business before the war and the 'specials' they created were called Emerysons. With more ideas than money, these ventures were perennially under-funded. In 1953 and now based in Twickenham, he built an F2 Emeryson with a tubular chassis, coil spring/double-wishbone independent front suspension and a de Dion rear axle with coil springs and trailing arms. Emery acquired a 2-litre Alta engine from Cooper, bored it out to 2,471cc and mated it to an ENV pre-selector gearbox. The car's bodywork was low thanks to a complex propshaft layout.

Emery had the temerity to lead Stirling Moss's Maserati 250F for a couple of laps of a *Formule Libre* race at Crystal Palace on a day when Moss was making a show of it for the crowd. Second on aggregate that day, Emery entered the British GP, qualified on the penultimate row and retired after 12 laps after a couple of plug changes failed to cure ignition trouble.

Paul's brother, Peter, also used the Emeryson moniker.

BOB GERARD

Bob Gerard continued to campaign his under-powered 2.2-litre Cooper T23-Bristol in British national races. Fourth in the 1956 International Trophy at Silverstone and second in another non-championship race at Aintree, he was the last classified finisher (11th) in the British GP at Silverstone after a lonely race.

Bob Gerard, Cooper T23-Bristol (*International Trophy, Silverstone*)

DRIVER PERFORMANCE (EXCLUDING INDIANAPOLIS 500)

DRIVER	CAR-ENGINE	RA	MC	B	F	GB	D	I
Elie Bayol	Gordini 32	–	[11] 6	–	–	–	–	–
Jean Behra	Maserati 250F	[4] 2	[4] 3	[4] 7	[7] 3	[13] 3	[8] 3	[5] R
Joakim Bonnier	Maserati 250F	–	–	–	–	–	–	[NT] R
Jack Brabham	Maserati 250F	–	–	–	–	[28] R	–	–
Tony Brooks	BRM P25	–	[13] DNS	–	–	[9] R	–	–
Eugenio Castellotti	Lancia-Ferrari D50	[2] R	[3] 4	[5] R	[2] **2**	[8] 10	[3] R	[2] **8**
Colin Chapman	Vanwall VW3	–	–	–	[5] DNS *	–	–	–
Louis Chiron	Maserati 250F	–	[NT] DNQ	–	–	–	–	–
Peter Collins	Ferrari 555 Supersqualo	[9] R	–	–	–	–	–	–
	Lancia-Ferrari D50	–	[9] 2	[3] **1**	[3] **1**	[4] 2	[2] R	[7] 2
Hermano da Silva Ramos	Gordini 16	–	[14] 5	–	–	–	–	–
	Gordini 32	–	–	–	[14] 8	[26] R	–	[21] R
Emmanuel de Graffenried	Maserati 250F	–	–	–	–	–	–	[19] 7
Alfonso de Portago	Lancia-Ferrari D50	–	–	–	[9] R	[12] 2+10	[10] R	[9] R
Paul Emery	Emeryson Mk1-Alta	–	–	–	–	[23] R	–	–
Jack Fairman	Connaught B-Alta	–	–	–	–	[21] 4	–	[16] 5
Juan Manuel Fangio	Lancia-Ferrari D50	[1] **1** FL	[1] 4+2 FL	[1] **R**	[1] **4** FL	[2] **1**	[1] **1** FL	[1] 8+2
Ron Flockhart	BRM P25	–	–	–	–	[17] R	–	–
	Connaught B-Alta	–	–	–	–	–	–	[24] 3
Paul Frère	Lancia-Ferrari D50	–	–	[8] 2	–	–	–	–
Olivier Gendebien	Ferrari 555 Supersqualo-Lancia	[10] 5	–	–	–	–	–	–
	Lancia-Ferrari D50	–	–	–	[11] R	–	–	–
Bob Gerard	Cooper T23-Bristol	–	–	–	–	[22] 11	–	–
Gerino Gerini	Maserati 250F	[NT] 4	–	–	–	–	–	[17] 10
Chico Godia	Maserati 250F	–	–	[14] R	[17] 7	[25] 8	[16] 4	[18] 4
José Froilán González	Maserati 250F	[5] **R**	–	–	–	–	–	–
	Vanwall VW1	–	–	–	–	[6] R	–	–
Oscar González	Maserati 250F	[NT] 6	–	–	–	–	–	–
'Horace Gould'	Maserati 250F	–	[16] 8	[15] R	–	[14] 5	[13] R	–
Bruce Halford	Maserati 250F	–	–	–	–	[20] R	[11] DSQ	[22] R
Mike Hawthorn	Maserati 250F	[8] 3	–	[13] DNS	–	–	–	–
	BRM P25	–	[10] DNS	–	–	[3] **R**	–	–
	Vanwall VW2	–	–	–	[6] 10	–	–	–
Chico Landi	Maserati 250F	[11] 4	–	–	–	–	–	–
'Les Leston'	Connaught B-Alta	–	–	–	–	–	–	[20] R
Umberto Maglioli	Maserati 250F	–	–	–	–	[24] R	[7] R	[13] R
Robert Manzon	Gordini 16	–	[12] R	–	–	–	–	–
	Gordini 32	–	–	–	[15] 9	[18] 9	[15] R	[23] R
Carlos Menditéguy	Maserati 250F	[6] **R**	–	–	–	–	–	–
André Milhoux	Gordini 32	–	–	–	–	–	[22] R	–
Stirling Moss	Maserati 250F	[7] **R**	[2] **1**	[2] 3 FL	[8] 5	[1] **R** FL	[4] 2	[6] **1** FL
Luigi Musso	Lancia-Ferrari D50	[3] 1	[8] R	–	–	–	[5] R	[3] **R**
Cesare Perdisa	Maserati 250F	–	[7] 7	[9] 3	[13] 5	[15] 7	[6] DNS	–
André Pilette	Gordini 32	–	[NT] 6	–	–	–	[18] DNS	–
	Lancia-Ferrari D50	–	–	[16] 6	–	–	–	–
	Gordini 16	–	–	–	[19] 11	–	–	–
Luigi Piotti	Maserati 250F	[12] R	–	–	–	–	[19] DNS	[15] 6
Louis Rosier	Maserati 250F	–	[15] R	[10] 8	[12] 6	[27] R	[14] 5	–
Roy Salvadori	Maserati 250F	–	–	–	–	[7] R	[9] R	[14] 11
Giorgio Scarlatti	Ferrari 500	–	[17] DNQ	–	–	–	[17] R	–

DRIVER PERFORMANCE CONTINUED

DRIVER	CAR-ENGINE	RA	MC	B	F	GB	D	I
Harry Schell	Vanwall VW1	–	5 R	6 4	4 R	–	–	–
	Vanwall VW2	–	–	–	NT 10	5 R	–	10 R
	Maserati 250F	–	–	–	–	–	12 R	–
Archie Scott Brown	Connaught B-Alta	–	–	–	–	10 R	–	–
Piero Scotti	Connaught B-Alta	–	–	12 R	–	–	–	–
André Simon	Maserati 250F	–	–	–	20 R	–	–	–
	Gordini 16	–	–	–	–	–	–	25 9
Piero Taruffi	Maserati 250F	–	–	–	16 R	–	–	–
	Vanwall VW1	–	–	–	–	–	–	4 R
Desmond Titterington	Connaught B-Alta	–	–	–	–	11 R	–	–
Maurice Trintignant	Vanwall VW2	–	6 R	7 R	–	–	–	–
	Bugatti T251	–	–	–	18 R	–	–	–
	Vanwall VW4	–	–	–	–	16 R	–	11 R
Alberto Uría	Maserati 250F	13 6	–	–	–	–	–	–
Luigi Villoresi	Maserati 250F	–	–	11 5	10 R	19 6	21 R	8 R
Ottorino Volonterio	Maserati 250F	–	–	–	–	–	20 NC	–
Wolfgang von Trips	Lancia-Ferrari D50	–	–	–	–	–	–	12 DNS

*Qualifying time set by Harry Schell. **SHARED DRIVES** Argentine GP: Luigi Musso/Juan Manuel Fangio (Lancia Ferrari D50) 1; Chico Landi/Gerino Gerini (Maserati 250F) 4; Alberto Uría/Oscar González (Maserati 250F) 6; Juan Manuel Fangio/Luigi Musso (Lancia Ferrari D50) R. Monaco GP: Peter Collins/Juan Manuel Fangio (Lancia Ferrari D50) 2; Juan Manuel Fangio/Eugenio Castellotti (Lancia Ferrari D50) 4; Elie Bayol/André Pilette (Gordini 32) 6. Belgian GP: Cesare Perdisa/Stirling Moss (Maserati 250F) 3. French GP: Cesare Perdisa/Stirling Moss (Maserati 250F) 5; Mike Hawthorn/Harry Schell (Vanwall VW2) 10. British GP: Alfonso de Portago/Peter Collins (Lancia Ferrari D50) 2; Eugenio Castellotti/Alfonso de Portago (Lancia Ferrari D50) 10. German GP: Alfonso de Portago/Peter Collins (Lancia Ferrari D50) R; Luigi Musso/Eugenio Castellotti (Lancia Ferrari D50) R. Italian GP: Peter Collins/Juan Manuel Fangio (Lancia Ferrari D50) 2; Juan Manuel Fangio/Eugenio Castellotti (Lancia Ferrari D50) 8; Umberto Maglioli/Jean Behra (Maserati 250F) R; Luigi Villoresi/Joakim Bonnier (Maserati 250F) R.

FORMULA 1 RACE WINNERS

ROUND	RACE (CIRCUIT)	DATE	WINNER
1	Gran Premio de la República Argentina (Buenos Aires)	Jan 22	Luigi Musso/Juan Manuel Fangio (Lancia-Ferrari D50)
–	Gran Premio de la Ciudad de Buenos Aires (Mendoza)	Feb 5	Juan Manuel Fangio (Lancia-Ferrari D50)
–	Glover Trophy (Goodwood)	Apr 2	Stirling Moss (Maserati 250F)
–	Gran Premio di Siracusa (Syracuse)	Apr 15	Juan Manuel Fangio (Lancia-Ferrari D50)
–	BARC 200 (Aintree)	Apr 21	Stirling Moss (Maserati 250F)
–	Daily Express International Trophy (Silverstone)	May 5	Stirling Moss (Vanwall VW2)
–	Gran Premio di Napoli (Posillipo)	May 6	Robert Manzon (Gordini 16)
2	Grand Prix de Monaco (Monte Carlo)	May 13	Stirling Moss (Maserati 250F)
3*	Indianapolis 500 (Indianapolis)	May 30	Pat Flaherty (Watson-Offenhauser)
4	Grand Prix de Belgique (Spa-Francorchamps)	Jun 3	Peter Collins (Lancia-Ferrari D50)
–	Aintree 100 (Aintree)	Jun 24	'Horace Gould' (Maserati 250F)
5	Grand Prix de l'Automobile Club de France (Reims)	Jul 7	Peter Collins (Lancia-Ferrari D50)
6	British Grand Prix (Silverstone)	Jul 14	Juan Manuel Fangio (Lancia-Ferrari D50)
–	Vanwall Trophy (Snetterton)	Jul 22	Roy Salvadori (Maserati 250F)
7	Grosser Preis von Deutschland (Nürburgring)	Aug 5	Juan Manuel Fangio (Lancia-Ferrari D50)
–	Grand Prix de Caen (Caen)	Aug 26	Harry Schell (Maserati 250F)
8	Gran Premio d'Italia e Europa (Monza)	Sep 2	Stirling Moss (Maserati 250F)
–	BRSCC Formula 1 Race (Brands Hatch)	Oct 14	Archie Scott Brown (Connaught B-Alta)

*Run to USAC National Championship rules

DRIVERS' CHAMPIONSHIP

	DRIVERS	POINTS	
1	Juan Manuel Fangio	30	(34.5)*
2	Stirling Moss	27	(28)*
3	Peter Collins	25	
4	Jean Behra	22	
5	Pat Flaherty	8	
6	Eugenio Castellotti	7.5	
7=	Paul Frère	6	
	Chico Godia Sales	6	
	Sam Hanks	6	
10	Jack Fairman	5	
11=	Ron Flockhart	4	
	Don Freeland	4	
	Mike Hawthorn	4	
	Luigi Musso	4	
15=	Johnnie Parsons	3	
	Cesare Perdisa	3	
	Alfonso de Portago	3	
	Harry Schell	3	
19=	Olivier Gendebien	2	
	'Horace Gould'	2	
	Dick Rathmann	2	
	Louis Rosier	2	
	Hermano da Silva Ramos	2	
	Luigi Villoresi	2	
25=	Gerino Gerini	1.5	
	Chico Landi	1.5	
27	Paul Russo	1	

*Best five results count

Juan Manuel Fangio (Maserati 250F) takes a final GP victory at the Nürburgring

1957
FANGIO'S FIFTH AND FINAL WORLD CHAMPIONSHIP

Stirling Moss takes over Tony Brooks's Vanwall during the British GP

Juan Manuel Fangio moved to Maserati for his last full season and won his fourth World Championship in a row, and his fifth overall. However, Vanwall completed 1957 as F1's pacesetters and lead driver Stirling Moss was championship runner-up for the third successive year.

The season began with petrol rationed across Europe due to the Suez oil crisis. Fuel was only granted for racing in Britain in February, forcing the International Trophy to be postponed until September. Rationing was finally lifted in Britain on 15 May.

Swiss authorities maintained the country's circuit-racing ban after the parliament's lower house voted 66–46 against in March. All GP race organisers except Italy met in Brussels before the European season and agreed a reduced scale of start and prize money. The Italian teams refused these terms and the Belgian (2 June) and Dutch (16 June) GPs were cancelled and the German GP threatened. No World

Vanwall owner Tony Vandervell celebrates victory at Aintree with drivers Tony Brooks and Stirling Moss

The harbour at Monte Carlo after the Lancia-Ferrari D50s of Mike Hawthorn and Peter Collins were eliminated at the chicane

Championship races were held for a couple of months during the summer and *Motor Sport*'s Denis Jenkinson bemoaned that the crisis was 'due entirely to the sordid question of finance'. The promotors eventually relented. Regulations stipulated that a minimum of six GPs had to be held, so Pescara was elevated to championship status, its 16-mile road course the longest in F1 history. The Spanish GP was scheduled for 20 October but was also cancelled.

The start of the French GP was delayed by 20 minutes when a bridge connecting the pits to the main grandstand collapsed, with two people seriously injured. Aintree held the British GP once more and the £7,000 prize fund (a record for the UK) was paid in guineas, as this was the home of the famous Grand National horse race.

A drivers' union – the Union des Pilotes Professionale et Internationale (UPPI) – was formed in May with Louis Chiron elected president. This later became the Grand Prix Drivers' Association (GPDA).

Fangio secured his fifth world title by winning the German GP

Jean Behra, Maserati 250F (German GP)

OFFICINE ALFIERI MASERATI

Ferrari hoped Juan Manuel Fangio would stay, but the World Champion began 1957 competing on a race-by-race basis for the highest bidder, rather than sign a season-long contract with anyone. He accepted Maserati's offer for the Argentine races on the condition that Carlos Menditéguy, who had recovered from his Sebring injuries, was offered a drive. Jean Behra remained for a third year. With Vanwall not ready for the *Temporada*, Stirling Moss drove a fourth works Maserati 250F.

Technical chief Giulio Alfieri introduced a lightweight 250F with smaller-diameter tubular frame, revised and tapered body, wider brake drums and steering mounted on the chassis rather than to the engine as before. The offset transmission and angled engine

introduced at Monza in 1956 were shelved. The lightweight 250F was officially referred to as the 250F-T2 and three such cars were built.

A new 60-degree V12 engine was developed throughout the season but proved slower and less drivable than the existing 'six' and was seldom raced. This 2,490cc unit had twin overhead camshafts per cylinder bank with six specially designed Weber twin-choke carburettors. Dual ignition and dry-sump lubrication were retained. Initially, the new engine was fitted into a modified 1956 chassis and, from Monaco, mated to a five-speed gearbox. Pirelli reversed its decision to withdraw and supplied tyres to Maserati and Vanwall for one further season.

Fangio, Behra and Moss drove new 250Fs in Argentina with Menditéguy in a 1956 chassis. Utterly dominant in the Argentine GP, all seven Maseratis (including three privateers) finished with Fangio, Behra and Menditéguy 1–2–3 for the works team. After his throttle linkage broke at the shambolic start, Moss lost nine laps for repairs but on resuming he set the fastest race lap and unlapped himself twice while recovering to finish eighth. In the non-championship Buenos Aires GP, where 103.1°F was recorded in the shade, Fangio beat Behra on aggregate. Moss led heat one but suffered sunstroke and withdrew, then during heat two he took over Menditéguy's car only to spin when caught out by Maserati's normal central throttle pedal. Aside from the racing, the city of Rosario celebrated Fangio's fourth title by presenting him with a trophy that matched his height (5ft 8in) and weight (187lb).

Fangio was so impressed by the new 250F that he signed a contract for the year's other championship GPs, with Menditéguy also

Juan Manuel Fangio, Maserati 250F (Monaco GP)

Carlos Menditéguy, Maserati 250F (British GP)

retained. The V12 appeared at the first European race at Syracuse but did not start. The works 'sixes' of Behra and Harry Schell, who chose to sign with Maserati rather than Vanwall, both retired.

Behra dominated at Pau but missed the Monaco GP after breaking his wrist during practice for the Mille Miglia. Five cars were taken to the Principality with Fangio, Menditéguy and Schell in 250F-T2s. Giorgio Scarlatti and Hans Herrmann shared an older model with the Italian chosen to race when he proved quicker in practice. The V12 ran in practice but 'died' at low revs and was discarded again. Fangio became the first man to win the Monaco GP twice when he led from lap five until the finish. Schell challenged for third until he damaged his car against a kerb at Ste Dévote while Menditéguy was running in that position when he crashed into a lamppost at the chicane, breaking his nose. Schell took over Scarlatti's car only to retire from fifth place.

The financial dispute between the Italian teams and promoters prevented any more F1 races for almost two months, by which time Behra had recovered. He joined Fangio and Schell in the new cars at the French GP with Menditéguy relegated to an old chassis once more. Fangio was quickest in practice in his six-cylinder car and second quickest with the V12, which was now mounted in a new 250F-T2 chassis with twin air ducts on the bonnet, but once again remained unraced.

'The old man' was the master of the extended Rouen-les-Essarts with his 250F power-sliding through its sweeping curves as he eased

to another victory, winning by 50.8sec. The specialist press were in awe. *Autosport* called him 'the most accomplished racing driver of all time' and *The Autocar* agreed: 'He is still the outstanding driver of our time – or of any time.' Behra qualified second and jumped the start but was soon passed by Luigi Musso (Lancia-Ferrari) and Fangio. Suffering from fumes due to a broken exhaust, Behra was fifth in the closing stages when an oil line fractured and covered him from head to foot. He stopped by the finish and waited 10 minutes for Fangio to win before pushing his car over the line without losing a position, but he was then relegated to sixth when his final lap was disqualified for having taken too long. Schell's overheating and very slow 250F

Stirling Moss, Maserati 250F (Argentine GP)

Joakim Bonnier, Maserati 250F (Italian GP)

SCUDERIA CENTRO SUD

Scuderia Centro Sud acquired a second Maserati 250F and sent both cars to Argentina, along with its elderly 2-litre Ferrari 500. Both 250Fs finished the GP, Harry Schell a distant fourth and Joakim Bonnier seventh. Driving the old Ferrari, Alejandro de Tomaso, who had recently announced his engagement to sports car driver Isabelle Haskell, survived a couple of spins to claim ninth.

Thereafter Centro Sud entered only the 250Fs. Piero Taruffi finished fourth in Syracuse despite a broken shock absorber. At Pau Schell and the bespectacled Masten Gregory finished second and fourth respectively, both lapped, and Gregory followed up with fifth in Naples. Gregory made his World Championship début in Monaco,

where André Simon joined him but did not qualify. As faster rivals fell by the wayside, Gregory diced with Jack Brabham's Cooper-Climax and inherited third place when the Australian broke down with three laps to go.

Simon's car was repainted Swedish blue and yellow for Bonnier at the British GP, where he qualified on the penultimate row and was the first retirement. Gregory was joined by Hans Herrmann for the German GP, where the organisers were keen on national racing colours being observed so the 250Fs wore America's white and blue and Germany's plain white. Herrmann retired from the midfield while Gregory came eighth. There was another new colour scheme – silver with a blue-and-yellow stripe on the bonnet – when Bonnier

Alejandro de Tomaso, Ferrari 500 (Argentine GP)

Masten Gregory, Maserati 250F (Pescara GP)

replaced Herrmann for the last two GPs, at Pescara and Monza, but he retired from both. Gregory finished fourth at Pescara following an eventful race: he almost hit a kilometre post when he spun and then locked up as he pitted, 'making a mechanic do an Olympic high jump' as Gregor Grant reported in *Autosport*. Both cars were rebuilt before the Italian GP, where Gregory capped an excellent season with another fourth place, putting him sixth in the final standings.

Bonnier and Gregory finished fourth and fifth in the International Trophy at Silverstone before the Swede joined BRM for the final non-championship races of the season.

OTHER MASERATI PRIVATEERS

'Horace Gould' sent his 250F to Maserati's Modena works after his accident at Caen in August 1956 and it was repaired in time for him to take part in New Zealand's season of racing that winter. He returned to Europe at Pau, where transmission problems ruined his race although he was able to finish, a much-lapped eighth and last. With low gearing fitted at Naples, 'Gould' led the works Ferraris off the line before finishing fourth. Sixth during the early laps at Monaco, when pursued by a train of faster cars, his 250F was soon battle-scarred following contact with frustrated rivals and a split fuel tank brought his retirement. He departed early from the French GP and finished sixth in the lesser Reims event. A bizarre incident during practice for the British GP forced 'Gould' to miss the race: having stopped to help extinguish a fire on Bob Gerard's Cooper-Climax,

Hans Herrmann, Maserati 250F (German GP)

the stricken car rolled over and injured his foot. A distant fifth at Caen, he gained an entry for the German GP when BRM withdrew, only for his rear axle to fail. There were mechanics still on the grid at the start of the Pescara GP and 'Gould' hit one in the ensuing chaos but continued round the first lap, only to crash into a vineyard at the chicane at the end of the lap, retiring the bent 250F in the pits. He was the slowest qualifier for the Italian GP and finished 10th, while his final appearance of 1957, Silverstone's International Trophy, yielded sixth place.

'Horace Gould', Maserati 250F (German GP)

Bruce Halford, Maserati 250F (Italian GP)

Bruce Halford's ex-'Bira' Maserati 250F also had a complete overhaul during the winter. Third at Caen, he travelled to the Nürburgring without an entry for the German GP but was able to race after BRM withdrew, finishing 11th and last of the F1 entries. Seventh when his differential broke at half distance at Pescara, Halford borrowed a works car for the Italian GP but it had fuel-feed problems during practice and blew up after 47 laps of the race. He was back in his own car for the non-championship races at Silverstone and Modena, an unobtrusive seventh in both.

Ivor Bueb raced Gilby Engineering's aged ex-Roy Salvadori 250F in Britain's major F1 events. Last on the grid having missed final practice for the British GP, Bueb made numerous pitstops trying to sort its recalcitrant engine on the way to eighth place. He was fourth in his heat and ninth in the final of the International Trophy at Silverstone.

Swiss Ottorino Volonterio acquired a two-year-old Maserati 250F and ran it three times. In his first race, at Naples, the engine suffered a cracked cylinder block and put him out after four laps. Herbert MacKay-Fraser qualified it for the non-championship Reims GP but was killed beforehand during the supporting F2 race. For the Italian GP Volonterio entered André Simon, who qualified on the last row and ran among the backmarkers before handing the car to its owner when he refuelled; Volonterio was immediately black-flagged as the stewards debated whether he had done the required 12 laps in practice but he was eventually allowed to continue, finishing 11th, 15 laps down.

Ivor Bueb, Maserati 250F (British GP)

André Simon/Ottorino Volonterio, Maserati 250F (Italian GP)

Mike Hawthorn, Lancia-Ferrari D50 (German GP)

SCUDERIA FERRARI

Scuderia Ferrari's negotiations with Juan Manuel Fangio broke down in early December so Peter Collins was announced as team leader. Eugenio Castellotti, Luigi Musso and Alfonso de Portago (an all-round sportsman who beat the 25-year-old course record for bobsleigh's Cresta Run on 30 December 1956) remained while Cesare Perdisa arrived from Maserati. Mike Hawthorn was originally committed to BRM but confirmed his return to Ferrari in the last week of December. The old Lancia-Ferrari D50 was retained but proved no match for Maserati or Vanwall despite various modifications. Pirelli and Firestone tyres were tested during the winter following the Monza *débacles* of 1955 and 1956 but Ferrari's contract with Englebert was renewed. Eraldo Sculati fell out of favour with *Il Commendatore* so was replaced as team manager by technical chief Girolamo Amorotti.

Six cars were entered for the Argentine GP with José Froilán González making his annual reappearance. Castellotti, Collins and Hawthorn had new chassis that were 4in shorter and featured new spaceframes. These revisions were overseen by Ing Vittorio Bellentani with 33-year-old Carlo Chiti new to the design department. Four Solex carburettors were angled at 20 degrees to improve breathing and the V8 engine now developed 290bhp. The side tanks were enlarged and a smaller tail unit was added to improve weight distribution. New suspension was tried as Bellentani sought to eradicate low-speed understeer. The steering arms were strengthened following the failures during the 1956 Italian GP.

Fourth-placed Castellotti was the top Lancia-Ferrari man in

qualifying and both he and Collins led before Maranello's challenge wilted in the heat. Collins, Musso and Hawthorn all suffered clutch failure and Castellotti, who spun on lap 16, shed a rear wheel following hub failure after 75 laps. González handed his car to de Portago, who finished fifth, while Perdisa's car was sixth, Collins and Wolfgang von Trips both having taken turns behind the wheel.

Soundly beaten in the non-championship Buenos Aires GP, the Lancia-Ferraris were heavily revised for Syracuse. The engines were returned to 1956 specification with vertical carburettors while heavier-gauge tubing was used on Collins's car to reduce chassis flex. Front suspension was now by coil springs and longer unequal wishbones due to the narrower front of the chassis. The most visible

Peter Collins, Lancia-Ferrari D50 (French GP)

Ivor Bueb, Connaught B-Alta (Monaco GP)

CONNAUGHT ENGINEERING

Kenneth McAlpine could not afford to invest any more money into Connaught so Rodney Clarke faced financial reality and closed the competition department on 29 May. 'In view of the continued lack of adequate monetary assistance for our motor racing activities,' the statement read, 'and in light of the unstable financial conditions in Formula 1 racing at this particular time, we have reluctantly decided that we must close down the motor racing side of Connaught Engineering.' Connaught continued to operate in the general motor trade from its works in Portsmouth Road, Send.

Connaught began 1957 by entering a pair of B-types in European races in the hope of surviving on start money. SU fuel injection was developed during the winter and Harry Weslake modified the

Stuart Lewis-Evans, Connaught B-Alta (Monaco GP)

engine's cylinder heads and strengthened its con rods. Three B-types were sent to Syracuse, where Ivor Bueb finished fifth, Jack Fairman retired and 'Les Leston' crashed in practice. Bueb and 'Leston' finished third and fifth at Pau, albeit lapped at least three times. For a fine display at Goodwood, there was angular new bodywork for the B-type of Bernie Ecclestone's protégé, Stuart Lewis-Evans, who used the still unpainted 'toothpaste tube' to lead home Fairman and Ron Flockhart in standard cars as Connaughts finished 1–2–3 in the Glover Trophy. Lewis-Evans reverted to normal bodywork to run second among the Lancia-Ferraris in Naples before a front hub failed.

Lewis-Evans, in the 'toothpaste tube' again, and Bueb entered the Monaco GP with both cars converted back to Weber carburettors and sporting short noses to limit damage in Monte Carlo's tight confines. Bueb qualified last and was forced into the spare when his race car lost gearbox oil on the way to the start. He ran at the back, pitted when the exhausts fell off, made another long stop to blank off the split rear fuel tank and finally retired. Lewis-Evans stayed out of trouble to finish fourth.

Having returned to base, the team was informed of its closure 10 days after Monaco. The cars and other assets were auctioned by Goddard, Davison & Smith Ltd on 17–19 September with only the incomplete C-type not achieving its reserve. This had a lighter spaceframe with new de Dion rear axle and inboard brakes. The car was eventually completed in May 1959 and sold to Paul Emery. Among those to buy the six Connaught B-types was Bernie Ecclestone of Compton & Ecclestone, who acquired chassis B3 (the 'toothpaste tube') and B7 for £2,100 and £1,950 respectively.

Ron Flockhart, BRM P25 (French GP)

BRITISH RACING MOTORS (BRM)

Seven hundred members of the Owen Racing Motor Association attended an open meeting at Kensington Town Hall on Monday 7 January when Sir Alfred Owen announced that two BRMs would enter all European GPs during 1957 with Roy Salvadori and long-standing test driver Ron Flockhart soon confirmed as drivers. Peter Berthon reported that the engine's valve springs had been strengthened and transmission issues solved.

Testing at Monza in October 1956 resulted in higher cockpit sides and a longer wheelbase, although the P25's handling remained a problem. Alec Issigonis and Alex Moulton reworked the rear suspension, with transverse leaf springs replacing the oleopneumatic struts when the revised P25s appeared at Goodwood on Easter Monday. Salvadori's brakes locked solid at Woodcote on the opening lap of the Glover Trophy while Flockhart spun twice on the way to third. They struggled at Monaco, where *Autosport* reported that 'the gremlins of Bourne struck again'. Salvadori did not qualify and Flockhart retired from fifth, so Colin Chapman was hired as a consultant to sort out the erratic handling. He prescribed coil springs all round, with hydraulic dampers and Watt's links at the rear, but gains were offset by extra strain on the drive shafts and the de Dion system's pot-type universal joints.

Frustrated by the lack of progress, Salvadori left before the French GP, where Herbert MacKay-Fraser made his début and ran a promising sixth during the early laps before his transmission failed. Flockhart hit oil at Rouen's Courbe de l'Etoile on lap three and rolled into a concrete parapet, the double Le Mans winner hospitalised

Herbert MacKay-Fraser, BRM P25 (French GP)

Jack Fairman, BRM P25 (British GP)

'Les Leston', BRM P25 (British GP)

with an injured hip and burns to an arm and legs after being thrown clear. A week later MacKay-Fraser was killed driving a streamlined Lotus in the F2 race at Reims.

Turned down by Archie Scott Brown, BRM signed Jack Fairman and 'Les Leston' for the British GP at Aintree, where both spun before suffering near simultaneous engine failures. Maserati released Jean Behra and Harry Schell for the following week's minor race at Caen and they entertained the crowd by swapping positions at the front of a small field; Schell's engine failed but Behra gave BRM a much-needed boost with victory. Despite that encouragement, BRM withdrew from the last three championship races before three cars

were entered for the International Trophy at Silverstone. Without works opposition from the continent or from Vanwall, Behra, Schell and the recovered Flockhart eased to a BRM 1–2–3. Joakim Bonnier and Flockhart raced at Modena but both proved slow and did not finish. The Moroccan GP organisers were keen for a French driver to take part so Maurice Trintignant was chosen and finished in a strong third place while Flockhart retired when he hit a bird and damaged the throttle.

Although it had been another frustrating season for Britain's great under-achievers, there had been moments of promise.

COOPER CAR COMPANY/ ROB WALKER RACING

The Cooper Car Company saw the new Formula 2 as a potential market so Owen Maddock drew a single-seater derivative of the type 40 'Bob-tail' sports car. The Cooper T41 first appeared at Silverstone for a support race for the 1956 British GP, fully six months before the new category came into effect. Powered by the 1.5-litre Coventry Climax FWB engine, the T41 had a narrower steel tubular frame, transverse-leaf/double-wishbone independent suspension and a four-speed Citroën gearbox. Driving the only pukka F2 car in the field that day, Roy Salvadori eased to the first of his four national race wins that year.

Over the winter Maddock refined the design as the type 43,

Jack Brabham, Cooper T43-Climax (Pescara GP)

which was 2in longer with chassis and bodywork lightly modified. This was powered by the new 1,475cc twin-cam Climax FPF four-cylinder dry-sump engine in standard F2 trim. In addition to entering a works team and selling customer cars, Cooper opened a new racing drivers' school at Brands Hatch on 20 March 1957. Jack Brabham raced the 1.5-litre twin-cam T43 for the first time at Goodwood on Easter Monday, finishing fourth in the F1 Glover Trophy and beaten into second place in the supporting F2 race by Tony Brooks in Rob Walker's T41.

Eager to re-enter F1, staunch privateer Rob Walker ordered a T43 that new chief mechanic Alf Francis fitted with an enlarged 1,960cc Climax FPF engine and auxiliary fuel tanks on either flank. When the engine was bench-tested nine days before its planned début with Brabham at Monaco, it offered 175bhp at 6,500rpm. As there was no time for a proper shakedown test, Brabham tried the car on the Kingston bypass (A3) near Cooper's Surbiton factory to check systems before it was despatched to the Principality. The Australian arrived late so Peter Collins briefly tried the car during first practice, but Brabham took over for second practice and immediately crashed at Massenet when the brakes locked. 'Les Leston' drove the regular 1.5-litre works F2 T43 but blew the engine and did not qualify, so Walker took over the tiny green car and had his 2-litre engine installed in it overnight. After Brabham qualified 13th, the giant-killing Cooper was the sensation of the race, reaching a remarkable third place before a fuel pump mounting broke at the Old Station Hairpin in the closing stages. He coasted down to the harbourside and pushed the car to the line to claim sixth place.

With Cooper cleaning up in F2, three T43s (including a spare) were taken to Rouen-les-Essarts for the French GP with Brabham in Walker's enlarged car and amateur Mike MacDowel in the 1.5-litre works machine, which was fitted with disc brakes. Rouen's fast sweeps exposed their relative lack of power and both qualified towards the back and initially ran last; after four laps Brabham crashed but took over MacDowel's car to finish a distant seventh.

The factory team added a second 2-litre car at Aintree and Salvadori, having left BRM, returned to duty. He drove a tremendous race and only lost a fourth-place finish when the gearbox casing split, but he was able to push the car across the line to claim fifth and a couple of championship points. The Walker T43 was also now fitted with disc brakes but its clutch failed when Brabham lay sixth. Salvadori's works 1,960cc car inherited second at the following week's Caen GP where guest driver Tony Brooks had another clutch fail on the Walker car, prompting Francis to switch to a Maserati-made version. Cooper and Walker entered the F2 class of the German GP and Salvadori led these runners (ahead of a couple of F1 Maseratis) before both he and Brabham retired. For Pescara 1.5-litre engines were fitted for the anticipated F2 class, but this evaporated and, against the F1 field, the little Coopers were outclassed on the long straights as a consequence, and also bottomed alarmingly on the Abruzzi bumps. Salvadori crashed into a kilometre post near Cappelle and Brabham, works-entered on this occasion, finished last.

Cooper missed the Italian GP as it prepared for the following

Mike MacDowel/Jack Brabham, Cooper T43-Climax (French GP)

week's International Trophy. Brooks qualified Walker's 1,960cc T43 on pole position at Silverstone only to snap the crown wheel and pinion at the start of his heat. Brabham missed qualifying but drove through the field to claim second place in heat two, and in the final he passed Joakim Bonnier's Maserati for fourth before developing a terminal oil leak. Salvadori's works car won the F2 class with Coopers filling the top eight positions. The non-championship Moroccan GP was disappointing as Salvadori retired and Brabham's Walker T43 was disqualified because his gearbox had been repaired away from the pits. It was a low-key finish but these cars would soon be turning heads.

Roy Salvadori, Cooper T43-Climax (British GP)

Bob Gerard, Cooper T43-Bristol (British GP)

BOB GERARD CARS

Leicester-based Bob Gerard acquired a Cooper T43 that he modified to accept his tall 2,246cc Bristol six-cylinder engine by moving the central cross member forward, with the Cooper/Citroën gearbox lowered to suit and the exhausts exiting vertically. Gerard's 'special' was the penultimate qualifier for the British GP at Aintree after a troubled practice but he finished sixth, albeit lapped eight times.

GERMAN FORMULA 2 CLASS

The Automobilclub von Deutschland invited a works-only F1 entry, although two private Maseratis were admitted when BRM withdrew. This was bolstered by a concurrent race for the newly introduced 1,500cc F2 class, which attracted a nine-car field.

Porsche sent two sports-bodied 550RS Spyders for Edgar Barth and Umberto Maglioli. Barth was the quickest F2 driver in qualifying and emerged from his dice with Roy Salvadori's Cooper-Climax to win the class. Maglioli's engine failed on lap 14 when second behind his team-mate. Carel Godin de Beaufort also drove an 500RS, entered by his Ecurie Maarsbergen and resplendent in Dutch orange, and finished third in class and 14th overall.

There were another four Cooper-Climaxes in addition to the regular cars of Roy Salvadori and Jack Brabham (see previous pages). Brian Naylor's T43 finished second in class while Dick Gibson damaged the suspension on his similar car when he hit a bank on lap two and retired next time around. Ridgeway Managements sent a T43 for hillclimber Tony Marsh and a T41 for Australian Paul England, who raced in Europe for just one month. Marsh stripped a crown wheel during practice and lost three laps for repairs to broken suspension using a wishbone from Salvadori's retired car. Marsh, who won the 1957 British F2 title, was the last driver still circulating at the finish of the race. Like Gibson, *Autosport* reported that England was 'a little overawed by the whole undertaking'. He retired from last place after four laps.

Carel Godin de Beaufort, Porsche 550RS (German GP)

Edgar Barth, Porsche 550RS (German GP)

Umberto Maglioli, Porsche 550RS (German GP)

Dick Gibson, Cooper T43-Climax (German GP)

Brian Naylor, Cooper T43-Climax (German GP)

Tony Marsh, Cooper T43-Climax (German GP)

Paul England, Cooper T41-Climax (*BRSCC F2 race, Mallory Park*)

The Belgian GP at Spa-Francorchamps finally starts with Stirling Moss's Vanwall to the fore

1958

HAWTHORN DENIES MOSS FOR BRITAIN'S FIRST CROWN

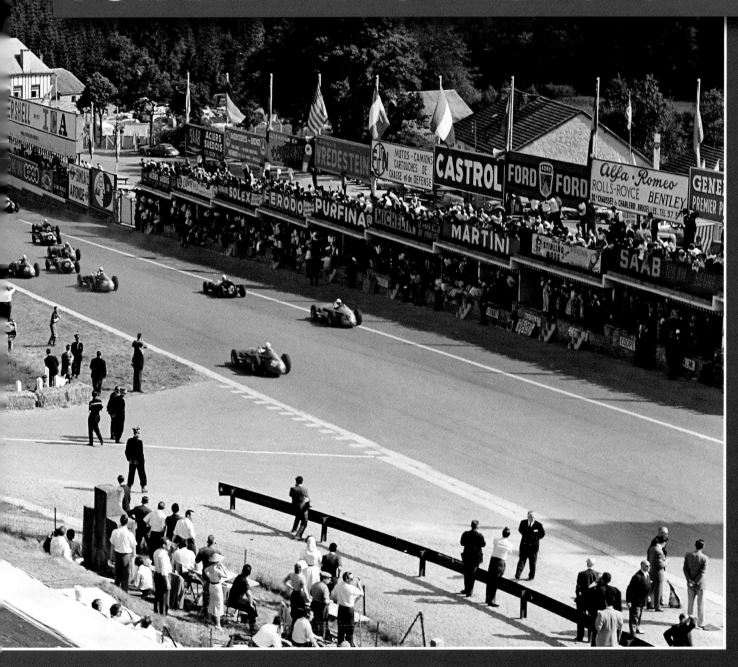

Title contenders Stirling Moss and Mike Hawthorn round Monte Carlo's Station hairpin

Mike Hawthorn on the way to second place at Spa-Francorchamps

A number of new initiatives were ratified for the coming season when the FIA's sporting commission met on 7 October 1957. Maximum engine capacities remained unchanged but commercial fuel was now mandatory, with aviation fuel soon standard. The new Constructors' Cup was introduced with no points awarded for the Indianapolis 500 and just the leading car of each marque scoring points. The best six results counted for each championship. Shared drives were no longer rewarded with points. Finally, race duration was reduced to between 300kms and 500kms or a minimum of two hours, which purists saw as a retrograde move.

The 1958 season was a tragic if successful campaign for Ferrari. Luigi Musso and Peter Collins were both killed while racing and Mike Hawthorn lost his life in a road accident on 22 January 1959. Furthermore, Vanwall's Stuart Lewis-Evans was fatally burned during the final championship round.

The Portuguese GP was included on the calendar for the first time on the long Porto street circuit, complete with cobbled streets, tramlines and varying track width. Originally slated for 29 June or 6 July, it was eventually postponed to 24 August. There was confusion over whether the races in Argentina would go ahead when the last ship left Europe for Buenos Aires in December. The Italians seemingly were never in doubt but the British believed the events had been

The new Lotus team in the paddock at Silverstone with a type 12 (bodywork removed) and two type 16s

cancelled: neither Vanwall nor BRM sent cars, leading the Royal Automobile Club to protest the Argentine GP's inclusion in the championship, while the Italians and South Americans threatened to leave the FIA if the race was stripped of points status. In fact the GP was only confirmed as the opening championship round 11 days after it happened, following a meeting in Monaco on 30 January at which the Moroccan GP was also elevated to the championship. The whole process led *The Autocar* to describe the FIA as 'astoundingly slow and unwieldy'. The Argentine fiasco, and the fact that four cars were delayed on the high seas, led to the smallest field in championship history – just 10 cars.

Silverstone was always keen to improve its facilities and *Autosport* reported that the 'BRDC Members' enclosure and refreshment tent was a popular innovation' at the British GP. Less welcome was the announcement at the end of the year that the *Daily Express* was ending its sponsorship after 10 years. A welcome aspect of the year was Peter Ustinov's *Grand Prix of Gibraltar* gramophone record, a parody with drivers 'Juan Manuel Fandango' and 'Girling Foss' among his imitations. However, *Motor Sport* had its reservations: 'Alas, the fun has rather dated,' it noted two years later, 'jokes at the expense of Gordini making one feel ancient and, by jove, the thing does go on and on.'

Maria Teresa de Filippis became the first woman to race in F1

Mike Hawthorn, Ferrari Dino 246 (Moroccan GP)

Peter Collins, Ferrari Dino 246 (Monaco GP)

SCUDERIA FERRARI

Enzo Ferrari held a lunch at Modena's Ristorante Fini on 21 December 1957 at which he announced Peter Collins, Mike Hawthorn and Luigi Musso as his unchanged F1 line-up. Wolfgang von Trips, Olivier Gendebien and Phil Hill were retained as junior drivers and for sports cars. Promoted to chief engineer in May, Carlo Chiti worked with the legendary Vittorio Jano to refine the 1957 F2 car's tubular spaceframe with a small-diameter superstructure. Suspension on the Ferrari Dino 246 was by coil springs at the front and transverse leaf/de Dion tube to the rear while Houdaille lever-arm dampers were standard. Ferrari experimented with rear coil springs on Hawthorn's car during practice at the Nürburgring and subsequent races. Drum brakes were usual although Hawthorn persuaded Ferrari to try discs, which he raced in the last two GPs. The 2,417cc V6 engine developed 270bhp at 8,300rpm. The carburettors (first Weber, then Solex) protruded through the low-line bonnet, covered by a Perspex 'bubble'. Englebert continued as tyre supplier. The Dino 246 was a bulky car and could not match the nimble rear-engine Coopers in the corners, but it was powerful and had an advantage on faster circuits.

Four Dino 246s were entered for the Argentine GP although von Trips's chassis arrived after the race! Hawthorn and Collins qualified on the front row but Collins's driveshaft snapped at the start. Hawthorn led briefly before understeer and fading oil pressure

Luigi Musso, Ferrari Dino 246 (Belgian GP)

forced him to pit. Musso trailed Stirling Moss's Cooper-Climax, the Italian convinced that Moss would change tyres, but when he realised late in the day that the little Cooper would not be stopping he gave chase from 30secs behind and finished just 2.7secs adrift. Hawthorn passed Fangio and Jean Behra to claim third place, despite contact with Carlos Menditéguy's spun Maserati.

Ferrari sent singleton entries to the spring non-championship races at Goodwood, Syracuse and Silverstone, which Hawthorn, Musso and Collins respectively won against national fields.

With redesigned drum brakes, Ferrari struggled in qualifying for the Monaco GP. That said, Hawthorn recovered from being hit at the start to charge from eighth place to assume the lead when Behra's brakes faded. He duelled with Moss before the Vanwall retired and set a new lap record only for a broken fuel pump to deny victory. Musso again finished second to take the points lead, with Collins third. Driving a fourth Dino, von Trips was on course to claim fourth, despite pain caused by his broken brake pedal, when his rough-sounding engine seized nine laps from home.

Three Ferrari entries were accepted for the Dutch GP, where the cars understeered and were slow on the straights. Gearbox failure caused Collins to spin at Scheivlak and both Hawthorn (fifth) and Musso (seventh) were lapped by Moss's dominant Vanwall.

At the fast Spa-Francorchamps circuit, which better suited the Dino 246, long air intakes replaced the carburettor covers and Hawthorn led Musso in a scarlet qualifying 1–2. The start was a shambles as all the cars were left on the grid for an age. *Autosport* reported that 'Collins's car was boiling like a kettle' but he fought with Tony Brooks for the lead for five laps until his overheating engine forced him to retire. Hawthorn slowed when Musso crashed into a house near Stavelot, thinking it was *Mon Ami Mate* Collins, and fearing the worst. He sped up as soon as he saw both team-mates by the side of the track and chased Brooks to the finish, setting the fastest race lap on the final tour despite his engine exploding as he exited La Source. Hawthorn coasted across the line to claim second. Driving a fourth car painted yellow at the behest of the organisers, Gendebien ran third until Stuart Lewis-Evans rammed him at La Source, but after losing three minutes for repairs the Belgian climbed back through the field to finish sixth.

Ferrari ended the run of British victories at Reims, where Hawthorn qualified on pole, led from start to finish and set the fastest lap. Von Trips was third but Collins, who spun down to 18th due to a loose air intake wedging under his brake pedal, lost fourth when he ran out of fuel on the last lap and pushed his car over the line to salvage fifth. Musso was second when he lost control at the fast first corner and barrel-rolled into a field. A dominant day ended on a sombre note when news broke that the 33-year-old had succumbed to his injuries in hospital.

Von Trips replaced Musso for the British GP but retired on his first visit to Silverstone. Collins took the lead at Stowe on the opening lap and led to the finish, while Hawthorn, who had tried

Wolfgang von Trips, Ferrari Dino 246 (Monaco GP)

Olivier Gendebien, Ferrari Dino 246 (Belgian GP)

Dunlop tyres in practice, was second and set the fastest race lap to assume the points lead for the first time.

With the Dino 246 now handling better and showing improved reliability, Collins and Hawthorn ran 1–2 in Germany after Moss's retirement. Brooks passed both red cars on lap 11 and the Ferraris were chasing the Vanwall when Collins crashed at Pflanzgarten at over 100mph and was thrown clear and into a tree when the car somersaulted. Hawthorn saw the accident and retired, officially due to clutch issues. Collins's death was confirmed during that evening's prize giving. Motor racing had lost its 'golden boy' in another tragic race for Ferrari. Lacking oil and brakes, von Trips finished fourth. Phil Hill's Dino 156 was lying fifth in the F2 class when delayed by a lurid spin near Adenau and dropping to ninth.

Moss dominated a dull race in Portugal that only came to life in the closing stages. Having crucially set a new lap record and running second, Hawthorn spun on the last lap at the uphill Boavista straight. He rolled the Ferrari against the direction of traffic, but on the pavement, as he started the engine. Hawthorn's second place was only confirmed at 11pm when Moss, who had stopped to watch the drama during his lap of honour, gave evidence to the stewards on his behalf. Just two Ferraris were sent to Porto and von Trips claimed fifth in the coil-spring car.

All four Ferraris entered for the Italian GP qualified in the top seven with Hawthorn on the front row and Hill, von Trips and Gendebien filling the next line. Both Hawthorn and von Trips used

Phil Hill, Ferrari Dino 246 (Moroccan GP)

a new 2,451cc version of the V6 engine in the race. The opening lap could have been disastrous for von Trips, who collided with Harry Schell's BRM at the first Lesmo and crashed into the trees, breaking his left leg. Gendebien stalled on the grid and was hit by Jack Brabham's Cooper, bending the Ferrari's de Dion tube. Phil Hill made a tremendous start to his first F1 race and led the first four laps before his left rear tyre delaminated in the Parabolica. He set a new lap record (the first 200kph lap during a road race) as he climbed back through the field to lead once more before finishing third after his scheduled stop for rear tyres. Using disc brakes in a race for the first time, Hawthorn was on course for a victory that would have clinched the title when his clutch started slipping, leaving Brooks to steal the win and prolong the title fight to the final race in Casablanca.

All three Ferraris had old-specification engines for the Moroccan GP, where Phil Hill drove flat-out from the start in the hope of breaking Moss's Vanwall. Forced down the escape road as he challenged Moss for the lead entering lap two, Hill regained second before deferring to let Hawthorn through and thus finished third once more. Hawthorn qualified on pole position and drove a conservative race to claim second and the world title. Driving the coil-spring car that was now fitted with Girling disc brakes, Gendebien spun on oil at the Brickyard corner and was hit by François Picard's F2 Cooper-Climax, an incident that left the Frenchman seriously injured.

Hawthorn beat Moss by a single point once the best six scores were counted and Ferrari finished as runner-up in the inaugural Constructors' Cup. 'Well, I'm bloody glad it's over!' was Hawthorn's reaction on the BBC evening news. A private luncheon with Queen Elizabeth and the Duke of Edinburgh at Buckingham Palace and accolades from the British racing establishment followed, before Hawthorn announced his immediate retirement from the sport on 9 December. Within two months he too would be gone, killed in a road accident outside Guildford.

Phil Hill, Ferrari Dino 156 (German GP)

Stirling Moss, Vanwall VW5 (Moroccan GP)

VANWALL

The Automóvil Club Argentina only confirmed on 15 December 1957 that its races would be held as scheduled, and this late announcement, plus the switch to aviation fuel, meant that Vanwall was not ready for the opening championship round. Team leader Stirling Moss made alternative arrangements with Rob Walker but Vanwall team-mates Tony Brooks and Stuart Lewis-Evans were left temporarily unemployed.

Vanwall modified its engines for the new fuel regulations and the auxiliary side tanks were redundant due to reduced race distances and improved consumption. The team switched from Pirelli to Dunlop tyres as the Italian company made a belated withdrawal. New alloy wheels were introduced at the start of the season but older Borrani wire fronts were generally preferred. High oil temperatures were

Stuart Lewis-Evans, Vanwall VW9 (British GP)

initially a problem so a new tank was placed behind the radiator at Reims with access via a hinged flap in the bonnet. A whole new system was introduced in Portugal with a separate oil radiator beneath an air intake in the bonnet.

The team concentrated on championship races so made its 1958 début at Monaco, where the cars featured a short nose. Preparation was impeded when an air freighter bringing an engine for the spare car and new Bosch fuel injection systems crashed near Paris. Brooks qualified on pole position but all three Vanwalls failed before half distance. Ill on Saturday and only eighth on the grid, Moss recovered to pass Mike Hawthorn's Ferrari for the lead only to have his engine drop a valve within five laps.

With just eight days available before the Dutch GP, the cars were flown back to London, overhauled in Acton and then freighted to Calais and onwards to Zandvoort by transporter. Vanwall confirmed its single-lap pace, especially on smooth tracks, by locking out the three-car front row with Lewis-Evans quickest. Moss was superb come race day: he took the lead from second on the grid and led throughout, shattering the lap record and lapping the Ferraris on the way to victory. Brooks was hit at the start and retired early while Lewis-Evans had a valve drop into a piston when third.

Moss led Brooks at the start of the Belgian GP only to break his engine when he missed a gear exiting Stavelot for the first time. Brooks then battled with Peter Collins's Ferrari for a couple of laps before winning the fastest road race yet held in Europe with Spa-Francorchamps débutant Lewis-Evans third. Both remaining Vanwalls were lucky to finish for Brooks was stuck in third gear and Lewis-Evans had a broken wishbone as they limped across the line.

Tony Brooks, Vanwall VW5 (Belgian GP)

Vanwall's mid-season dip in form then hampered Moss's title challenge. Handicapped by lack of pace and overheating during practice for the French GP, neither Brooks nor Lewis-Evans finished although Moss salvaged second place behind the dominant Hawthorn so that the countrymen shared the championship lead. Moss took another pole at the British GP only for his engine to fail when running second. Lewis-Evans lost a race-long duel with Roy Salvadori so finished fourth while an off-form Brooks was seventh on another disappointing day.

Just two Vanwalls were entered at the Nürburgring due to a lack of engines. With previous handling difficulties at the circuit sorted, Brooks and Moss qualified 2–3. Moss was leading by 18 seconds on lap four when he retired at Schwalbenschwanz with, stated *Motor Sport*, 'his magneto refusing to emit any more sparks'. Initially fourth, Brooks passed both Hawthorn and Collins to win his second GP of 1958. It was a sad day, however, for Collins succumbed that evening to injuries he sustained when he crashed while chasing the green car.

Having retired from the previous two GPs, Moss converted pole position into a much-needed victory in Portugal with Lewis-Evans third in qualifying and the race. Brooks spun and stalled at the end of the uphill Boavista straight on lap 36. Restarting against the flow of traffic or a push start meant disqualification, so he was out. Hawthorn had just set a new fastest lap and Vanwall's Derek Wootton showed Moss 'HAW-REC' (HAWthorn RECord) on his board. Moss read it as 'HAW-REG' (HAWthorn REGular) so did not attempt to retake the fastest lap and gain a bonus point that proved crucial in the destiny of the World Championship.

Moss tried a Cosworth-designed Plexiglas-enclosed cockpit during qualifying for the Italian GP but reverted to standard configuration for the race. All three Vanwalls started from the four-car front row and fought with the Ferraris for the lead before Moss's gearbox broke and Lewis-Evans stopped with an overheating engine. That left Hawthorn in the lead and on course to clinch the title in front of the *Tifosi*. But Brooks recovered from a 40sec pitstop to pass him with 10 laps to go, securing the inaugural constructors' title for Vanwall and preserving Moss's championship hopes until the final race in Morocco.

Moss needed to win the Moroccan GP and set the fastest race lap with Hawthorn third or lower. Moss achieved his part of the equation by leading from start to finish despite hitting Wolfgang Seidel's erratic Maserati. Brooks fought Hawthorn for third before his engine blew up, leaving the Ferrari man to finish in a conservative second place and claim the title. Worse still, Lewis-Evans's transmission seized during the closing stages and he crashed in flames. Badly burned as he was extricated from the inferno, he was flown to England aboard a chartered Vickers Viscount but died six days later in an East Grinstead burns unit.

Moss, who *Autosport* reported 'made certain of his umpteenth BRDC Gold Star' by winning four GPs to Hawthorn's one, was championship runner-up for a fourth successive season. Third in the standings, Brooks married Pina Resegotti in Pavia on 22 October.

In failing health and badly affected by the death of Lewis-Evans, Tony Vandervell announced Vanwall's shock withdrawal from motor racing on 12 January 1959. The team did start a single GP in 1959 and 1960 but this important British marque would never be a force again.

Roy Salvadori, Cooper T45-Climax (Portuguese GP)

COOPER CAR COMPANY

Cooper confirmed Roy Salvadori and Jack Brabham as its works F1 drivers for the coming season in October 1957 and the new Cooper T45-Climax was revealed to the press at the start of January. The frame and engine were lowered by 1½ inches, coil springs and double wishbones replaced transverse leaf springs at the front and the modified Citroën/ERSA gearbox was housed in a new Brabham-designed casing. A ZF limited-slip differential was used for the first time. Girling drum brakes were fitted at launch but discs were soon an alternative. When stretched to 2,207cc, the Climax FPF four-cylinder engine developed 194bhp at 6,250rpm.

After missing the Argentine GP, Cooper's F1 campaign began on Easter Monday at Goodwood, where the T45s of Brabham and Salvadori finished 2–3 in the Glover Trophy behind Mike Hawthorn's Ferrari. Second in non-championship races at Aintree (Brabham) and Silverstone (Salvadori), both qualified in the top four at Monaco. Salvadori caused mayhem at the start by entering the Gasworks hairpin too fast and running wide. Using the 2.2-litre Climax engine for the first time, Brabham finished fourth despite stopping to have the anti-roll bar reattached. Salvadori broke a track rod when he hit a couple of Vanwalls at the start and lost three laps in the pits for repairs before eventually retiring with gearbox trouble.

Jack Brabham, Cooper T45-Climax (Belgian GP)

Bruce McLaren, Cooper T45-Climax (German GP)

Jack Fairman, Cooper T45-Climax (Moroccan GP)

It was Salvadori's turn to use the single larger engine at Zandvoort and he finished fourth. Brabham had surreptitiously used the '2.2' to qualify fifth but trailed home eighth in the 1,960cc car. The high speeds of Spa-Francorchamps counted against the tiny green cars, which both used the smaller engine for this race. Salvadori ran as high as fourth but was delayed by a slipping clutch and Brabham, who had missed first practice through illness, had a blown head gasket. The Australian was sixth at Reims, where Salvadori had the 2.2-litre engine and lost a points score when the clutch failed but at least registered a finish by pushing the stricken car across the line.

The Cooper T45-Climax handled beautifully around Silverstone and Salvadori used the enlarged engine to claim an excellent third place with Brabham sixth. Ian Burgess, who ran Cooper's racing school at Brands Hatch, retired a third T45 with another clutch problem on his GP début. Salvadori continued his fine form with the 2.2-litre T45 in Germany, where he inherited second; Brabham entered the F2 division at the Nürburgring and was joined by Bruce McLaren, who impressed by finishing fifth on the road to win the class. Relegated to the back of the grid for not completing enough laps in practice, Brabham crashed into Joakim Bonnier's Maserati on the opening lap.

Brabham was handed the larger engine in Portugal but neither Cooper-Climax featured, Brabham seventh and Salvadori ninth with deranged suspension. They swapped engines once more at Monza

where Salvadori inherited a distant fifth-place finish after several stops to cure overheating. Brabham broke his suspension when he crashed into Olivier Gendebien's stalled Ferrari at the start. Four works T45s were entered for the final championship round in Morocco: Salvadori in the 2.2-litre T45, Jack Fairman in the smaller F1 car with Brabham and McLaren in the F2 class. Salvadori passed Fairman for seventh while Brabham clinched *the Autocar* British F2 Championship by leading McLaren in a works 1–2 among the smaller cars. Despite not using engines of the full 2.5 litres permitted in the regulations, Salvadori was fourth in the World Championship with Cooper-Climax third in the constructors' standings.

Ian Burgess, Cooper T45-Climax (British GP)

Maurice Trintignant, Cooper T45-Climax (Dutch GP)

ROB WALKER RACING

Stirling Moss agreed to race for Rob Walker in F1 events when Vanwall was absent so a late entry was made when the Argentine GP was confirmed as part of the World Championship and Tony Vandervell stayed away. Alf Francis modified the 1,960cc Climax FPF's carburation to run on aviation fuel and fitted radius rods to the Cooper T43 to improve handling. The car was air-freighted to Buenos Aires where its reduced capacity meant little was expected. Accidentally poked in the eye by his wife and wearing an eye patch as a consequence, Moss qualified seventh. His car stuck in second gear for a lap early in the race before the 'box somehow freed itself, after which Moss ran non-stop to a shock win, slowing during the final laps to conserve his worn-through Dunlop rears. Luigi Musso's Ferrari closed relentlessly but Moss held on to a famous victory by

just 2.7sec. 'Probably the most sensational upset in post-war motor racing,' enthused Peter Garnier in *The Autocar*.

Moss beat Jack Brabham by 0.2sec in the Aintree 200 with Walker's new Cooper T45, now powered by a Francis-modified Climax FPF featuring larger pistons that stretched capacity to 2,010cc. Vanwall entered the championship at Monaco so Maurice Trintignant replaced Moss although Walker's T45 had the 1.96-litre engine once more. Ron Flockhart handled the Argentina-winning T43 but did not qualify. Trintignant qualified fifth and benefited as others faltered to score Walker's second successive GP victory.

This unprecedented back-to-back success for a privateer entrant was so unexpected that Walker did not even have an entry for the following week's Dutch GP but Trintignant was immediately invited to Zandvoort where he finished outside the points. Walker missed the

Stirling Moss, Cooper T43-Climax (Argentine GP)

Wolfgang Seidel, Cooper T43-Climax (German GP)

Maurice Trintignant, Cooper T43-Climax (British GP)

next two rounds before returning at the British GP with Trintignant's T43 a misfiring eighth at the finish. Moss used the T45 to win a minor race at Caen before Trintignant completed the World Championship campaign in Walker's navy blue-and-white colours. Third in the German GP with the T45 powered by the 2,207cc Climax FPF engine, he was forced into the spare 2-litre T43 for the Portuguese GP when he hit a kerb in practice and bent the T45's frame; in the race shock-absorber problems restricted him to eighth. Trintignant's Cooper T45-Climax retired from the final two GPs of the season and he was seventh in the final standings.

Walker entered another T43 in the F2 sections of the German and Moroccan GPs. Wolfgang Seidel spun several times at the Nürburgring and was last when the suspension failed after nine laps. François Picard was running in the midfield at Ain Diab when

Olivier Gendebien spun on oil. Picard crashed into the Ferrari and was airlifted with serious injuries. He made a full recovery after a lengthy stay in hospital but did not race again.

BRITISH RACING MOTORS (BRM)

Both Jean Behra and Harry Schell tested at Folkingham on 18–19 November 1957 and were announced as BRM's lead drivers on 10 December. The four-cylinder BRM P25 was modified to run on AvGas with a five-bearing crankshaft replacing the previous four-bearing version but the revised engine proved underpowered. Tony Rudd introduced a new spaceframe chassis with detachable bodywork and modified the front suspension. The new chassis was stiffer and lighter than its predecessor and testing suggested that the revised front end

François Picard, Cooper T43-Climax (Moroccan GP)

Jean Behra, BRM P25 (Dutch GP)

was worth 1.5sec a lap around Silverstone. Shorter race durations plus improved consumption allowed for smaller fuel tanks.

BRM missed the Argentine GP and a pair of old-specification P25s arrived at Goodwood for the Easter Monday meeting. Behra led the Glover Trophy from the start but crashed into the chicane while Schell's brakes jammed after seven troubled laps. Behra qualified a singleton BRM on pole for the Aintree 200 but lost second place to another brake failure. The Frenchman gave the first 1958-specification P25 its début in the International Trophy and led before a stone shattered his goggles. He finished fourth after stopping for another pair and for glass and blood to be removed from one of his eyes. Ron Flockhart's old car was lying third when he crashed at Copse, avoiding Bruce Halford's spun Maserati and attending marshals.

Maurice Trintignant, BRM P25 (French GP)

Two new cars were available for Monaco, where a confident Behra qualified on the front row despite hitting the wall at Tabac. He led from the start only for fading brakes (again) to end a fine drive and deny a breakthrough victory for driver and marque alike. Schell finished fifth after a long pitstop for engine attention, including a change of spark plugs. The team travelled direct to Zandvoort for the following week's Dutch GP, where Flockhart was due to race the spare car but an administrative error meant only two BRMs were entered. Stirling Moss dominated with Schell and Behra second and third respectively. Despite the celebrations, Behra complained of a down-on-power engine and suspected preferential treatment for his team-mate. Relationships between the drivers grew ever more strained during 1958.

The BRMs handled well at Spa-Francorchamps but were handicapped by disappointing horsepower. Behra was shaken during Thursday practice when oil sprayed onto his left rear tyre, causing a frightening spin in the 160mph Masta kink and narrow avoidance of trees and a house. Behra made a good start but was passed by a reduced-capacity Cooper and a Lotus in a straight line. He was fourth when he gave up, making the spurious claim of falling oil pressure. Schell qualified seventh, ahead of his off-form team-mate once more, and finished fifth.

Maurice Trintignant joined Behra and Schell for the French GP as three 1958-specification cars were available for the first time. Two P25s had under-bonnet intakes for the Weber carburettors with the newest example having the oil cooler repositioned to the right of the engine. Schell qualified third, which prompted an angry Behra to demand the Franco-American's car for the race. Schell led away but lost the lead to

Harry Schell, BRM P25 (French GP)

Mike Hawthorn on the opening lap and Behra battled with Moss for second before all three retired as morale sagged and the poisonous atmosphere reached breaking point.

Cylinder heads were modified for the British GP to improve mid-range torque with the oil cooler now to the left of the engine. The unfortunate Flockhart had been injured when he hit an ambulance during a sports car race at Rouen-les-Essarts so Masten Gregory took over the third P25 for the British GP but he too was hurt while practising for a support race. Schell continued to outshine Behra and he qualified second, 'using all the road and quite a lot of the grass' observed Denis Jenkinson in *Motor Sport*. However, rising oil temperatures and falling pressures restricted him to another fifth-place finish while Behra retired from the midfield after hitting a hare and puncturing a tyre. Two cars were immediately flown to Caen for the following day's non-championship race, the scene of BRM's first F1 victory 12 months earlier, but both retired.

BRM had not raced or tested at the Nürburgring and the P25 could not handle the bumps and jumps. Behra crashed through a hedge when he tried Schell's car on Friday and eventually gave up after four laps with what 'Jenks' described as 'driver boredom'. Had he continued, Behra would have finished second, such was the rate of attrition in the German GP. Schell made a tremendous start from the third row and was second by the time the cars disappeared around the *Nordkehre* but he suffered another brake failure.

In Portugal Behra held the upper hand for once. He qualified and finished fourth and was only denied second place when his engine lost its edge; Schell was sixth. On the opening lap of the

Ron Flockhart, BRM P25 (Moroccan GP)

Italian GP, Schell somersaulted into the trees at Monza's first Lesmo corner when hit by Wolfgang von Trips's Ferrari. Behra challenged for the lead before pitting for brake adjustment and was fifth when his clutch failed. Joakim Bonnier drove a third car in Italy and emerged unscathed when it caught fire. The oil system was modified once again for the final race at Casablanca and there were twin air intakes on the bonnet. Behra qualified an excellent fourth but the frustrated Frenchman stormed away from his pit, and BRM, when he coasted in with a dead engine. Bonnier, again in a third car, and Schell both scored points, fourth and fifth respectively. Finally recovered from his Rouen injuries, Flockhart returned in a fourth P25 but retired.

Schell shared fifth position in the final drivers' standings while BRM claimed a distant and disappointing fourth in the Constructors' Cup.

Joakim Bonnier, BRM P25 (Moroccan GP)

Cliff Allison, Lotus 12-Climax (Belgian GP)

TEAM LOTUS

Colin Chapman formed Lotus Engineering on 1 January 1952 with a small works behind his father's pub (The Railway Hotel) in Tottenham Lane, Hornsey. He soon became renowned for lightweight sports-racing cars and the Lotus 11 was a class winner at the 1956 and 1957 Le Mans 24 Hours. The new F2 category was introduced for 1957 and Chapman launched his contender – the Lotus 12 – at the 1956 London Motor Show. He designed a light tubular spaceframe with double wishbone/coil spring front suspension, de Dion rear axle with radius rods and Girling disc brakes at all four corners, mounted inboard at the rear. The 1,475cc double-overhead-cam Climax FPF was originally driven through a BMC gearbox. Richard Ansdale soon designed a proprietary five-speed Lotus unit that was problematic and dubbed 'queerbox' by unhappy drivers. Keith Duckworth, a young graduate from Imperial College, London, then introduced a

new gearbox arrangement that improved matters but he left to form Cosworth Engineering in 1958. Magnesium alloy wheels also helped to save weight – Chapman's obsession – and the third type 12 to be built featured an ingenious strut arrangement for the rear suspension, featuring coil springs, dampers and radius arms. Williams & Pritchard fashioned the sleek, low bodywork from Chapman's drawings and Frank Costin's interpretation.

The Lotus 12 was no match for contemporary Cooper designs during 1957 but Chapman was not deterred. He announced Lotus's F1 graduation on 10 December 1957 using updated type 12s, initially powered by the enlarged 1,960cc Climax FPF. Cliff Allison signed as lead driver, supported by Graham Hill, who had run Lotus's gearbox department before Duckworth.

Team Lotus made a disappointing championship début in the 1958 Monaco GP. Allison finished sixth (and last) having pitted to have a

Graham Hill, Lotus 12-Climax (Dutch GP)

Graham Hill, Lotus 16-Climax (Moroccan GP)

Cliff Allison, Lotus 16-Climax (German GP)

section of loose exhaust removed and spun into the straw bales at Massenet. Hill crashed at Le Portier when a half-shaft broke. Now using the 2,207cc version of the Climax engine, Allison was sixth in Holland and a surprise fourth at Spa-Francorchamps. That Belgian result could have been so much better as the three leading cars all had problems by the finish and could not have completed another lap. Hill retired his overheating car after numerous pitstops for water during the Dutch GP and blew his 1.96-litre engine in Belgium.

The Lotus men were the slowest two qualifiers for the French GP at Reims, where Hill had a new Lotus 16-Climax, and both exited the race with engine failures. The type 16 was a refinement of the previous design with its 1.96-litre Climax FPF both inclined (to reduce frontal area) and offset (so that the prop-shaft was to the driver's left). The spaceframe was wider with suspension and disc brakes similar to those of the type 12, although the rear radius rods on the Lotus 16 were longer. Costin again turned Chapman's sketches into plans for Williams & Pritchard to fabricate the distinctive aluminium bodywork. Unfortunately, the Lotus 16 had inadequate cooling for engine and driver alike and was not a success.

Allison continued with the type 12 with enlarged engine at the British GP and qualified an encouraging fifth. Alan Stacey drove a third car – the second Lotus 16-Climax to be built – but all three Lotuses retired, the proximity of the gearbox having burned Hill's backside for 17 uncomfortable laps. Denis Jenkinson observed in *Motor Sport* that 'once again the Hornsey team did not exactly inspire anyone'. Allison switched to the 1,960cc Lotus 16 in Germany and started from the back after missing scrutineering. Eighth by the end of lap one, he was on course to finish second when his radiator sprung a leak. He finished 10th on the road (fifth in the F1 class) after stopping twice for water.

Hill's Lotus 16 was fitted with an F2 engine that overheated and then failed during practice, forcing him to spin. He then crashed Allison's race car and eventually retired from the GP when an oil pipe broke.

The Portuguese GP was a disaster as Allison wrote off his new car in practice on the Boavista straight and Hill crashed out of the race. Allison borrowed a Scuderia Centro Sud Maserati 250F but gave up after 15 laps at the back of the field. At Monza Hill had a 2.2-litre type 16 with larger cockpit and revised exhausts while Allison was forced to use an F2 engine in his Lotus 12; the cars misfired throughout another troubled race but at least they finished, as tail-enders in sixth (Hill) and seventh (Allison) places. Both had 1.96-litre engines for the Moroccan GP and finished outside the points once more, Allison's old car 10th and Hill a much delayed 12th in the type 16 after further overheating problems.

It had been a very disappointing début campaign for Lotus.

Alan Stacey, Lotus 16-Climax (British GP)

Juan Manuel Fangio, Maserati 250F (French GP)

SCUDERIA SUD AMERICANA

The annual 'Juan Manuel Fangio to retire' stories began circulating as soon as the 1957 season had finished. With the five-time World Champion still undecided, his manager Marcello Giambertone leased two of the lightweight 1957 Maserati 250Fs for the Argentine *Temporada* and entered them for Fangio and Carlos Menditéguy under the Scuderia Sud Americana banner. Fangio qualified on pole position and led for 25 laps before dropping to fourth following a tyre stop. Menditéguy finished seventh after a couple of pitstops and contact with Mike Hawthorn's Ferrari after a spin. After winning the non-championship Buenos Aires GP, Fangio hit headlines when Fidel Castro loyalists kidnapped him before the sports car Cuban GP.

Released after the event, Fangio returned in a *Piccolo* 250F for

his final GP appearance at Reims. This brand-new chassis was first tested by Guerino Bertocchi at Modena, driven by Masten Gregory during practice for the Belgian GP and then taken to the Nürburgring on the day after the race for Stirling Moss. It was 1½ inches shorter than a standard 250F with lightweight, small-diameter tubes used in the new spaceframe. The front wishbones were fabricated in tube and sheet steel with Koni telescopic dampers inside coil springs at the rear. The straight-six engine was mounted further back and driven through a new five-speed gearbox. It was prepared and run by works mechanics but still officially entered by Scuderia Sud Americana. Fangio ran in the early slipstreaming battle for second before clutch and braking trouble restricted him to fourth at the finish. His retirement from F1 was confirmed by Giambertone on 23 July.

TEMPLE BUELL

Unsuccessful in an attempt to sign Stirling Moss for 1958, wealthy American Temple Buell effectively took over the Maserati *Piccolo* project when Juan Manuel Fangio retired from F1, the cars maintained and run from the works factory in Modena as before. Masten Gregory was originally intended as driver but he dislocated his shoulder when he crashed an Ecurie Ecosse Lister-Jaguar at Woodcote while practising for the British GP support race. Fangio's Reims car, repainted in American blue and white, was entered into the Portuguese GP for Carroll Shelby, who lost a fine sixth-place finish on the penultimate lap when he locked his brakes and spun.

Carlos Menditéguy, Maserati 250F (Argentine GP)

1958

Masten Gregory, Maserati 250F (Moroccan GP)

A second *Piccolo* chassis was built in time for the Italian GP, where Buell entered Shelby and the fit-again Gregory. However, Scuderia Centro Sud had prior claim to Shelby, who was forced to drive Guglielmo Dei's older 250F. Gregory was mighty with Buell's *Piccolo* 250F during the early laps and challenged Mike Hawthorn for the lead despite increasing pain from his shoulder. Having already parked his slow Centro Sud 250F, Shelby relieved Gregory at his tyre stop on lap 47 and finished fourth. Originally disqualified as Shelby had not been entered in the car, Gregory/Shelby were reinstated a week later although shared drives no longer scored points.

For the championship finale in Morocco, Gregory had the choice of both new Maseratis, which sported an unusual new nose/radiator arrangement. He drove a steady race into sixth despite shock-absorber problems.

Carroll Shelby, Maserati 250F (British GP)

'HORACE GOULD'

Maserati's withdrawal eventually forced 'Horace Gould' to quit his privateer existence. He began 1958 by shipping his venerable Maserati 250F to Argentina where he finished ninth and last. Fourth in the non-championship race at Syracuse, he did not qualify a Scuderia Centro Sud 250F at Monaco. At the Dutch GP he handed his car to Masten Gregory, who *Motor Sport* reported was 'on holiday in the pits', but a broken fuel-pump drive ended the American's promising climb through the field. 'Gould' withdrew from F1 although he would make a brief return in the 1960 Italian GP.

'Horace Gould', Maserati 250F (Argentine GP)

Maurice Trintignant, Maserati 250F (Belgian GP)

Wolfgang Seidel, Maserati 250F (Belgian GP)

SCUDERIA CENTRO SUD

Guglielmo Dei's Scuderia Centro Sud entered up to three Maserati 250Fs throughout the 1958 World Championship. The cars failed to arrive in time for the Argentine GP when the ship broke down in the Atlantic so the team's first appearance was at Syracuse, where both Masten Gregory and Wolfgang Seidel retired, the American losing third place as a consequence. Both finished Silverstone's non-championship race in May with Gregory continuing to show promise by taking third place in a strong field.

Three 250Fs were entered for the Monaco GP although Gregory was away winning the Spa sports car race with Ecurie Ecosse's Lister-Jaguar. The Maserati 250F was clearly past its prime and Luigi Taramazzo, Gerino Gerini and 'Horace Gould' all failed to qualify. Not invited to enter the Dutch GP, Centro Sud's three 250Fs were sent to Spa-Francorchamps for Gregory, Seidel and Maurice Trintignant, the Frenchman finishing seventh. Normally the quickest Maserati driver, Gregory had trouble firing his engine before the start and retired on the first lap. Seidel's silver car was pushed away after four troubled laps with a broken rear axle.

It was all-change for the French GP for Gerini was back in the car Trintignant had driven in Belgium. Two rebuilt and immaculate blue-and-white 250Fs were on hand for Americans Carroll Shelby and Troy Ruttman (the 1952 Indianapolis 500 winner) to make their GP débuts. The cars only arrived in time for final practice and Shelby's engine never ran cleanly although Gerini and Ruttman finished ninth and 10th. At Silverstone, Shelby was ninth despite being covered in oil from his down-on-power and smoking engine and Gerini's gearbox

Gerino Gerini, Maserati 250F (French GP)

broke when running last. Ruttman had visited John Eason-Gibson of the British Racing Drivers' Club to arrange an entry but only two Centro Sud 250Fs were accepted.

With engine troubles having reduced the team's serviceable equipment, Ruttman drove a singleton entry in Germany but he did not start due to another failure. Centro Sud sent two 250Fs to the Portuguese GP where both nominated drivers – Ruttman and Casimiro Oliveira – failed to arrive, so the redundant cars were handed to Maria Teresa de Filippis and Cliff Allison after they crashed in practice. Both withdrew early after unhappy runs at the back of the field. Ruttman was later suspended for a year by the United States Automobile Club for walking out on Centro Sud and bringing the sport into disrepute. Gerini and Shelby returned at Monza for another disastrous GP as Centro Sud's season continued to unravel. Shelby spun at high speed when a stub axle failed in practice and he parked the undrivable spare car after just a lap of the race. Push-started off the grid, Gerini crashed at the Parabolica after two laps.

Replacing Shelby for the final race in Morocco and running last, Seidel was hit by Stirling Moss's leading Vanwall when he swerved unexpectedly while being lapped for the second time. Gerini finished among the F2 cars, 11th of the F1 cars still circulating.

JOAKIM BONNIER

Joakim Bonnier acquired two Maserati 250Fs during 1958 – Chico Godia's old car and the ex-Menditéguy/Scarlatti lightweight version. His début in the former car at Syracuse resulted in a distant second

Troy Ruttman, Maserati 250F (French GP)

Cliff Allison, Maserati 250F (Portuguese GP)

Joakim Bonnier, Maserati 250F (French GP)

Hans Herrmann, Maserati 250F (Moroccan GP)

Phil Hill, Maserati 250F (French GP)

Giulio Cabianca, Maserati 250F (Italian GP)

place behind Luigi Musso's Ferrari. The final qualifier in Monaco, he crashed out of fifth place when he clipped a kerb in Casino Square. The car was rebuilt for the following week's Dutch GP at Zandvoort, where he lost the use of at least two gears during a troubled run. Bonnier took delivery of the newer 250F before the Belgian GP and finished outside the points at Spa-Francorchamps and in France. Second in the non-championship race at Caen, Bonnier retired from the GPs in Britain, Germany and Portugal (where he was unwell) before accepting a drive with BRM for the last two championship rounds.

Bonnier entered his older car for Phil Hill to make his GP début at Reims, the Le Mans winner finishing seventh after an unobtrusive race. Hans Herrmann experienced engine problems in Germany and Italy (when running sixth) and finished ninth in Morocco. Sports car driver Giulio Cabianca drove Bonnier's second car at Monza and the retirement rate was such that he was fifth by the time he too suffered engine failure. Ulf Norinder also tried that 250F during practice for the Italian GP.

OTHER MASERATI PRIVATEERS

Moto Guzzi 500cc rider Ken Kavanagh acquired the third lightweight Maserati 250F and planned to enter himself in selected championship rounds during 1958. He took the car to Argentina where Jean Behra raced it into fifth place after a spin and unscheduled pitstop to adjust the suspension. Kavanagh retired from the Buenos Aires GP before finishing sixth in Syracuse. He qualified for the Belgian GP but did not start after a con rod breakage holed the engine during practice. That was his last appearance of the year and he returned to bikes after crashing out of the 1959 Glover Trophy at Goodwood. With BRM absent, Harry Schell also hired a private 250F for the Argentine GP, driving Luigi Piotti's 1957 car into sixth at the finish without pitting.

Chico Godia began the season by finishing eighth in Argentina having run non-stop in his old Maserati 250F. He sold that car to Joakim Bonnier and acquired the newer lightweight version that Juan Manuel Fangio had raced in that year's *Temporada*. Third on his début with his new car at Syracuse, he did not qualify in Monaco and was not invited by the Dutch organisers. The Spaniard then suffered engine failure in Belgium before his final GP appearance in France. He started 11th at Reims thanks to a qualifying time set by Fangio but crashed after 28 laps.

Maserati may have officially withdrawn its works team in 1958 but the company was happy to run paying customers with Nello Ugolini directing operations and Guerino Bertocchi responsible for preparation. The car Mendíteguy had driven in Argentina was taken over by Giorgio Scarlatti from Syracuse, where he qualified second (3.3sec slower than Luigi Musso's dominant Ferrari) and retired. He was just one of two Maserati drivers to qualify for the Monaco GP but his run ended in a spectacular engine failure as he approached Ste Dévote for the 29th time. A week later in Holland, Scarlatti spun into a wire fence behind the pits and was last when the rear axle failed.

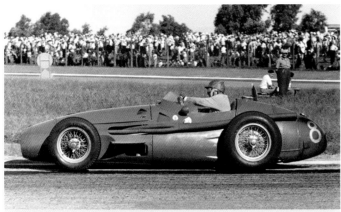

Harry Schell, Maserati 250F (Argentine GP)

Chico Godia, Maserati 250F (Belgian GP)

Giorgio Scarlatti, Maserati 250F (Dutch GP)

Maria Teresa de Filippis, Maserati 250F (Belgian GP)

Jean Behra, Maserati 250F (Argentine GP)

Jack Fairman, Connaught B-Alta (British GP)

Maria Teresa de Filippis became the first woman to race in the World Championship. Persuaded by Luigi Musso to buy a Maserati 250F, the V12 car now fitted with a six-cylinder engine, she finished fifth on début in the non-championship race at Syracuse. A non-qualifier for the Monaco GP after a piston failure, she finished 10th in Belgium. De Filippis crashed into a lamppost during practice for the Portuguese GP so borrowed Scuderia Centro Sud's 250F but withdrew after six slow laps. She was running fifth in Italy when a broken con rod denied a points finish. Gino Munaron also tried her car during practice at Monza.

Monte Carlo-based businessman André Testut never looked like qualifying his 250F for the Monaco GP and local veteran Louis Chiron went 1.6sec quicker when he tried the car but that was still 4.8sec from making the grid.

B.C. ECCLESTONE

Bernie Ecclestone had intended to sell his recently acquired Connaught B-types in New Zealand. However, the 1957–58 Tasman races proved unsuccessful for Roy Salvadori and Stuart Lewis-Evans so Ecclestone ran the cars in the early English non-championship events of 1958. Archie Scott Brown and Lewis-Evans, the latter in the rebodied 'toothpaste tube', were fifth and sixth at Goodwood, but Silverstone's International Trophy brought no success. Ecclestone obtained two entries for the Monaco GP but took only 'toothpaste tube', which neither Bruce Kessler nor Paul Emery could qualify, Kessler's best time 4.5sec slower than required. Both Connaughts were taken to Silverstone for the British GP where Ivor Bueb ('toothpaste tube') and Jack Fairman retired early on.

Ecclestone drove a couple of slow laps during practice in Monte Carlo and at Silverstone but did not attempt to qualify on either occasion. The 1958 season ended with the death of Lewis-Evans, who was managed by Ecclestone, and for some years thereafter F1's future 'ringmaster' concentrated on non-sporting business affairs.

Ivor Bueb, Connaught B-Alta (British GP)

PORSCHE SYSTEM ENGINEERING

Dr Ferry Porsche announced a limited F2 programme in April and a single Porsche 718RSK was entered in the F2 class of the German GP. Designed by Wilhelm Hild, this sports racer had fully enclosed wheels, a central seating position and a spaceframe chassis. Fitted behind the driver, the 1,498cc double-overhead-cam flat-four engine was driven through a five-speed gearbox. Suspension was by trailing links and torsion bars at the front and double wishbones/coil springs to the rear, with telescopic dampers all-round.

Nominated driver Edgar Barth was injured in the previous week's Freiburg hillclimb so Stuart Lewis-Evans, temporarily unemployed as Vanwall was running just two cars at the Nürburgring, practised before Barth was declared fit. Thirteenth overall on the grid, the East German's Porsche was the second F2 car to finish when sixth on the road and 6.1sec behind Bruce McLaren's class-winning Cooper-Climax.

Edgar Barth, Porsche 718RSK (German GP)

ECURIE MAARSBERGEN

As was often the case, the organisers of the Dutch GP relaxed its selective works-only entry policy to add some local interest. From 1958, the main beneficiary was Carel Godin de Beaufort who entered his 1.5-litre Porsche 718RSK two-seater sports car. He ran reliably at the back to finish 10th and last, six laps down. He also raced an older Porsche 550RS in the F2 class of the German GP but retired after three laps.

OFFICINE SPECIALIZATE COSTRUZIONE AUTOMOBILI (OSCA)

The Maserati brothers were concentrating on sports car racing by now and sports-bodied OSCAs were often entered in F2 races during 1958. Two such 1.5-litre, four-cylinder cars were entered for the Monaco GP for Giulio Cabianca and Luigi Piotti, but neither came close to qualifying and Piotti's efforts included a spin on oil at Mirabeau. OSCA's best F2 result of the year was Cabianca's third place at Pau.

Carel Godin de Beaufort, Porsche 718RSK (Dutch GP)

Ian Burgess, Cooper T43-Climax (German GP)

Tony Marsh, Cooper T45-Climax (German GP)

Brian Naylor, Cooper T45-Climax (German GP)

FORMULA 2 CLASS

The German and Moroccan Grands Prix both included a concurrent race for F2 cars. Works Ferrari, Cooper, Lotus and Porsche entries are detailed earlier in this chapter, along with those of Rob Walker Racing and Carel Godin de Beaufort's Ecurie Maarsbergen. In addition, numerous privateers made up the numbers in these championship races.

Cooper was the most popular F2 marque in 1958, invariably with Climax power. When not running Cooper's racing school at Brands Hatch, Ian Burgess was campaigning a T43 in F2 for High Efficiency Motors, a Chessington-based precision tool-making company owned by former bike racer C.T. 'Tommy' Atkins. At Snetterton in July Burgess beat a young pupil called Bruce McLaren but the roles were reversed a week later in the German GP, where the tutor finished third in class behind McLaren's winning T45.

Tony Marsh, British Hillclimb Champion for the previous three years, acquired a new T45 that he brought home eighth overall and fourth in class at the Nürburgring. Brian Naylor, recovered from injuries sustained at Aintree in the spring, experienced teething problems with his T45 throughout the German GP weekend and retired at the end of lap one with a broken fuel pump. Dick Gibson and Christian Goethals both retired T43s, the latter driver entered by Ecurie Eperon d'Or.

Ivor Bueb was the first privateer to buy a Lotus 12-Climax that

Dick Gibson, Cooper T43-Climax (*Silver City Trophy, Snetterton, 1959*)

he entered under the Ecurie Demi-Litre moniker. He retired from the German GP with two laps to go.

Stirling Moss's father (Alfred) and manager (Ken Gregory) announced plans for a new F2 team in January 1958. The British Racing Partnership (BRP) ordered a new Cooper T45-Climax to be driven by Stuart Lewis-Evans when Vanwall commitments allowed and otherwise by Tommy Bridger. The Moroccan GP was a tragic event as Lewis-Evans was seriously burned when his Vanwall caught fire and Bridger was one of those to crash when oil spilled onto the course. The T45s of local amateurs Robert la Caze and André Guelfi were the last two F2 finishers, third and fourth in class respectively.

Christian Goethals, Cooper T43-Climax (German GP)

Tommy Bridger, Cooper T45-Climax (Moroccan GP)

Robert la Caze, Cooper T45-Climax (Moroccan GP)

André Guelfi, Cooper T45-Climax (Moroccan GP)

Ivor Bueb, Lotus 12-Climax (German GP)

DRIVER PERFORMANCE (EXCLUDING INDIANAPOLIS 500)

DRIVER	CAR-ENGINE	RA	MC	NL	B	F	GB	D	P	I	MA
Cliff Allison	Lotus 12-Climax	–	13 6	11 6	13 4	20 R	5 R	–	–	16 7	16 10
	Lotus 16-Climax	–	–	–	–	–	–	24 5	–	–	–
	Maserati 250F	–	–	–	–	–	–	–	13 R	–	–
Edgar Barth	Porsche 718RSK	–	–	–	–	–	–	13 F2	–	–	–
Jean Behra	Maserati 250F	4 5	–	–	–	–	–	–	–	–	–
	BRM P25	–	2 **R**	4 3	10 R	9 R	8 R	9 R	4 4	8 R	4 R
Joakim Bonnier	Maserati 250F	–	16 R	15 10	14 9	16 8	13 R	21 R	14 R	–	–
	BRM P25	–	–	–	–	–	–	–	–	10 R	8 4
Jack Brabham	Cooper T45-Climax	–	3 4	5 8	8 R	12 6	10 6	19 F2	8 7	15 R	19 F2
Tommy Bridger	Cooper T45-Climax	–	–	–	–	–	–	–	–	–	22 F2
Tony Brooks	Vanwall VW10	–	1 R	–	–	–	–	–	–	–	7 R
	Vanwall VW7	–	–	3 R	–	–	–	–	–	–	–
	Vanwall VW5	–	–	–	5 **1**	5 R	9 7	–	5 R	2 **1**	–
	Vanwall VW9	–	–	–	–	NT R	–	–	–	–	–
	Vanwall VW4	–	–	–	–	–	–	2 **1**	–	–	–
Ivor Bueb	Connaught B-Alta	–	–	–	–	–	17 R	–	–	–	–
	Lotus 12-Climax	–	–	–	–	–	–	16 F2	–	–	–
Ian Burgess	Cooper T45-Climax	–	–	–	–	–	16 R	–	–	–	–
	Cooper T43-Climax	–	–	–	–	–	–	11 F2	–	–	–
Giulio Cabianca	OSCA	–	26 DNQ	–	–	–	–	–	–	–	–
	Maserati 250F	–	–	–	–	–	–	–	–	20 R	–
Louis Chiron	Maserati 250F	–	21 DNQ	–	–	–	–	–	–	–	–
Peter Collins	Ferrari Dino 246	3 R	9 3	10 R	4 **R**	4 5	6 1	4 **R**	–	–	–
Carel Godin de Beaufort	Porsche 718RSK	–	–	17 11	–	–	–	–	–	–	–
	Porsche 550RS	–	–	–	–	–	–	15 F2	–	–	–
Maria Teresa de Filippis	Maserati 250F	–	23 DNQ	–	19 10	–	–	–	15 R	21 R	–
Bernie Ecclestone	Connaught B-Alta	–	NT DNP	–	–	–	21 DNS	–	–	–	–
Paul Emery	Connaught B-Alta	–	24 DNQ	–	–	–	–	–	–	–	–
Jack Fairman	Connaught B-Alta	–	–	–	–	–	19 R	–	–	–	–
	Cooper T45-Climax	–	–	–	–	–	–	–	–	–	11 8
Juan Manuel Fangio	Maserati 250F	1 **4** FL	–	–	–	8 4	–	–	–	–	–
Ron Flockhart	Cooper T43-Climax	–	17 DNQ	–	–	–	–	–	–	–	–
	BRM P25	–	–	–	–	–	–	–	–	–	15 R
Olivier Gendebien	Ferrari Dino 246	–	–	–	6 6	–	–	–	5 R	–	6 R
Gerino Gerini	Maserati 250F	–	20 DNQ	–	–	15 9	18 R	–	–	19 R	17 11
Dick Gibson	Cooper T43-Climax	–	–	–	–	–	–	18 F2	–	–	–
Chico Godia	Maserati 250F	9 8	18 DNQ	–	18 R	11 R *	–	–	–	–	–
Christian Goethals	Cooper T43-Climax	–	–	–	–	–	–	23 F2	–	–	–
'Horace Gould'	Maserati 250F	10 9	28 DNQ	–	–	–	–	–	–	–	–
Masten Gregory	Maserati 250F	–	–	14 R	9 R	–	–	–	–	11 4	13 6
André Guelfi	Cooper T45-Climax	–	–	–	–	–	–	–	–	–	25 F2
Mike Hawthorn	Ferrari Dino 246	2 **3**	6 R FL	6 5	1 2 FL	1 **1** FL	4 2 FL	1 **R**	2 2 FL	3 **2**	1 2
Hans Herrmann	Maserati 250F	–	–	–	–	–	–	20 R	–	18 R	18 9
Graham Hill	Lotus 12-Climax	–	15 R	13 R	15 R	–	–	–	–	–	–
	Lotus 16-Climax	–	–	–	–	19 R	14 R	22 F2	12 R	12 6	12 12
Phil Hill	Maserati 250F	–	–	–	–	13 7	–	–	–	–	–
	Ferrari Dino 156	–	–	–	–	–	–	10 F2	–	–	–
	Ferrari Dino 246	–	–	–	–	–	–	–	–	7 **3** FL	5 3
Ken Kavanagh	Maserati 250F	–	–	–	20 DNS	–	–	–	–	–	–
Bruce Kessler	Connaught B-Alta	–	22 DNQ	–	–	–	–	–	–	–	–
Robert la Caze	Cooper T45-Climax	–	–	–	–	–	–	–	–	–	23 F2
Stuart Lewis-Evans	Vanwall VW5	–	7 R	1 R	–	–	–	–	–	–	–
	Vanwall VW4	–	–	–	12 3	–	–	–	–	–	3 R
	Vanwall VW9	–	–	–	–	10 R	7 4	–	–	–	–
	Porsche 718RSK	–	–	–	–	–	–	NT DNP	–	–	–
	Vanwall VW6	–	–	–	–	–	–	–	3 3	4 R	–
Tony Marsh	Cooper T45-Climax	–	–	–	–	–	–	14 F2	–	–	–
Bruce McLaren	Cooper T45-Climax	–	–	–	–	–	–	12 F2	–	–	21 F2
Carlos Menditéguy	Maserati 250F	6 7	–	–	–	–	–	–	–	–	–
Stirling Moss	Cooper T43-Climax	7 **1**	–	–	–	–	–	–	–	–	–
	Vanwall VW7	–	8 **R**	–	–	–	–	–	–	–	–
	Vanwall VW10	–	–	2 **1** FL	3 R	6 2	1 R	3 R FL	1 **1**	1 **R**	–
	Vanwall VW5	–	–	–	–	–	–	–	–	–	2 **1** FL
Gino Munaron	Maserati 250F	–	–	–	–	–	–	–	NT DNP	–	–

DRIVER PERFORMANCE CONTINUED

DRIVER	CAR-ENGINE	RA	MC	NL	B	F	GB	D	P	I	MA
Luigi Musso	Ferrari Dino 246	[5] 2	[10] 2	[12] 7	[2] R	[2] R	—	—	—	—	—
Brian Naylor	Cooper T45-Climax	—	—	—	—	—	—	[25] F2	—	—	—
Ulf Norinder	Maserati 250F	—	—	—	—	—	—	—	—	[NT] DNP	—
François Picard	Cooper T43-Climax	—	—	—	—	—	—	—	—	—	[24] F2
Luigi Piotti	OSCA	—	[27] DNQ	—	—	—	—	—	—	—	—
Troy Ruttman	Maserati 250F	—	—	—	—	[18] 10	—	[26] DNS	—	—	—
Roy Salvadori	Cooper T45-Climax	—	[4] R	[9] 4	[11] 8	[14] 11	[3] 3	[6] 2	[11] 9	[14] 5	[14] 7
Giorgio Scarlatti	Maserati 250F	—	[14] R	[16] R	—	—	—	—	—	—	—
Harry Schell	Maserati 250F	[8] 6	—	—	—	—	—	—	—	—	—
	BRM P25	—	[11] 5	[7] 2	[7] 5	[3] R	[2] 5	[8] R	[7] 6	[9] R	[10] 5
Wolfgang Seidel	Maserati 250F	—	—	—	[17] R	—	—	—	—	—	[20] R
	Cooper T43-Climax	—	—	—	—	—	—	[17] F2	—	—	—
Carroll Shelby	Maserati 250F	—	—	—	—	[17] R	[15] 9	—	[10] R	[17] 4	—
Alan Stacey	Lotus 16-Climax	—	—	—	—	—	[20] R	—	—	—	—
Luigi Taramazzo	Maserati 250F	—	[19] DNQ	—	—	—	—	—	—	—	—
André Testut	Maserati 250F	—	[25] DNQ	—	—	—	—	—	—	—	—
Maurice Trintignant	Cooper T45-Climax	—	[5] 1	[8] 9	—	—	—	[7] 3	[9] 8	[13] R	[9] R
	Maserati 250F	—	—	—	[16] 7	—	—	—	—	—	—
	BRM P25	—	—	—	—	[7] R	—	—	—	—	—
	Cooper T43-Climax	—	—	—	—	—	[12] 8	—	—	—	—
Wolfgang von Trips	Ferrari Dino 246	—	[17] R	—	—	[21] 3	[11] R	[5] 4	[6] 5	[6] R	—

*Qualifying time set by Juan Manuel Fangio. **SHARED DRIVES** French GP: Stuart Lewis Evans/Tony Brooks (Vanwall VW9) R. Italian GP: Masten Gregory/Carroll Shelby (Maserati 250F) 4.

FORMULA 1 RACE WINNERS

ROUND	RACE (CIRCUIT)	DATE	WINNER
1	Gran Premio de la República Argentina (Buenos Aires)	Jan 19	Stirling Moss (Cooper T43-Climax)
–*	Gran Premio de la Ciudad de Buenos Aires (Buenos Aires)	Feb 2	Juan Manuel Fangio (Maserati 250F)
–	Glover Trophy (Goodwood)	Apr 7	Mike Hawthorn (Ferrari Dino 246)
–	Gran Premio di Siracusa (Syracuse)	Apr 13	Luigi Musso (Ferrari Dino 246)
–	BARC 200 (Aintree)	Apr 19	Stirling Moss (Cooper T45-Climax)
–	Daily Express International Trophy (Silverstone)	May 3	Peter Collins (Ferrari Dino 246)
2	Grand Prix de Monaco (Monte Carlo)	May 18	Maurice Trintignant (Cooper T45-Climax)
3	Grote Prijs van Nederland (Zandvoort)	May 26	Stirling Moss (Vanwall VW10)
4**	Indianapolis 500 (Indianapolis)	May 30	Jimmy Bryan (Epperly-Offenhauser)
5	Grand Prix de Belgique et d'Europe (Spa-Francorchamps)	Jun 15	Tony Brooks (Vanwall VW5)
6	Grand Prix de l'Automobile Club de France (Reims)	Jul 6	Mike Hawthorn (Ferrari Dino 246)
7	British Grand Prix (Silverstone)	Jul 19	Peter Collins (Ferrari Dino 246)
–	Grand Prix de Caen (Caen)	Jul 20	Stirling Moss (Cooper T45-Climax)
8	Grosser Preis von Deutschland (Nürburgring)	Aug 3	Tony Brooks (Vanwall VW4)
9	Grande Premio de Portugal (Porto)	Aug 24	Stirling Moss (Vanwall VW10)
10	Gran Premio d'Italia (Monza)	Sep 7	Tony Brooks (Vanwall VW5)
11	Grand Prix du Maroc (Ain Diab)	Oct 19	Stirling Moss (Vanwall VW5)

*Formule Libre **Run to USAC National Championship rules

DRIVERS' CHAMPIONSHIP

	DRIVERS	POINTS
1	Mike Hawthorn	42 (49)*
2	Stirling Moss	41
3	Tony Brooks	24
4	Roy Salvadori	15
5=	Peter Collins	14
	Harry Schell	14
7=	Luigi Musso	12
	Maurice Trintignant	12
9	Stuart Lewis-Evans	11
10=	Jean Behra	9
	Phil Hill	9
	Wolfgang von Trips	9
13	Jimmy Bryan	8
14	Juan Manuel Fangio	7
15	George Amick	6
16=	Tony Bettenhausen	4
	Johnny Boyd	4
18=	Cliff Allison	3
	Jo Bonnier	3
	Jack Brabham	3
21	Jim Rathmann	2

*Best six results count

MANUFACTURERS' CHAMPIONSHIP

	MANUFACTURERS	POINTS
1	Vanwall	48 (57)*
2	Ferrari	40 (57)*
3	Cooper-Climax	31
4	BRM	18
5	Maserati	6
6	Lotus-Climax	3

*Best six results count. No points awarded for Indianapolis 500; points only awarded to first car to finish for each manufacturer

Jack Brabham's rear-engined Cooper leads Tony Brooks (Ferrari), Harry Schell (BRM), Jean Behra (Ferrari) and Graham Hill (Lotus) at Zandvoort

1959

COOPER'S REAR-ENGINED REVOLUTION IS COMPLETE

Avus's high-banked Nordkurve presented a unique challenge in 1959; eventual winner Tony Brooks leads Stirling Moss at the start of heat one

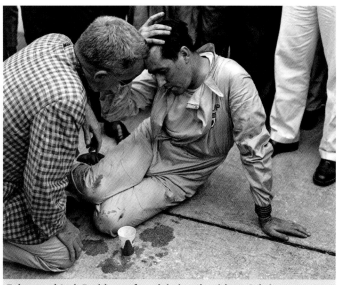

Exhausted Jack Brabham after claiming the title at Sebring

The 1959 season confirmed a seismic shift in F1 car design. Rather than the front-engine battle for supremacy between Vanwall and Ferrari, nimble rear-engine Coopers held sway. With engine capacity stretched to a full 2.5 litres, Cooper added power to road-holding and won both World Championships. Mike Hawthorn announced his retirement on 9 December 1958 and Vanwall withdrew a month later, so neither reigning champion offered a title defence. BRM finally scored its first GP win after nine years of hyperbole and disappointment.

Citing financial grounds, the Automóvil Club Argentina cancelled its races in September 1958 so the championship started late in Monaco. The FIA now demanded that regulations for World Championship races should be issued two months before the event, something that Holland's Koninklijke Nederlandsche Automobiel Club (KNAC) did not adhere to. The Belgian GP was scheduled for June but was cancelled by the end of April. The German GP made an unpopular switch to the Automobil-Verkehrs-und Übungsstraße (AVUS) to the south-west of Berlin. This was either side of a motorway with a dangerous, steep banked corner to the north and a hairpin to the south; *Autosport* judged the race 'completely pointless'. Punctures on the Nordkurve were a concern so the race was split into two 30-lap heats to allow a tyre change. Jean Behra was killed during the supporting sports car race and for 1960 the race returned to the Nürburgring, albeit for F2.

The Portuguese GP also moved from Porto to Monsanto Park to the north-west of Lisbon. Originally due to be held on 11 October, the Moroccan GP was postponed for two weeks and then cancelled. Alec Ulmann of Sebring worked tirelessly to host the first championship GP in the United States: it was announced for the day after the established 12-hour sports car race (22 March) but soon postponed to the end of the season, with Saturday 12 December finally chosen, three months after the penultimate championship round.

Colin Chapman has an altercation with the authorities at Monza

Jean Behra, Stirling Moss and Jack Brabham motor past Monaco's most famous tobacconist

Jack Brabham, Cooper T51-Climax (Portuguese GP)

Masten Gregory, Cooper T51-Climax (British GP)

COOPER CAR COMPANY

Rob Walker had delivered Cooper's first victories in 1958 but before the 1959 season few predicted that the works team would emerge as World Champions. Coventry Climax managing director Leonard Lee agreed to extend the existing FPF engine to 2,495cc to exploit the full permitted capacity. At Surbiton, Owen Maddock developed the existing Cooper as the T51, which was available in F1 or F2 trim with disc brakes now standard. Cooper could not afford both Jack Brabham and Roy Salvadori so chose Brabham with the help of increased backing from Esso. Masten Gregory replaced Salvadori, who had accepted an attractive offer from Aston Martin, while promising New Zealander Bruce McLaren was promoted as third driver.

Coopers dominated the first F1 race of 1959 at Goodwood's Easter Monday meeting, although Stirling Moss's private T51 beat Brabham. After winning the International Trophy at Silverstone – the works team's F1 breakthrough – the Australian qualified on the outside of the front row at Monaco and ran in the top three throughout the race, inheriting victory after the retirements of Jean Behra and Moss. Gregory's 2.5-litre T45 dropped out early and McLaren finished fifth (with a 2.2-litre T51) despite crashing into Harry Schell at the chicane.

Just two Coopers were accepted for the depleted Dutch GP field so McLaren watched as Brabham and Gregory disputed the lead with Joakim Bonnier's BRM. Both led before losing gears and having to settle for second and third respectively. Extreme heat during the French GP caused the track to break up dangerously. Second

Bruce McLaren, Cooper T51-Climax (Monaco GP)

when hit in the face by a stone, Gregory pitted suffering from heat stroke and concussion; mechanics were unable revive him and the healthy T51 had to be retired. Brabham tried streamlined bodywork in practice but raced his normal car into third. For this race and thereafter, McLaren reverted to the 1958 chassis used by Gregory in Monaco: powered by the '2.2' for the last time and, another bloodied by flying stones, he claimed another fifth when just 0.2sec behind Olivier Gendebien's Ferrari.

In the British GP at Aintree Brabham consolidated his championship advantage by leading from start to finish without stopping for tyres. McLaren, with his own 2,495cc engine for the first time, chased second-placed Moss across the line in his most impressive drive so far, while Gregory was seventh after an unscheduled stop for water. The German GP was a bad day for Surbiton as all three works Coopers retired, but Gregory did dice with the Ferraris in the first heat. The American was second in Portugal (his best F1 result) but Brabham did not score after an incident-filled afternoon. He narrowly missed a young boy who had ran across the track and then misjudged lapping Mário Cabral and crashed into a concrete telegraph pole, injuring his knee when thrown clear.

Brabham finished third in Italy to maintain his points lead but Moss's back-to-back victories had set up a three-way title decider in America, with Ferrari's Tony Brooks also in the hunt. McLaren suffered clutch failures in Portugal. Gregory injured his shoulder during the RAC Tourist Trophy so Giorgio Scarlatti drove his regular T51 at Monza and finished 12th after losing a couple of laps in the pits having the gear linkage repaired.

Giorgio Scarlatti, Cooper T51-Climax (Italian GP)

Bruce McLaren, Cooper T45-Climax (Portuguese GP)

Masten Gregory, Cooper T45-Climax (Monaco GP)

It was three months before the United States GP at Sebring, during which time Brabham finished second in non-championship races at Oulton Park and Snetterton. With Gregory still unfit, Cooper entered just two cars, both fitted with new Climax engines with revised cylinder heads. The title excitement fizzled out during the early laps when Moss retired and Brooks was delayed. Brabham led McLaren and Maurice Trintignant (Rob Walker Racing) in a Cooper 1–2–3 but ran out of fuel on the last lap, leaving McLaren to beat the Frenchman by 0.6sec and become the youngest GP winner so far, a record that would stand until 2003. Brabham, new World Champion, pushed his car a mile to the finish line and collapsed, exhausted. The rear-engine innovators had won the Constructors' Cup and changed F1 forever.

ROB WALKER RACING

Vanwall's shock withdrawal on 12 January left Stirling Moss without an F1 drive for 1959. He turned down Ferrari's offer and agreed to race for Rob Walker at Monaco, initially as a one-off. Awarded the Order of the British Empire in the New Year's honours list, Moss met with his father Alfred, manager Ken Gregory, Walker and Alf Francis to decide what to drive. A couple of new Cooper T51 chassis were subsequently delivered to Walker's Pippbrook Garage in Dorking and new 2.5-litre Climax FPFs were on order. In addition agreement was reached with Sir Alfred Owen to borrow a BRM four-cylinder engine. Concerned about the stress that increased

power would place on Cooper's Citroën/ERSA gearbox, Francis and Moss commissioned a new five-speed unit from Valerio Colotti. An old friend of Francis's from their Maserati days, Colotti had formed the independent design agency Studio Tecnica-Meccanica (Tec-Mec) in Modena. Francis helped assemble the prototype gearbox at the workshop of another ex-Maserati acquaintance, Giorgio Neri, and then modified a T51 in Dorking, moving the seat moved forward to accommodate the BRM engine. Unfortunately, the Colotti transmission proved a weakness until a manufacturing fault was discovered and rectified.

The unique Cooper-BRM was ready in April and Moss, having already won the Glover Trophy with the 2,495cc Cooper T51-Climax, led the Aintree 200 with his new car before a gearbox locator sheared. Moss chose Climax power for Monaco and the Cooper-BRM was quietly shelved. He qualified on pole, passed Jean Behra's Ferrari and built a commanding lead until the gearbox broke after 81 laps. It was a similar story at Zandvoort, where he recovered from a poor start to take the lead on lap 60, only for the Colotti unit to fail again.

Moss raced a BRM P25 for the British Racing Partnership in France and England before returning to Walker and further gearbox woes at the German GP, where he had a new Cooper T51-Climax with revised cylinder heads that added 12–15bhp. In Portugal, with just six points to his name so far (all achieved in the BRP BRM at Aintree), Moss dominated qualifying and lapped the field when the gearbox lasted for once. The manufacturing issue was identified

Stirling Moss, Cooper T51-Climax (Portuguese GP)

before the Italian GP, where tyre wear was the major concern and so 'knock-off' rear wheels were fitted to speed any tyre stop that was required. Moss slipstreamed the Ferraris to conserve fuel and rubber and ran non-stop to victory as the Ferraris all changed tyres.

Back-to-back victories thrust Moss back into the title fight and he won the Oulton Park Gold Cup only to suffer minor injuries in a road accident on his way back to London. Moss had new self-designed coil spring rear suspension on his T51 for the title decider at Sebring. Needing maximum points, he led away but his challenge evaporated after just five laps when the gearbox broke once more. Moss finished third overall behind Jack Brabham and Tony Brooks as another title eluded him.

Hosting a dinner to celebrate being named Champion of France in Paris during the last days of 1958, Maurice Trintignant announced that he had re-signed with Walker, driving a 2.5-litre Cooper T51-Climax throughout the F1 season. Delayed in Monaco and Holland by a sticking throttle, he finished third in the Principality after a race of attrition. He was second in France when he spun at the Thillois hairpin and lost points by stopping three times to have water poured over him. The consistent Frenchman finished the next three GPs in the top five, albeit lapped on each occasion.

Slow but reliable in Italy, Trintignant saved his finest performance of 1959 for the United States GP. He set the fastest race lap as he closed on the works Cooper-Climaxes of Brabham and Bruce McLaren and inherited second place when the new World Champion ran out of fuel, 0.6sec from victory.

Maurice Trintignant, Cooper T51-Climax (United States GP)

Tony Brooks, Ferrari Dino 246 (United States GP)

SCUDERIA FERRARI

Angered by criticism in the Italian press and from the Vatican following the deaths of Luigi Musso and Peter Collins, Enzo Ferrari told the audience at his annual luncheon on 9 December 1958 that he would not hire Italian drivers (a promise that held true for two seasons) or compete in his home country (this was never adhered to). He also confirmed Mike Hawthorn's retirement that day and announced the signings of Jean Behra, Cliff Allison and American newcomer Dan Gurney, while Phil Hill and Olivier Gendebien remained under contract. Ferrari approached Tony Brooks when Vanwall withdrew, and he was added to the *Scuderia*'s driving roster by the end of February.

Jean Behra and test driver Martino Severi began testing the

1959-specification Ferrari Dino 246 at the Modena Aerautodromo in January, Behra temporarily living in the town's Reale Hotel. This update had the 2,451cc type 256 engine that had been introduced at the 1958 Italian GP and bonnet-top air intakes. Chief engineer Carlo Chiti moved the five-speed gearbox underneath, rather than in front of, the differential, Dunlop disc brakes and Koni telescopic dampers were used, and the exhausts exited beneath the rear suspension. Although Modena-based Fantuzzi fabricated new, sleeker bodywork, Ferrari had lost its straight-line speed advantage over Cooper. It switched from Englebert to Dunlop tyres.

Ferrari began 1959 as favourites and Behra led Brooks in a non-championship 1–2 at Aintree only for Jack Brabham's Cooper-Climax to dominate the International Trophy. Three 246s were entered at

Dan Gurney, Ferrari Dino 246 (Portuguese GP)

Phil Hill, Ferrari Dino 246 (Portuguese GP)

Jean Behra, Ferrari Dino 246 (Monaco GP)

Monaco with fashionable stubby nose cowlings designed to avoid damage in the inevitable close contact around those famous streets. Behra qualified second and led the opening 21 laps before his engine blew up. Brooks finished second despite oversteer and being sick in his cockpit while Hill's much-battered 246 finished fourth following repeated spins. Allison was a late qualifier in the F2 Dino 156 only to be collected when Wolfgang von Trips's Porsche spun at Ste Dévote on lap two.

The Ferraris proved a handful and were lapped in Holland for a second year. Behra preferred the F2 chassis fitted with full 2.5-litre engine. He proved a 'mobile chicane' as he ran third in the early laps and eventually faded to fifth at the finish. Brooks retired while Hill and Allison finished outside the points, the Englishman having started at the back after Romolo Tavoni reached agreement with rival team managers shortly before the race.

Outright power prevailed at Reims, where Brooks qualified on pole and led throughout to win the European GP for the third consecutive year, following victories at Aintree and the Nürburgring – previous races honoured by that meaningless title – in 1957 and 1958 respectively. Hill withstood high cockpit temperatures to finish second while Gendebien's additional 246 beat Bruce McLaren into fourth by just 0.2sec. Gurney made an impressive début but retired, as did Behra in a huge cloud of blue smoke. Frustrated by that failure, Behra punched Tavoni as they argued in the pits and was fired, although Ferrari claimed he departed on good terms. Four weeks later Behra was killed at Avus during the 1,500cc sports car race that supported the German GP.

A strike of Italian metalworkers prevented Ferrari from racing in the British GP but the cars enjoyed the long straights at Avus. Reserve driver once more, Allison set the fastest qualifying time but had to line up at the back when allowed to start following Porsche's withdrawal. The 246s of poleman Brooks, Gurney and Hill toyed with the opposition once Masten Gregory's Cooper-Climax expired and finished 1–2–3 in that order. Allison's clutch failed after just three laps of heat one.

With Surbiton back in the ascendency on the twisty Porto street circuit, Gurney was third despite crushing the nose of his 246 against the back of Maurice Trintignant's Rob Walker Cooper-Climax. Brooks suffered a misfire and poor brakes while a furious Hill was the innocent victim of namesake Graham Hill's spin. Brooks's title hopes

Cliff Allison, Ferrari Dino 246 (Dutch GP)

Olivier Gendebien, Ferrari Dino 246 (Italian GP)

Wolfgang von Trips, Ferrari Dino 246 (United States GP)

Cliff Allison, Ferrari Dino 156 (Monaco GP)

faded still further when a piston failed at the start of the Italian GP, a race in which Ferrari's more severe tyre wear compared with the lighter Coopers proved decisive. Moss and Brabham did not stop but Hill, Gurney, Allison and Gendebien did, finishing 2–4–5–6 after changing rear tyres. Denis Jenkinson was not complimentary about Ferrari's tyre strategy in *Motor Sport*: 'The recent Italian GP at Monza saw the Scuderia Ferrari make their biggest tactical errors ever, and they have made some pretty big ones.'

Four Ferraris were entered at Sebring, where Brooks, who flew in after the christening of his new daughter, retained an outside chance of the title. Gurney was dropped as he considered an alternative offer for 1960. Brooks and von Trips, who was making his first start for Ferrari in a year, both had short chassis; Allison a normal 246 and Hill an F2 car with its new twin-cam V6 bored out to 2.4-litres. *The Autocar* reported that Hill's hybrid chassis was 'very un-Ferrari-like in its blue finish'. All four had new independent rear suspension via double wishbones and coil springs with telescopic Koni dampers, but handling remained erratic.

Brooks was denied third on the grid when Harry Schell successfully argued a better time, although the Franco-American's short cut in achieving it had gone unnoticed. Brooks's title hopes dipped at the first corner when he collided with von Trips and stopped to check for damage. He recovered to finish third but that was not enough. Allison crashed while chasing the leading Coopers, Hill retired and von Trips's engine failed with a couple of laps to go. He pushed the dead car over the line to claim sixth. Brooks and Ferrari both finished as runners-up in their respective championships.

BRITISH RACING MOTORS (BRM)

The Owen Racing Organisation was quick to sign Harry Schell, Joakim Bonnier and Ron Flockhart for 1959 to drive the BRM P25, which was updated with Dunlop disc brakes. Schell qualified on pole for Goodwood's Glover Trophy and led from the start before being passed by both Stirling Moss and Jack Brabham. Moss tested the P25s the next day and set the first 100mph lap of the Sussex venue. He qualified a works BRM on pole position for the International Trophy but spun out of the lead when his front brakes failed at Copse. Flockhart inherited third at Silverstone that day in the sister P25.

Fading brakes accounted for all three P25s in Monaco before BRM finally tasted victory in a *Grande Épreuve* three weeks later at Zandvoort. Using 15-inch wheels to improve handling, Bonnier qualified on pole and beat the Cooper-Climaxes of Brabham and Masten Gregory after an error-free drive, prompting joyous scenes in the BRM pit and at Bourne.

Flockhart and Schell were 6–7 at Reims after having goggles smashed by flying stones as the track broke up, while Bonnier damaged his radiator when he spun and pushed his car to the pits to retire. At Aintree Schell was fourth in the British GP after a spectacular spin at Tatt's, while both Bonnier (throttle linkage) and Flockhart (spun) retired. Bonnier was fifth on aggregate after a plug change in Germany while Schell pushed his clutchless car over the line to claim seventh having 'scrounged a cigarette from a spectator' and waited for the winner.

Joakim Bonnier, BRM P25 (Monaco GP)

Harry Schell, BRM P25 (Portuguese GP)

Ron Flockhart, BRM P25 (British GP)

Hans Herrmann, BRM P25 (German GP)

In Portugal's heat Schell was fifth despite yet more brake problems but Flockhart was denied points by gearbox maladies. When Bonnier's fuel pump packed up at the end of the *Auto Estrada* section that day, the Swede proceeded to set up a makeshift watering station by the side of the track for dehydrated colleagues. Exhausted drivers stopped for a drink or to be doused by Bonnier's water-filled helmet at what *Autosport* dubbed 'Bonnier's bar'. All three BRMs finished outside the points at Monza, with Schell seventh and Bonnier eighth, and Flockhart won the minor Silver City Trophy at Snetterton with Bruce Halford third on a one-off with the team.

BRM withdrew from the United States GP to prepare for 1960 but there was an important nod to the future during practice for the Italian GP. Both Bonnier and Schell tried the rear-engine BRM P48, which had been built in six weeks. Peter Berthon placed the four-cylinder engine originally supplied to Rob Walker behind the driver. The de Dion rear axle was replaced with new double wishbone/coil spring suspension and 100lbs was saved. Initially slower than the regular cars, the P48 would not be raced until April 1960.

BRM finally scored its first GP victory and finished third in the constructors' standings during a landmark season.

BRITISH RACING PARTNERSHIP (BRP)

Sir Alfred Owen did not mind how BRM scored its breakthrough GP victory so he reached a deal with Alfred Moss and Ken Gregory of the British Racing Partnership for Stirling Moss to drive a P25 in the French and British GPs. Chief mechanic Tony Robinson prepared the

Stirling Moss, BRM P25 (French GP)

light green car at BRP's Highgate workshops with engines maintained by BRM at Bourne. Having driven a works car in the International Trophy, Moss qualified fourth in France but after losing his clutch he had to retire when he spun and stalled at Thillois. Two weeks later, he recovered from a precautionary fuel stop at Aintree to retake second position from Bruce McLaren and narrowly hold off the New Zealander at the finish.

Moss returned to Rob Walker Racing for the German GP at Avus, where Hans Herrmann drove the BRM P25. Eighth in heat one, Herrmann barrel-rolled out of the second race on the approach to Avus's southern hairpin. The chassis was written off and BRP did not continue with the project.

BRP also entered a couple of F2 Cooper T51-Borgwards during 1959, including the 1.5-litre class of the British GP. Chris Bristow led throughout and finished 10th overall while Ivor Bueb was last due to gearbox trouble. Bristow, who had signed an 18-month contract with BRP in June, later won a British F2 round at Brands Hatch but Bueb died on 1 August following injuries sustained at Clermont-Ferrand.

TEAM LOTUS

Team Lotus entered its sophomore F1 season with an updated version of the front-engine type 16 with new recruit Len Terry responsible for detailed changes to Colin Chapman's original design. The spaceframe and bodywork were modified, with an enlarged cockpit, and coil-spring suspension was employed front and rear. A firewall between engine and driver helped reduce cockpit temperatures. Coventry

Chris Bristow, Cooper T51-Borgward (British GP)

Ivor Bueb, Cooper T51-Borgward (British GP)

Graham Hill, Lotus 16-Climax (British GP)

Innes Ireland, Lotus 16-Climax (Dutch GP)

Climax's 2,495cc FPF double-overhead-cam engines were ordered and Stan Elsworth joined from Vanwall as chief mechanic. Graham Hill remained but Cliff Allison moved to Ferrari. Plans for Keith Hall to replace him were scuppered when the Newcastle-based wholesaler retired to concentrate on business. Lotus continued to sell sports-racing cars but the works Team Lotus concentrated solely on racing single-seaters.

Poor reliability and questionable speed continued to hamper Lotus. After the Italian GP, *Motor Sport*'s Denis Jenkinson was moved to question the marque's F1 future. 'One wonders if this was the last GP for Lotus. Organisers must be getting tired of their dismal performances.'

Alan Stacey, Lotus 16-Climax (British GP)

The transporter broke down on the way to Monte Carlo so Lotus missed the first two days of practice. Hill qualified at the back after a troubled Saturday and in the race an oil line broke at Mirabeau after 21 laps, causing a fire that Hill was able to put out. Driving the second car for the only time, Pete Lovely did not qualify after spinning at Tabac.

There was encouragement at Zandvoort where Innes Ireland finished a faultless fourth on début. Hill qualified and ran fifth in the early stages but came seventh after a spin and unscheduled trackside stop to investigate smoke from his engine. Both retired in France. At Aintree Hill finished ninth following another mid-race spin that scattered the photographers while Alan Stacey, deputising as Ireland was feeling the after-effects of a crash during Rouen's F2 race, came home eighth.

Hill and Ireland both retired from the next three championship rounds, including a hopeless Portuguese GP outing. Team Lotus missed first practice when its transporter broke down again on the way to Lisbon and both cars retired by lap six, Hill spinning on his own oil on the *Auto Estrada* and collecting the Ferrari of a furious Phil Hill in the process. 'Once again Team Lotus failed completely,' wrote Gregor Grant in *Autosport*.

It was all too much for Graham Hill, who signed for BRM for 1960 and was consequently dropped for the final race at Sebring. His replacement, Stacey, lasted a lap but Ireland finished fifth despite a spin and only have one usable gear by the end. Lotus moved into expanded new premises in Cheshunt in October 1959.

Bruce Halford, Lotus 16-Climax (Monaco GP)

JOHN FISHER

Bruce Halford sold his Maserati 250F in the winter of 1958/59 and raced John Fisher's F2 Lotus 16-Climax during 1959. He narrowly qualified for the Monaco GP but lasted little more than a lap of the race when Wolfgang von Trips crashed on oil at Ste Dévote and eliminated the entire F2 class. A heavy crash at Clermont-Ferrand following a puncture severely damaged the car and hospitalised Halford. Years later Halford helped restore the car to compete in historic racing and won the 1982 Monaco GP support race 23 years after his brief appearance in the main event.

ASTON MARTIN

Having spent $20,500 to acquire Aston Martin in February 1947, David Brown saw racing as integral to rebuilding the famous old marque's prestige. Initially that was in sports cars, a programme that culminated in victory in the Le Mans 24 Hours and World Sportscar Championship in 1959. A prototype F1 car had been tested in 1957 although production was delayed as the team concentrated on endurance racing. Reg Parnell was hired as team manager when he retired from the cockpit in 1957 and Aston Martin finally confirmed an F1 testing exercise in a statement on 8 October 1958. Roy Salvadori signed as expected but Tony Brooks chose Ferrari rather than Aston. Aston's F1 plans were still unconfirmed by the Sebring 12 Hours of March 1959, although Carroll Shelby was happy to tell the press there that he would drive the second car.

Built at the company's factory at the London Air Park aerodrome in Feltham, the Aston Martin DBR4/250 tested at Goodwood with Stirling Moss at the wheel on 3 March 1959, two years after the car's conception. Just when Cooper was leading the rear-engine revolution, the Aston still had its engine mounted ahead of the driver. It was also the last new F1 car to be built with a de Dion rear axle. The double-wishbone/torsion-bar front suspension from the DBR3 sports car was replaced by wishbones and coil springs by the time the DBR4/250 raced for the first time. Its 2,493cc twin-overhead-cam straight-six engine had three double-choke Weber carburettors and drove through a five-speed gearbox until a new four-speed was introduced at the British GP. The tubular spaceframe chassis

Roy Salvadori, Aston Martin DBR4/250 (British GP)

Carroll Shelby, Aston Martin DBR4/250 (Portuguese GP)

was conventional and Girling disc brakes were mounted outboard front and rear. In a field dominated by Dunlop, Aston Martin used Avon tyres while BP supplied fuel and oil. The beautifully prepared DBR4/250 looked and sounded good, but it was overweight, underpowered and out-of-date.

Motor Sport described its début in the International Trophy as a 'sensationally satisfactory first appearance' as Salvadori finished second and Shelby only lost fourth when he retired with two laps to go. Aston Martin chose to miss Monaco so made its championship début at Zandvoort. The cars qualified in the midfield before making early exits from the race, Salvadori in a cloud of steam and Shelby due to a high-speed spin when his engine seized. After missing the French GP, Salvadori qualified an excellent second for the British GP but the oil tanks on both cars were overfilled for the race and both drivers had to stop when oil spilled into their cockpits. Salvadori went on to finish sixth despite a spin at Anchor Crossing on lap 41 while Shelby lost seventh when the magneto failed in the closing stages. The team skipped the German GP and in Portugal Salvadori and Shelby finished sixth and eighth respectively.

Aston Martin arrived at the Italian GP as World Sportscar Champions, following its title-winning performance in the RAC Tourist Trophy at Goodwood, where Salvadori received burns to his face and an arm in a pit fire and remained bandaged at Monza. The cars were so slow in Italy, where Shelby finished 10th and Shelby retired, that the team withdrew from the United States GP to concentrate on preparations for 1960.

VANWALL

Despite Tony Vandervell's shock withdrawal in January, he began eying a return during the summer. A 1958 chassis (VW5) was rebuilt with the engine and bodywork lowered and some weight was shed by using titanium parts. Stirling Moss declined the offer of the car for the French GP, preferring to drive the British Racing Partnership's BRM P25 instead. Scuderia Ferrari missed the British GP due to the Italian metalworkers' strike so Vandervell lent VW5 to long-term contracted driver Tony Brooks. It proved slow in qualifying at Aintree and Brooks suffered fuel-injection problems during the race so retired after 13 misfiring laps. A three-car team was planned for 1960 but one of Britain's most important marques disappeared after a single final appearance that year.

SCUDERIA CENTRO SUD

Needing to update its machinery, Scuderia Centro Sud ordered three Cooper T51s and arranged a supply of Maserati 250S sports car engines. This was a twin-cam straight-four that Maserati chief engineer Giulio Alfieri bored out to 2,489cc, fitted with Marelli magnetos, eight sparking plugs and two twin-choke Weber carburettors. A little heavier than the rival Climax FPF (by just 6lb), it was mated to a Maserati five-speed gearbox.

The Cooper-Maseratis were not due to be completed until June so Centro Sud entered old Maserati 250Fs in the early non-championship races with Hermano da Silva Ramos's distant fourth place in the Aintree

Tony Brooks, Vanwall VW5 (British GP)

Ian Burgess, Cooper T51-Maserati (German GP)

Fritz d'Orey, Maserati 250F (British GP)

Mário Cabral, Cooper T51-Maserati (Portuguese GP)

200 the only result of note. Centro Sud arrived late for the French GP with Cooper-Maseratis for new signing Ian Burgess and works OSCA driver Colin Davis, plus 250Fs for little-known South Americans Fritz d'Orey and Asdrúbal Bayardo. Over half a minute slower than anyone else, Bayardo did not qualify while his team-mates started from the back and failed to make an impression during the race. D'Orey was classified 10th and both T51s retired before the end of lap 14.

The new-car teething troubles continued in Britain where Burgess, who had qualified in the midfield, and Hans Herrmann suffered further mechanical failures. Running last following an oil leak in his 250F, d'Orey crashed into a gate at the Anchor Crossing when his brakes failed. Burgess was a reserve for the German GP so started when Porsche withdrew following Jean Behra's death. The Cooper-Maserati was unsuited to the high-speed Avus but Burgess soldiered on to finish sixth, lapped four times. Inexperienced local Mário Cabral took the car for the Portuguese GP and was being lapped when Jack Brabham crashed into a telegraph pole. Burgess and Davis returned at Monza, Davis a late replacement when Giorgio Scarlatti was offered a works drive. The underpowered cars both finished outside the top 10 when lapped four times or more. Centro Sud did not enter the United States GP.

HIGH EFFICIENCY MOTORS

High Efficiency Motors acquired a 1958 Cooper T45 that mechanic Harry Pearce modified to accommodate a Maserati 250S engine in a workshop behind Chessington's North Star public house. This engine

Colin Davis, Cooper T51-Maserati (Italian GP)

Hans Herrmann, Cooper T51-Maserati (British GP)

Jack Fairman, Cooper T43-Climax (British GP)

Roy Salvadori, Cooper T45-Maserati (Monaco GP)

Jack Fairman, Cooper T45-Maserati (Italian GP)

was marginally offset to the left and fitted with larger oil tank and radiator. Cooper's Citroën/ERSA four-speed gearbox was retained. Roy Salvadori signed as number one driver when his Aston Martin commitments allowed.

The car was ready for Goodwood's Easter Monday meeting and Salvadori qualified second in the wet for the Glover Trophy but spun during the race. He had just inherited fourth at Monaco when the transmission seized but pushed the Cooper-Maserati over the line to claim sixth. He retired on his next two GP appearances with the car in France and the United States and finished fourth in the Oulton Park Gold Cup. The engine misfire experienced in France forced owner C.T. 'Tommy' Atkins to withdraw the Cooper-Maserati from the British GP, where Salvadori drove for Aston Martin. Jack Fairman spun the team's Cooper T43-Climax at Becher's before the gearbox failed after 39 laps of the British GP. Fairman returned in the Cooper T45-Maserati at Monza where he stopped repeatedly to have a misfire cured before a piston failure ended his race.

OTHER COOPER PRIVATEERS

The Automobile Club de Monaco bolstered its field with eight F2 cars including four Cooper-Climaxes. Equipe Nationale Belge sent a pair of T51s for Lucien Bianchi and Alain de Changy while 'Jean Lucienbonnet' entered an older T45. All three failed to qualify and *Autosport* reported that 'de Changy did it all wrong,' on Friday, 'considerably bending the machine.' The unluckiest non-qualifier in Monaco was Ivor Bueb who missed the cut by just 0.1sec due to Cliff Allison's late efforts in the F2 Ferrari. Bueb was driving a Cooper T51-Climax entered by United Racing Stable, a team formed by Bob Gibson-Jarvie of United Dominions Trust and future Ferrari importer Colonel Ronnie Hoare. Bill Moss did not qualify the car for the British GP and United Racing Stable closed after a single season.

BRM missed the United States GP so Harry Schell drove a new 2.2-litre Cooper T51-Climax entered by his Ecurie Bleue. Allegedly having used a short cut, Schell set the third best qualifying time but was originally relegated to row four. Just before the start, he successfully argued his case and was pushed onto the front row, causing others, including title contender Tony Brooks, to be demoted,

much to the *chagrin* of Ferrari team manager Romolo Tavoni. Schell's clutch slipped badly from the start and he retired after seven laps. Mike Taylor entered the rather tired 2-litre Cooper T45-Climax he had raced in the British GP but was ill so local sports car driver George Constantine deputised only for the head gasket to blow after six laps.

Alejandro de Tomaso made his second and final World Championship appearance as a driver in the United States GP with a modified Cooper T43 powered by a 2-litre twin-cam OSCA engine with two twin-choke Weber carburettors. New bodywork was fabricated by Fantuzzi of Modena and a five-speed Colotti gearbox and Amadori alloy wheels were fitted. The car, although far from the slowest, was 28sec off the pace in qualifying and in the race its brakes failed when last.

George Constantine, Cooper T45-Climax (United States GP)

Harry Schell, Cooper T51-Climax (United States GP)

Alejandro de Tomaso, Cooper T43-OSCA (United States GP)

Wolfgang von Trips, Porsche 718 (Monaco GP)

PORSCHE SYSTEM ENGINEERING AND BEHRA-PORSCHE

Two very different Porsches entered the F2 class of the Monaco GP. First was a works single-seater version of the 718RSK sports car, which was powered by Porsche's air cooled 1,498cc flat-four engine. Developing 145bhp at 8,000rpm and fitted with a six-speed gearbox, the car had unaltered track and wheelbase dimensions but its conventional steel spaceframe was new and narrower. Out-dated drum brakes were retained and revised suspension was via trailing arms and torsion bars at the front and double wishbones, coil springs and telescopic dampers at the rear. A large fuel tank was placed left of the cockpit with auxiliary tank to the right while oil was

Carel Godin de Beaufort, Porsche 718RSK (Dutch GP)

housed in the nose. The prototype was tested at Malmsheim airfield before Wolfgang von Trips completed three successful laps of the Nürburgring in the week before Monaco. He qualified with ease but spun on oil at Ste Dévote on the second lap, eliminating all three F2 cars that started.

Jean Behra knew Valerio Colotti well from their days at Maserati and he commissioned Studio Tecnica-Meccanica to produce a light, new F2 car based on the Porsche 718RSK he had bought from the works. Colotti designed a new spaceframe and tight-fitting aluminium bodywork while retaining the RSK's engine and suspension. Maria Teresa de Filippis drove the Behra-Porsche at Monaco but did not qualify when four seconds slower than von Trips. Edgar Barth also tried it but proved no quicker.

Both cars were entered for the German GP with Behra free to drive his repainted blue machine following his departure from Ferrari after punching the team manager at Reims. Rain rendered the fearsome banked North Turn lethal and Behra was killed when he crashed during the supporting 1,500cc sports car race. The Behra-Porsche and von Trips's works 718 were withdrawn from the following day's GP.

ECURIE MAARSBERGEN

Carel Godin de Beaufort borrowed a works 1.5-litre Porsche 718RSK for the Dutch GP, 'showing every possible courtesy to the faster drivers' noted Autosport. He was lapped after just nine laps and finished 10th and last.

Harry Blanchard, Porsche 718RSK (United States GP)

BLANCHARD AUTOMOBILE COMPANY

The inaugural United States GP included 1959 SCCA Production F Champion Harry Blanchard and his 1.5-litre Porsche RSK sports car, complete with central driving position. Fresh from racing the car at the previous week's International Bahamas Speed Week in Nassau, Blanchard drove an unobtrusive race into seventh, receiving $500 from Martini & Rossi as the first (and only) American to finish. He shipped the Porsche to Buenos Aires for the following month's 1,000Kms but was killed after crashing into Heini Walter's similar car.

JBW CARS

Eager to attract the increased start money offered to manufacturers by continental promoters, Brian Naylor raced a series of JBW sports car specials during the 1950s that had been created for him by mechanic Fred Wilkinson ('JB' were Naylor's initials and 'W' stood for Wilkinson). Naylor drove a F2 Cooper-Climax during 1958, including his GP début at the Nürburgring. For 1959, Wilkinson used the Cooper as inspiration to construct the first JBW F1 car using the 2.5-litre four-cylinder engine and five-speed gearbox from a Maserati 250S sports car. Larger than the T45 or subsequent T51, but fitted with wire knock-off rear wheels, it retired from the International Trophy on its first appearance and did not start the Oulton Park Gold Cup. Naylor also entered the British GP where he qualified and ran in the midfield before the rear axle failed. There was talk of a short production run at the end of the year but Naylor's JBWs remained one-off specials.

OTHER MASERATI PRIVATEERS

Maserati remained financially challenged during 1959 as Adolfo and Omer Orsi sought to restructure and find investment.

During 1958 company director Nello Ugolini had managed the Trident's racing affairs on behalf of its private clients, including Temple Buell, but rumours of Buell's continued participation, complete with a superstar lead driver, came to naught so the experienced team manager intermittently entered Maserati 250Fs of varying ages under the Scuderia Ugolini banner. Giorgio Scarlatti retired from a couple of British non-championship events before failing to qualify at Monaco, his 250F having a revised short tail. He returned at the French GP where Carel Godin de Beaufort

Brian Naylor, JBW-Maserati (British GP)

Giulio Cabianca, Maserati 250F (Italian GP)

Giorgio Scarlatti, Maserati 250F (French GP)

Carel Godin de Beaufort, Maserati 250F (French GP)

drove a second Ugolini 250F. The slowest two to qualify, Scarlatti and de Beaufort were classified eighth and ninth respectively and did not reappear.

André Testut entered his 250F at Monaco for a second successive year with the same outcome. Now listed as entered by Monte Carlo Auto Sport, he was even slower than in 1958 so failed to qualify once more. Ottorino Volonterio lent his ancient 250F to OSCA sports car driver Giulio Cabianca for the Italian GP, who started and finished last. American amateur Phil Cade bought the 250F that de Beaufort had raced in France but could not start his home GP when it broke down during practice.

CAMORADI USA (TEC-MEC)

Former Maserati engineer Valerio Colotti was much in demand in 1959. He established Studio Tecnica-Meccanica in the centre of Modena when Maserati closed its works team at the end of 1957. Giorgio Scarlatti commissioned Colotti to design a lightweight replacement for his Maserati 205F but development was slow. Scarlatti eventually sold his interest in the project to Modena-based American Gordon Pennington.

The resulting Tec-Mec F415 had a small-diameter tubular spaceframe, Girling disc brakes and double wishbone/coil spring front suspension with wishbones and transverse leaf springs at the rear. The front-mounted 2,493cc straight-six engine from the 250F had three twin-choke Weber carburettors and drove through a five-speed gearbox in unit with the final drive. Like almost all of the field, it was fitted with Dunlop tyres. Colotti had sold his studio to Pennington by the time it finally made its one-off appearance in the United States GP entered by Lloyd 'Lucky' Casner's ambitious Camoradi organisation. Jim Rathmann was originally listed as driver but it was Brazilian Fritz d'Orey who drove the slow, front-engine car. The Tec-Mec lasted seven laps 'spewing oil on the concrete' (according to *Autosport*) before retiring.

Pennington soon lost interest and the Tec-Mec F415 did not race again until it was restored for historic racing by Donington Park and museum owner Tom Wheatcroft. Colotti later formed Gear Speed Developments with Alf Francis and the pair used their respective bases in Turin and Dorking.

CONNAUGHT ENGINEERING

More than two years had elapsed since Connaught had quit racing when the spaceframe C-type, now owned by Paul Emery, finally made its belated F1 début in the United States GP with SCCA racer Bob Said behind the wheel. This privateer effort was officially entered by Connaught Engineering and unfortunately for Rodney Clarke and his men it was a torrid weekend and a short race. The C-type, fitted with 'toothpaste tube' bodywork, 'went appallingly badly' (according to *The Autocar*) throughout practice but lined up 13th nonetheless. Said jumped the start and crashed on the north runway on the first lap.

Fritz d'Orey, Tec-Mec F415-Maserati (United States GP)

Bob Said, Connaught C-Alta (United States GP)

Rodger Ward, Kurtis-Offenhauser (United States GP)

LEADER CARD RACERS

Among the most unsuitable cars to start a World Championship GP was the Kurtis-Kraft midget that Indianapolis 500 winner and new USAC champion Rodger Ward drove at Sebring. Powered by a 1.7-litre double-overhead-cam four-cylinder Offenhauser engine with two-speed gearbox, it had a tubular spaceframe, rigid front axle and torsion bars to the rear. The Kurtis-Kraft had lever-operated Halibrand disc brakes and ran on 12-inch wheels. Small even next to a Cooper, the car was set up to slide on North America's short dirt tracks rather than hug a road course. Ward showed well in a road race at Lime Rock although the most relevant competition that day came from Chuck Daigh's outdated Maserati 250F. Entered by a regular USAC entrant, Bob Wilke's Leader Card Racers of Milwaukee, Wisconsin, Ward qualified 43.8sec slower than Stirling Moss's pole time and resigned himself with good grace to being lapped many times. He was ahead of Harry Blanchard's 1.5-litre Porsche sports car when the clutch failed at half distance.

BRITISH FORMULA 2 CLASS

The British GP grid was bolstered with F2 cars that were also classified in the overall results. Chris Bristow's British Racing Partnership Cooper T51-Borgward led the class throughout with Henry Taylor giving chase in Tim Parnell's Cooper T51-Climax, Parnell having failed to qualify a year-old T45. Ken Tyrrell managed

Mike Taylor, Cooper T45-Climax (British GP)

Peter Ashdown, Cooper T45-Climax (British GP)

Alan Brown Equipe's pair of similar Cooper T45-Climaxes for Mike Taylor and Peter Ashdown. Taylor's transmission failed after 15 laps while Ashdown, who spun at Anchor Crossing, and Ivor Bueb's second BRP Cooper T51-Borgward finished at the back. The Cooper-Climaxes of Trevor Taylor (Ace Garage's T51), Bill Moss (United Racing Stable T51) and Keith Greene (Gilby Engineering T43) were also left unemployed come race day.

Having sold some farmland to the government as the M1 motorway was built, David Piper combined with Bob Bodle's Dorchester Service Station to acquire an F2 Lotus 16-Climax. Second at Zeltweg in August, Piper completed 19 misfiring laps

of the British GP before the head gasket blew. Dennis Taylor's older Lotus 12-Climax also did not qualify for the race. The south London publican then returned to Formula Junior but was killed during the opening heat at Monaco in 1962.

Engineer/driver Michael Parkes attempted to make his GP début in the Fry-Climax he had helped build. Part-monocoque, part-frame, David Fry's ungainly one-off had a large central tail. It had been intended for Stuart Lewis-Evans, who had died from burns inflicted at the 1958 Moroccan GP, so Parkes was chosen for its début at Mallory Park in June. Fifth that day, he was another non-qualifier at Aintree and the project was soon abandoned.

Henry Taylor, Cooper T51-Climax (British GP)

David Piper, Lotus 16-Climax (British GP)

DRIVER PERFORMANCE (EXCLUDING INDIANAPOLIS 500)

DRIVER	CAR-ENGINE	MC	NL	F	GB	D	P	I	USA
Cliff Allison	Ferrari Dino 156	15 R	–	–	–	–	–	–	–
	Ferrari Dino 246	–	15 9	–	–	14 R	–	8 5	7 R
Peter Ashdown	Cooper T45-Climax	–	–	–	23 12	–	–	–	–
Edgar Barth	Behra-Porsche	NT DNQ	–	–	–	–	–	–	–
Azdrúbal Bayardo	Maserati 250F	–	–	22 DNQ	–	–	–	–	–
Jean Behra	Ferrari Dino 246	2 R	4 5	5 R	–	–	–	–	–
	Behra-Porsche	–	–	–	–	NT DNS	–	–	–
Lucien Bianchi	Cooper T51-Climax	19 DNQ	–	–	–	–	–	–	–
Harry Blanchard	Porsche 718RSK	–	–	–	–	–	–	–	16 7
Joakim Bonnier	BRM P25	7 R	1 1	6 R	10 R	7 5	5 R	11 8	–
Jack Brabham	Cooper T51-Climax	3 1 FL	2 2	2 3	1 1	4 R	2 R	3 3	2 4
Chris Bristow	Cooper T51-Borgward	–	–	–	16 10	–	–	–	–
Tony Brooks	Ferrari Dino 246	4 2	8 R	1 1	–	1 1 FL	10 9	2 R	4 3
	Vanwall VW5	–	–	–	17 R	–	–	–	–
Ivor Bueb	Cooper T51-Climax	17 DNQ	–	–	–	–	–	–	–
	Cooper T51-Borgward	–	–	–	18 13	–	–	–	–
Ian Burgess	Cooper T51-Maserati	–	–	19 R	13 R	15 6	–	16 14	–
Giulio Cabianca	Maserati 250F	–	–	–	–	–	–	21 15	–
Mário Cabral	Cooper T51-Maserati	–	–	–	–	–	14 10	–	–
Phil Cade	Maserati 250F	–	–	–	–	–	–	–	18 DNS
George Constantine	Cooper T45-Climax	–	–	–	–	–	–	–	15 R
Colin Davis	Cooper T51-Maserati	–	–	17 R	–	–	–	18 11	–
Carel Godin de Beaufort	Porsche 718RSK	–	14 10	–	–	–	–	–	–
	Maserati 250F	–	–	20 9	–	–	–	–	–
Alain de Changy	Cooper T51-Climax	20 DNQ	–	–	–	–	–	–	–
Maria Teresa de Filippis	Behra-Porsche	21 DNQ	–	–	–	–	–	–	–
Alejandro de Tomaso	Cooper T43-OSCA	–	–	–	–	–	–	–	14 R
Fritz d'Orey	Maserati 250F	–	–	18 10	20 R	–	–	–	–
	Tec-Mec F415-Maserati	–	–	–	–	–	–	–	17 R
Jack Fairman	Cooper T43-Climax	–	–	–	15 R	–	–	–	–
	Cooper T45-Maserati	–	–	–	–	–	–	20 R	–
Ron Flockhart	BRM P25	10 R	–	13 6	11 R	–	11 7	15 13	–
Olivier Gendebien	Ferrari Dino 246	–	–	11 4	–	–	–	6 6	–
Keith Greene	Cooper T43-Climax	–	–	–	NT DNQ	–	–	–	–
Masten Gregory	Cooper T45-Climax	11 R	–	–	–	–	–	–	–
	Cooper T51-Climax	–	7 3	7 R	5 7	5 R	3 2	–	–
Dan Gurney	Ferrari Dino 246	–	–	12 R	–	3 2	6 3	4 4	–
Bruce Halford	Lotus 16-Climax	16 R	–	–	–	–	–	–	–
Hans Herrmann	Cooper T51-Maserati	–	–	–	19 R	–	–	–	–
	BRM P25	–	–	–	–	11 R	–	–	–
Graham Hill	Lotus 16-Climax	14 R	5 7	14 R	9 9	10 R	15 R	10 R	–
Phil Hill	Ferrari Dino 246	5 4	12 6	3 2	–	6 3	7 R	5 2 FL	8 R
Innes Ireland	Lotus 16-Climax	–	9 4	15 R	NT DNP	13 R	16 R	14 R	9 5
Pete Lovely	Lotus 16-Climax	22 DNQ	–	–	–	–	–	–	–
'Jean Lucienbonnet'	Cooper T45-Climax	23 DNQ	–	–	–	–	–	–	–
Bruce McLaren	Cooper T51-Climax	13 5	–	–	–	–	–	–	–
	Cooper T45-Climax	–	–	10 5	8 3 FL	9 R	8 R	9 R	10 1
Bill Moss	Cooper T51-Climax	–	–	–	NT DNQ	–	–	–	–
Stirling Moss	Cooper T51-Climax	1 R	3 R FL	–	–	2 R	1 1 FL	1 1	1 R
	BRM P25	–	–	4 DSQ FL	7 2 FL	–	–	–	–
Brian Naylor	JBW-Maserati	–	–	–	14 R	–	–	–	–
Michael Parkes	Fry-Climax	–	–	–	NT DNQ	–	–	–	–
Tim Parnell	Cooper T45-Climax	–	–	–	NT DNQ	–	–	–	–
David Piper	Lotus 16-Climax	–	–	–	22 R	–	–	–	–

DRIVER PERFORMANCE CONTINUED

DRIVER	CAR-ENGINE	MC	NL	F	GB	D	P	I	USA
Bob Said	Connaught C-Alta	–	–	–	–	–	–	–	13 R
Roy Salvadori	Cooper T45-Maserati	8 6	–	16 R	–	–	–	–	11 R
	Aston Martin DBR4/250	–	13 R	–	2 6	–	12 6	17 R	–
Giorgio Scarlatti	Maserati 250F	18 DNQ	–	21 8	–	–	–	–	–
	Cooper T51-Climax	–	–	–	–	–	–	12 12	–
Harry Schell	BRM P25	9 R	6 R	9 7	3 4	8 7	9 5	7 7	–
	Cooper T51-Climax	–	–	–	–	–	–	–	3 R
Carroll Shelby	Aston Martin DBR4/250	–	10 R	–	6 R	–	13 8	19 10	–
Alan Stacey	Lotus 16-Climax	–	–	–	12 8	–	–	–	12 R
Dennis Taylor	Lotus 12-Climax	–	–	–	30 DNQ	–	–	–	–
Henry Taylor	Cooper T51-Climax	–	–	–	21 11	–	–	–	–
Mike Taylor	Cooper T45-Climax	–	–	–	24 R	–	–	–	–
Trevor Taylor	Cooper T51-Climax	–	–	–	NT DNQ	–	–	–	–
André Testut	Maserati 250F	24 DNQ	–	–	–	–	–	–	–
Maurice Trintignant	Cooper T51-Climax	6 3	11 8	8 11	4 5	12 4	4 4	13 9	5 2 FL
Wolfgang von Trips	Porsche 718	12 R	–	–	–	NT DNS	–	–	–
	Ferrari Dino 246	–	–	–	–	–	–	–	6 6
Rodger Ward	Kurtis-Offenhauser	–	–	–	–	–	–	–	19 R

FORMULA 1 RACE WINNERS

ROUND	RACE (CIRCUIT)	DATE	WINNER
–	Glover Trophy (Goodwood)	Mar 30	Stirling Moss (Cooper T51-Climax)
–	BARC 200 (Aintree)	Apr 18	Jean Behra (Ferrari Dino 246)
–	Daily Express International Trophy (Silverstone)	May 2	Jack Brabham (Cooper T51-Climax)
1	Grand Prix de Monaco (Monte Carlo)	May 10	Jack Brabham (Cooper T51-Climax)
2*	Indianapolis 500 (Indianapolis)	May 30	Rodger Ward (Watson-Offenhauser)
3	Grote Prijs van Nederland (Zandvoort)	May 31	Jo Bonnier (BRM P25)
4	Grand Prix de l'Automobile Club de France (Reims)	Jul 5	Tony Brooks (Ferrari Dino 246)
5	British Grand Prix (Aintree)	Jul 18	Jack Brabham (Cooper T51-Climax)
6	Grosser Preis von Deutschland (Avus)	Aug 2	Tony Brooks (Ferrari Dino 246)
7	Grande Premio de Portugal (Monsanto)	Aug 23	Stirling Moss (Cooper T51-Climax)
8	Gran Premio d'Italia (Monza)	Sep 13	Stirling Moss (Cooper T51-Climax)
–	International Gold Cup (Oulton Park)	Sep 26	Stirling Moss (Cooper T51-Climax)
–	Silver City Trophy (Snetterton)	Oct 10	Ron Flockhart (BRM P25)
9	United States Grand Prix (Sebring)	Dec 12	Bruce McLaren (Cooper T45-Climax)

*Run to USAC National Championship rules

DRIVERS' CHAMPIONSHIP

	DRIVERS	POINTS
1	Jack Brabham	31 (34)*
2	Tony Brooks	27
3	Stirling Moss	25.5
4	Phil Hill	20
5	Maurice Trintignant	19
6	Bruce McLaren	16.5
7	Dan Gurney	13
8=	Jo Bonnier	10
	Masten Gregory	10
10	Rodger Ward	8
11	Jim Rathmann	6
12=	Innes Ireland	5
	Harry Schell	5
	Johnny Thomson	5
15=	Tony Bettenhausen	3
	Olivier Gendebien	3
17=	Cliff Allison	2
	Jean Behra	2
	Paul Goldsmith	2

*Best five results count

MANUFACTURERS' CHAMPIONSHIP

	MANUFACTURERS	POINTS
1	Cooper-Climax	40 (53)*
2	Ferrari	32 (38)*
3	BRM	18
4	Lotus-Climax	5

*Best five results count. No points awarded for Indianapolis 500; points only awarded to first car to finish for each manufacturer